2. Memorize, preferably by using in short sentences, the following nine forms of each verb (or of each pattern verb, where several are alike).

(a) present indicative—all six forms
(b) future
(c) present subjunctive
(d) past indefinite

(b)–(d): 1st person singular

3. From these nine forms, the other forms and tenses may be derived (with few exceptions) as in the following two examples.

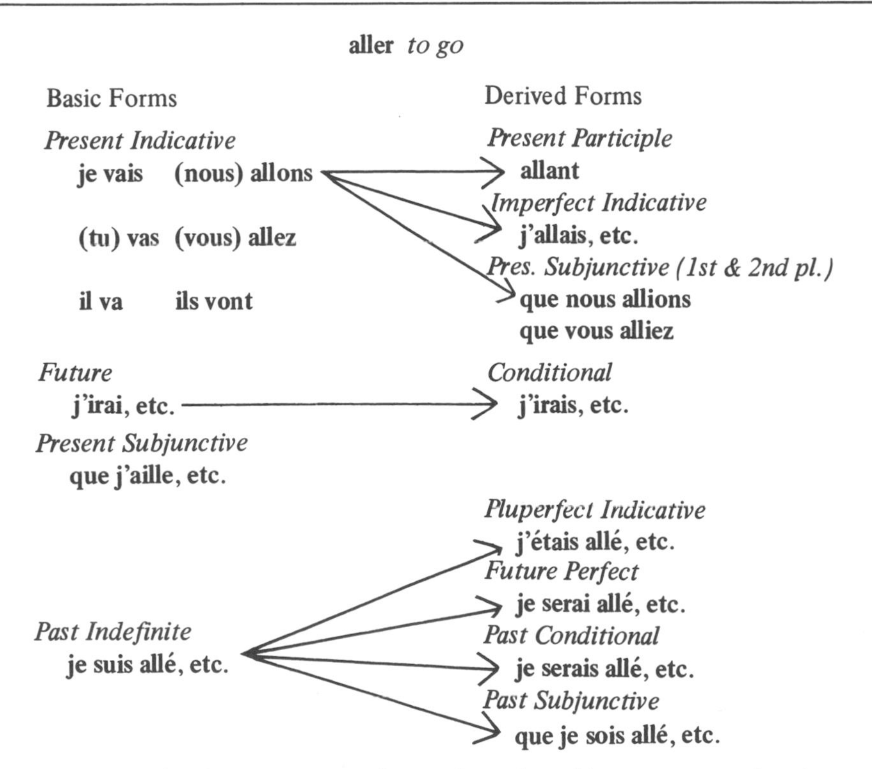


**Note**: For the three imperative forms, drop the subject pronouns given in parentheses in the Present Indicative above. In **-er** verbs (including **aller**) the final **-s** of the **tu** form is omitted in the imperative.

*(cf. pp. 181-193 for more detailed discussions.)*

*French for Review*

# *French for Review*

EDWARD T. HEISE *United States Naval Academy*

THE ODYSSEY PRESS *New York*

*Second Edition*

Published by The Odyssey Press
A Division of Western Publishing Company, Inc.


Printed in the United States
Library of Congress Catalog Card Number: 71-81806
A0987654321

# *Preface*

In this second edition of French for Review, as in the first, the emphasis remains upon learning through examples and exercises, with a minimum of verbal explanation. To this end, the number and variety of examples and drill materials have been substantially increased, and a new section of written exercises based upon the supplementary grammatical notes has been added. Many useful comments and suggestions from instructors who used the previous edition have been incorporated in the revision – especially in the recorded materials for language laboratory use or independent practice.

It is my strong conviction that an intermediate language course cannot re-introduce *all* the grammatical phenomena previously met in the beginning course without forfeiting time that could be put to a more effective use. An author's first task is to decide, on the basis of his experience, which items require specific, detailed review and drill, and which are relatively unimportant or are best learned through readings, conversational practice, footnotes, instructors' comments, etc. In this book, items of the first category form the principal material of the twelve lessons. Each subject reviewed is abundantly illustrated, and a large quantity of varied drill material is provided. The other items, for which special concentration seems less imperative at this time, are placed in the Supplementary Notes, where they may be studied and practiced if the need arises.

The following questions and answers will explain my plan and objectives.

1. What is the reason for reviewing grammar in the second year of college or the third year of high school?
   First, experience has shown that certain principles and patterns are inadequately understood and mastered in the beginning course, where the necessarily piecemeal presentation and the concurrent demands of pronunciation, vocabulary, and grammar leave the student with only a vague comprehension of the over-all picture. Second, students in intermediate courses often come from quite varied backgrounds – reflecting different standards of achievement and different degrees of emphasis on oral practice, grammar, reading, pronunciation, etc. Third, the summer vacation is generally a time of forgetting. Therefore, a quick review of the basic essentials is useful to refresh the memory, clarify what was only partially understood, and provide a more homogeneous background for the work which follows.

2. What method of presentation is most effective for an intermediate review?
   It has been my experience that an abundance of well-conceived examples is more effective than a long disquisition. Therefore, following the principle of *a mimimum of statement and a maximum of illustration,* the material is presented through numerous examples, chosen and arranged to demonstrate clearly each aspect of usage being studied.

   The student is expected to examine these examples, and, guided by the section headings and the Notes, to arrive at an understanding which will allow him to apply the patterns in the exercises of the lesson and in his own use of French. The aim is to stimulate the inductive reasoning powers of the student and thereby assure a more active assimilation and a longer retention. By limiting the vocabulary of the examples and drills, as much as possible, to words and idioms which are already familiar (from the beginning course), I have tried to reduce the vocabulary burden to a minimum so that a greater concentration on the patterns is possible.

3. Should the intermediate review concern itself with advanced grammar?
   At the beginning of the intermediate course, most students are neither ready for nor interested in the intriguing niceties of

advanced grammar. We are still laying the foundation; the superstructure must wait until the base is secure. It is not a question of *whether* certain items are important; it is a question of *when* they are important.

4. Can the twelve lessons be covered in twelve recitations?
   The division of the book into twelve lessons is not intended to suggest that it should be covered in twelve recitations. It reflects, rather, the desire to present the material in meaningful units. The lessons are of varying length and difficulty, and the number of recitations needed for coverage will depend upon the background, ability, and effort of a given class.

5. Should the explanations and directions be given in English or French?
   Because the explanations and drills are intended for preparation outside of class, I feel that giving the Notes and directions in English offers a greater guarantee of comprehension, a greater assurance of accuracy, and the prospect of a more efficient use of the student's study time. This should in no way prejudice the use of French in the classroom.

6. Should the grammatical patterns be introduced in a connected reading passage, in dialogue form, or through individual sentences?
   Given the principal aim of the book – to make the *patterns* of the language stand out clearly – it seems best to use individual sentences, since they offer possibilities of grouping and sequence which a dialogue or a connected passage cannot achieve.

7. Should a reading passage or a dialogue be added to each lesson?
   The lessons of this text are closely restricted in order to make the grammar review as brief and effective as possible; therefore, it seems undesirable to increase the length of the lessons by the addition of reading material or dialogues of very doubtful literary or inspirational value. An abundance and a great variety of excellent materials are available to supply this need and to allow the instructor to vary his choice according to the ages, abilities, and interests of his classes.

8. Should there be a section on pronunciation?
   Whereas continued improvement in pronunciation remains as important in the second year as in the first, it requires a different approach. In my experience, correction and drill as occasioned by student performance in class is the most effective procedure; it makes the practice meaningful and it avoids wasting time. Each oral exercise is a pronunciation drill, especially when classwork is supplemented by guided drill in the language laboratory.

9. What kinds of exercises should be used?
   I have used the following criteria for the exercises in each of the twelve lessons:
   (a) They are designed for teaching rather than testing.
   (b) They lend themselves to rapid oral drill.
   (c) They offer practice in the application of the principles illustrated by the Pattern Sentences.
   (d) They express thoughts which are realistic for a mature student.
   (e) They represent a variety of drill types.
   (f) Although many of them are of the "pattern" type, they involve enough mental challenge to prevent them from becoming boringly insipid.

10. Why are written exercises included?
    Many teachers believe that a more accurate comprehension and a longer retention result when the student has some practice in expressing in writing what he has already learned orally. In this text, the written exercises are distinctly supplementary and are placed in a separate section following the lessons proper as a reminder that they are not intended as classroom drills and that they should be assigned only after the material has been thoroughly covered in class.

11. In what order should the units be studied?
    In a review grammar, the order of presentation of the units is not of great importance, since the student has met them all before. In this book, the units are numbered for convenience of reference, but they can be studied in any desired order.

12. To what extent is vocabulary expansion an objective of the review course?

In order to maintain a single main objective and to keep the review short, I have attempted to use only words and idioms which most students will have met previously in their beginning course. However, not all of these will be familiar to every student, and many useful words and phrases will be added to the student's active vocabulary through repeated use in the oral drills. The specific objective of expanding the vocabulary range pertains more logically to other aspects of the intermediate course, which follow or accompany the review of grammar.

In summary, my aim is to review, through a study of useful colloquial sentences, the patterns and principles which seem most necessary for advancement toward fluency and accurate comprehension. An abundance of drill material is included, so that there may be ample practice for those classes that need it, and a choice of exercises for those who need less. The scope of the lessons is limited in order to allow a thorough concentration on the essential elements. I believe that this limited and concentrated approach offers the most effective use of the review portion of the intermediate course.

I am grateful to my colleague, Professor René F. Muller, for his careful reading of the manuscript and many useful suggestions. Responsibility for the accuracy of the text, of course, is mine.

E. T. H.

# *To the Student*

The objective of this book is to help you remember, organize, and master the basic concepts and patterns of French to which you were introduced in your previous study. In each of the following lessons you will find: (1) a series of sentences chosen and arranged to illustrate certain common patterns of French usage; (2) a few brief explanatory notes based upon the sentences; (3) several exercises designed to develop mastery of the aspect of usage being studied. I recommend the following study procedure for each lesson:

(a) Read *aloud* the Pattern Sentences, preferably imitating the pronunciation and intonation of the instructor or of a recording.
(b) Examine the sentences carefully, noting particularly the specific aspect of usage emphasized.
(c) Study the brief Notes which follow the sentences.
(d) Re-read the Pattern Sentences *aloud.*
(e) Covering the French versions of the sentences, see if you can express the ideas in French, using the English versions to prompt your recall. As an oral exercise, the lesson tape will provide immediate verification if you say your version during the pause which *precedes* each sentence – instead of during the pause which follows, as in (a).
(f) Prepare the other exercises. This should be easy if you have thoroughly mastered the Pattern Sentences.

If you find that you need more explanation than that offered by the examples and the Notes, consult the additional discussions which you will find in the Reference Materials, pp. 109-193.

Keep in mind that, whereas an understanding of grammar is very important in learning a language, it is even more important to get all the practice you can in using French. A course of approximately ninety-six class hours equals only eight twelve-hour days. The best possible use must be made of this class time, and you must supplement it by practice outside of class if you wish to achieve the ability to understand and express ideas in French. But once you have arrived at a basic mastery of the language, you will have attained a new dimension in your cultural experience and a new source of personal satisfaction – as well as a new skill which may be of great practical value.

# *Contents*

*French for Review*

# LESSON 1

## *Definite, Indefinite, and Partitive Articles*

| | DEFINITE | | INDEFINITE | | PARTITIVE | |
|---|---|---|---|---|---|---|
| MASC. SING. | **le (l')** | the | **un** | a, an | **du (de l')** | some, any |
| FEM. SING. | **la (l')** | | **une** | | **de la (de l')** | |
| PLURAL | **les** | | . . . | | **des** | |

(For contractions, see p. 112)

## PATTERN SENTENCES

*Articles used in French where also used in English (the general rule)*

1. **La bonne a acheté un gigot, du beurre et des légumes.** — The maid bought a leg of lamb, some butter, and some vegetables.
2. **En cherchant les souvenirs, un des touristes est allé à pied du Louvre au Panthéon.** *(Notice contractions.)* — While looking for the souvenirs, one of the tourists walked from the Louvre to the Pantheon.

*Definite Article expressed in French but omitted in English*

| | French | English |
|---|---|---|
| 3. | **La vérité est à désirer.** | Truth is to be desired. |
| 4. | **Que savez-vous de l'amour?** | What do you know about love? |
| 5. | **Les roses aiment le soleil.** | Roses love sunshine. |
| 6. | **Il a fait des recherches sur le crime et les criminels.** | He has done research on crime and criminals. |
| 7. | **Où se trouve le rayon des chemises?** | Where is the shirt counter? |
| 8. | **A quelle heure sert-on le déjeuner?** | (At) what time do they serve lunch? |
| 9. | **Qu'est-ce qu'elle a préparé pour le dîner?** | What has she prepared for dinner? |
| 10. | **Le colonel Javert vient d'arriver.** | Colonel Javert has just arrived. |
| 11. | **Le président Wilson avait un plan.** | President Wilson had a plan. |
| 12. | **Les plus belles saisons sont l'automne et le printemps.** | The most beautiful seasons are autumn and spring. |
| 13. | **Cette élève aime le français et le latin, mais elle n'aime pas la chimie et les mathématiques.** | That student likes French and Latin, but she doesn't like chemistry and mathematics. |
| 14. | **M. Dupont connaît bien l'Afrique – surtout le Maroc et la Tunisie.** | Mr. Dupont knows Africa well – especially Morocco and Tunisia. |
| 15. | **Le Texas est plus grand que la France.** | Texas is larger than France. |
| 16. | **Cet été nous allons ou au Canada ou au Mexique.** | This summer we are going either to Canada or Mexico. |
| 17. | **Votre oncle habite (dans la) rue Boyer, n'est-ce pas?** | Your uncle lives on Boyer Street, doesn't he? |
| 18. | **Non, il habite à présent (sur le) boulevard Flandrin, tout près de l'avenue Foch.** | No, he now lives on Flandrin Boulevard, very near Foch Avenue. |
| 19. | **Est-ce que le professeur de musique vient le mardi?** | Does the music teacher come on Tuesdays? |
| 20. | **Ces magasins ferment le dimanche.** | These stores close on Sundays. |
| 21. | **Le salon, la salle à manger, la cuisine et les chambres à coucher sont grands.** | The living room, dining room, kitchen, and bedrooms are large. |

| | |
|---|---|
| 22. **Le père, la mère, le fils et la fille travaillent dans le même bureau.** | The father, mother, son, and daughter work in the same officc. |

*Partitive article expressed in French but may be omitted in English*

| | |
|---|---|
| 23. **Ça prend du temps, n'est-ce pas?** | That takes time, doesn't it? |
| 24. **Apportez-moi de l'eau, du savon et des serviettes, s'il vous plaît.** | Bring me some water, soap, and towels, please. |
| 25. **Nous avons eu de la difficulté à le trouver.** | We had difficulty in finding it. |
| 26. **Partout on voyait des fleurs.** | Everywhere one saw flowers. |

*Indefinite article expressed in English but omitted in French*

| | |
|---|---|
| 27. **M. Dupont est avocat, n'est-ce-pas?** | Mr. Dupont is a lawyer, isn't he? |
| 28. **Cet homme là-bas est Américain.** | That man over there is an American. |
| 29. **S'il est évêque, il ne peut pas être presbytérien.** | If he is a bishop, he can't be a Presbyterian. |

*Partitive expressed by* de *alone*

| | |
|---|---|
| 30. **Je vous promets de beaux souliers de bal.** | I promise you some beautiful dancing shoes. |
| 31. **Nous sommes dc bons amis.** | We are good friends. |
| 32. **Elle n'a pas trouvé de bonbons dans la boîte.** | She didn't find any candy in the box. |
| 33. **Il n'y avait pas de valises près de la porte.** | There weren't any suitcases near the door. |
| 34. **Je n'ai jamais vu d'eau plus claire.** | I have never seen clearer water. |
| 35. **Vous aurez besoin d'argent pour le voyage.** | You will need money for the trip. |
| 36. **Cette bouteille est remplie de vinaigre.** | This bottle is filled with vinegar. |
| 37. **Les élèves de cette école serviront de guides pendant la visite.** | The pupils of this school will serve as guides during the visit. |

*Definite Article used in French where English uses Possessive*

| | |
|---|---|
| 38. **Ne fermez pas les yeux!** | Don't close your eyes! |
| 39. **Ma sœur a les cheveux bruns.** | My sister's hair is brown. (My sister has brown hair.) |
| 40. **Je n'ai même pas ouvert la bouche.** | I didn't even open my mouth. |
| 41. **M. Duval, le parapluie au bras, sort de la maison.** | Mr. Duval, with his umbrella on his arm, leaves the house. |
| 42. **Le voilà comme toujours – le chapeau rabattu sur les yeux et le revolver au poing.** | There he is as always – with his hat pulled down over his eyes and his revolver in his hand (fist). |
| 43. **Dites-leur de se laver bien la figure.** | Tell them to wash their faces well. |
| 44. **Il lui a pris la main.** | He took her hand. |
| 45. **A l'entrée, on vous ôte les chaussures et vous lave les pieds.** | At the entrance, they take off your shoes and wash your feet. |

*Exceptions and Special Cases*

| | |
|---|---|
| 46. **Elle porte les mêmes vêtements en été, en automne, en hiver et au printemps.** | She wears the same clothes in summer, (in) autumn, (in) winter, and (in) spring. |
| 47. **On trouve ces animaux en Norvège mais pas au Danemark.** | One finds those animals in Norway but not in Denmark. |
| 48. **Les pays de l'Europe avaient des colonies en Asie, en Afrique et en Amérique.** | The countries of Europe had colonies in Asia, (in) Africa, and (in) America. |
| 49. **Quand sont-ils revenus de France?** | When did they return from France? |
| 50. **Les vins de France sont bien appréciés.** | The wines of France (French wines) are highly esteemed. |
| 51. **La Bretagne est une ancienne province de France.** | Brittany is an ancient province of France (French province). |
| 52. **Cette jeune fille parle français et italien.** | This girl speaks French and Italian. |
| 53. **Avez-vous votre livre d'allemand?** | Do you have your German book? |

| | |
|---|---|
| 54. **Mon livre de chimie est écrit en français.** | My chemistry book is written in French. |
| 55. **Allez-vous à l'église ce matin?** | Are you going to church this morning? |
| 56. **Je ne l'ai pas vu à l'école.** | I didn't see him in school. |
| 57. **Nous avons passé l'année dernière en Amérique du Sud.** | We spent last year in South America. |
| 58. **Il se trouvait sans chemise, sans chaussettes, sans souliers et sans argent.** | He found himself without a shirt, without any socks, without shoes, and without any money. |
| 59. **Il n'avait ni chemise ni chaussettes.** | He had neither a shirt nor socks. |
| 60. **Elle lui a répondu avec dignité.** | She answered him with dignity. |

## NOTES

(a) Contrary to English usage, the definite article is used in the following cases in French:

(1) before abstract nouns, nouns used in a general sense, or to designate a category [ex. 3-7]
(2) before names of meals [ex. 8, 9]
(3) before titles used with names (except **monsieur, madame, mademoiselle**) [ex. 10, 11]
(4) before names of seasons [ex. 12]
(5) before names of languages and other subjects of study [ex. 13]
(6) before names of continents, countries, and other geographical divisions (except cities) [ex. 14-16] (See also Note (f).)
(7) before the words **rue, boulevard,** and **avenue** followed by the name [ex. 17, 18] (But in colloquial usage, both the preposition and the definite article are often omitted after such verbs as **habiter, demeurer, se trouver, arriver,** etc.)
(8) before days of the week to denote regular occurrence [ex. 19, 20]
(9) before each noun in a series [ex. 21, 22]

(b) The partitive article may not be omitted in French, although it frequently is in English. [ex. 23-26] (See also Notes (i), (j), and pp. 111-112.)

(c) In French the indefinite article is not used in statements of profession, nationality, religion, or similar cases where the predicate noun has principally an adjectival value. [ex. 27-29]

(d) The partitive is expressed by **de** alone (*i.e.* without the definite article) in the following cases:

(1) when an adjective precedes a plural noun [ex. 30, 31]
(2) before the object of a negative verb (including the complement of **il y a**) [ex. 32-34]
(3) when following expressions which already require the preposition **de** [ex. 35-37] (In this case the one **de** serves a double purpose.)

(e) The definite article is frequently used in French with parts of the body (and with articles of clothing in certain descriptive constructions [ex. 41, 42]) where a possessive adjective would be used in English. This occurs most commonly when the part of the body is the complement of a verb or is used in a descriptive parenthetical phrase. The possessive reference in French may be implicit in the context or may be expressed by an indirect object. [ex. 38 - 45]

(f) The definite article is used after the preposition **en** only in a few fixed expressions; therefore, the article generally used with geographical names (continents, countries, etc.) is omitted when those names follow **en**. (See Les. 11.) The article is also omitted with *feminine* geographical names after **de** meaning *from* and sometimes after **de** in adjective phrases. [ex. 46-51]

(g) The definite article is generally omitted with names of languages after **parler**, with names of languages and other subjects of study after **en**, and after **de** in adjective phrases. [ex. 52-54]

(h) A number of commonly used phrases include the definite article in French but not in English. Such phrases should be learned as units. [ex. 55-57]

(i) The partitive and indefinite articles are generally omitted after **sans** and **(ne ...) ni ... ni ...** . [ex. 58, 59]

(j) The partitive article is not normally used in adverbial phrases introduced by **avec**. [ex. 60]

## EXERCISES

A. *For each of the English versions of the Pattern Sentences give the French equivalent. (Cover the left-hand column.)*

B. *Each of the items listed below is to be substituted for* le café *in the question. The student will then give an appropriate answer modeled on the example.*

*Example:* Aimez-vous le café?
Oui, monsieur, j'aime beaucoup le café. Je prendrai du café au petit déjeuner.

| | | | |
|---|---|---|---|
| le thé | le beurre | la bouillie d'avoine | les œufs |
| les fruits | le jambon | la confiture | le pain grillé |
| la crème | les saucisses | le jus d'orange | le chocolat |
| les crêpes | les brioches | le bacon | les croissants |

C. *Complete each sentence, giving the French equivalent for "a Frenchman," "an Englishman," etc.*

Si cet homme habite à Paris, il est probablement ________.
Si cet homme habite à Londres, il est probablement ________.
Si cette femme habite à Heidelberg, elle est probablement ________.
Si cette femme habite à Madrid, elle est probablement ________.
Ce garçon est sans doute ________ puisqu'il vient de New York.
Ce garçon est sans doute ________ puisqu'il vient de Rome.
Cette jeune fille est sans doute ________ puisqu'elle vient de Moscou.
Cette jeune fille est sans doute ________ puisqu'elle vient de Montréal.

*(With a map of Europe, this exercise may be continued by listing on the blackboard: Suisse, Belge, Hollandais, Breton, Gascon, etc. The instructor points to a city and has the student give a sentence like those above.)*

**D.** *Use each of the following nouns in turn as subject and choose, from among the four endings given, the one which most appropriately completes the sentence.*

| | | | |
|---|---|---|---|
| l'amour | la haine | la miséricorde | |
| la diligence | l'ignorance | l'intempérance | ... est à désirer. |
| le lait | la bonté | la sagesse | ... est à éviter. |
| les œufs | le pain | le bonheur | ... est nourrissant. |
| le repos | les légumes | l'esclavage | ... sont nourrissants. |
| la pauvreté | le malheur | la liberté | |
| la beauté | les fruits | | |

**E.** *Supply the proper form of the definite article in the following sentences. Make the contractions* au, aux, du, *and* des *where appropriate.*

________ français est une de ________ langues vivantes. C'est ________ langue que nous étudions dans cette classe. ________ professeur explique à ________ élèves toutes ________ difficultés. Les élèves posent à ________ professeur des questions sur ________ leçon qu'ils ont étudiée. Ensuite ils font ________ exercices de ________ livre. Quelquefois ________ élèves vont à ________ tableau pour écrire ________ phrases. Mais plus souvent ________ classe répète oralement ________ phrases. Le professeur dit ≪Bien≫ à ________ élève qui fait bien ________ exercice, et il corrige ________ fautes de ________ élève qui ne le fait pas bien. Chaque membre de ________ classe doit parler français aussi à ________ maison, s'il veut bien parler.

**F.** *Each of the items below is to be substituted for* du café *in the question. As in the example, two students will answer, – the first affirmatively and the second negatively.*

*Example:* Voulez-vous du café, monsieur (madame, mademoiselle)?
Oui merci, donnez-moi du café, s'il vous plaît.
Non merci, je ne désire pas de café en ce moment.

| | | | |
|---|---|---|---|
| du lait | du vin | des gâteaux | des pommes frites |
| du raisin | de la bière | de la sauce | de la viande |
| de l'eau | du pain | du chocolat | du thé |
| des bonbons | de la salade | de la soupe | |

G. *Supply* de, du, de l', de la, *or* des *as required in the following sentences.*

1. Les élèves apportent ________ livres, ________ encre et ________ papier. 2. Ils n'apportent pas ________ sandwichs parce qu'on leur sert ________ soupe et ________ pain pour le déjeuner. 3. J'ai vu ________ bons films au cinéma l'année dernière. 4. Il n'y a pas ________ théâtre dans notre village. 5. Nous avons eu ________ difficulté à comprendre cela. 6. Il y a ________ jours où l'on n'a pas envie de travailler. 7. Elle m'a demandé ________ argent pour acheter ________ café et ________ lait. 8. On leur a servi ________ viande et ________ pommes frites, mais il n'y avait pas ________ vin.

H. *Answer each question affirmatively, giving a complete sentence. Repeat, answering in the negative.*

1. Aimez-vous le café?
2. Voudriez-vous du café?
3. Est-ce que la beauté est toujours appréciée?
4. Votre bonne aime-t-elle le travail?
5. Votre bonne a-t-elle acheté de la viande?
6. Connaissez-vous le lieutenant Colbert?
7. Etudient-ils le russe cette année-ci?
8. Aime-t-il beaucoup le chocolat?
9. Allez-vous prendre du chocolat?
10. Est-ce que ces magasins sont ouverts le dimanche?
11. Est-ce que l'automne est la saison qu'ils préfèrent?
12. Le pain et le sel sont-ils les symboles de l'hospitalité?
13. Vous ont-ils offert du vin et des gâteaux? (*Use* ne ... ni ... ni *if answer is negative.*)
14. Est-ce qu'on a servi de bons gâteaux?
15. Votre père est-il médecin?
16. Voulez-vous de l'eau chaude?
17. Les avez-vous vus à l'école?
18. Se lave-t-il toujours les mains et la figure sans résistance?
19. Cette belle jeune fille est-elle Américaine?
20. A-t-elle besoin d'argent à présent?
21. Est-ce que ça vous fait mal à la jambe?
22. Connaît-il bien la France, l'Espagne et le Portugal?
23. A-t-il voyagé en France, en Espagne et au Portugal?

**I.** *Read aloud, substituting names from the list below for* France *or* Canada. *(Remember: Names ending in* –e [*except* Mexique] *are feminine.)*

(a) La France est un beau pays. Ils aiment la France. Ils viennent de France. Ce sont des produits de France. Nous allons en France.
(b) Le Canada est un beau pays. Ils aiment le Canada. Ils viennent du Canada. Ce sont des produits du Canada. Nous allons au Canada.

| | | | |
|---|---|---|---|
| la Grèce | le Danemark | l'Angleterre | la Norvège |
| la Suisse | l'Espagne | le Portugal | la Chine |
| le Pérou | le Mexique | l'Italie | le Japon |
| le Maroc | les Etats-Unis | la Belgique | la Hollande |
| l'Allemagne | la Yougoslavie | le Brésil | la Russie |

**J.** *Read aloud, supplying the appropriate prepositions and articles where needed.*

1. L'été prochain nous allons visiter ________ Angleterre, ________ Belgique et ________ Danemark. 2. Nous passerons un mois ________ Angleterre, quinze jours ________ Belgique et huit jours ________ Danemark. 3. Pour le voyage de retour, nous partirons ou ________ Danemark ou ________ Belgique. 4. Ils cherchent ________ bonheur dans un pays lointain. 5. Préférez-vous ________ grandes villes ou ________ campagne? 6. On ne sert pas ________ cocktails dans un café. 7. On me dit aussi qu'il y a des restaurants où l'on ne sert pas ________ thé. 8. On nous a servi ________ café et ________ excellentes pâtisseries. 9. Qu'est-ce qui forme la frontière entre ________ Europe et ________ Afrique? 10. Est-ce que le lac Huron se trouve ________ Canada, ________ Etats-Unis, ou entre les deux? 11. S'il a vraiment besoin ________ argent, je lui en donnerai. 12. Nous avons passé ________ temps à chercher ________ souvenirs. 13. J'ai trouvé ________ livres que j'aime beaucoup. 14. Y a-t-il ________ viande dans ce potage? 15. Voulez-vous acheter pour moi ________ pain, ________ légumes et ________ glace? 16. Il y a d'excellentes boutiques sur ________ boulevard Haussmann. 17. Elles ont accepté avec ________ enthousiasme.

K. *Repeat each sentence, substituting in turn the subjects in parentheses.*

Pierre se lave les mains. (Nous, Vous, Marie, Tu, Je, Les garçons)
Je lui lave les mains. (Sa mère, Nous, Tu, Marie, Vous, Ses sœurs)
Marie s'est coupé le doigt. (Vous, Je, Nous, Pierre, Tu, Les garçons)
On lui a coupé le doigt. (Je, Tu, Quelqu'un, Pierre, Vous, Nous)

*(Repeat, using other parts of the body:* les cheveux, le cou, les oreilles, les genoux, le front, le nez, la figure, le menton, *etc.)*

*Supplementary Written Exercises for Lesson 1 are on p. 102.*

# LESSON 2

## *Meaning of Colloquial*

## *Verb Tenses of the Indicative**

### PATTERN SENTENCES

#### Simple Tenses

*Present Indicative* **(Présent de l'Indicatif)**†

| | |
|---|---|
| 1. **Je les attends tous les jours.** | I wait for them every day. |
| 2. **Ils finissent leur travail en ce moment.** | They are finishing their work right now. |
| 3. **Comprend-elle la question?** | Does she understand the question? |
| 4. **Etes-vous prêt?** | Are you ready? |
| 5. **Nous avons assez de temps pour cela.** | We have enough time for that. |
| 6. **Je ne vais pas à l'école aujourd'hui.** | I am not going to school today. |

* See pp. 161-164 for literary tenses.

† The names of the tenses are given in both languages so that students may easily identify them, no matter which names they learned in their preceding course.

*Imperfect Indicative* **(Imparfait de l'Indicatif)**

| | |
|---|---|
| 7. **Les attendiez-vous tous les jours?** | Did you wait for them every day? |
| 8. **Nous finissions toujours notre travail avant de rentrer à la maison.** | We always used to (We would always) finish our work before returning home. |
| 9. **Elle ne comprenait jamais ses explications.** | She never understood his explanations. |
| 10. **Etais-tu dans le bâtiment quand tu es tombé?** | Were you in the building when you fell? |
| 11. **Nous avions des amis nommés Durand.** | We had some friends named Durand. |
| 12. **J'allais à l'école quand j'ai vu l'accident.** | I was going to school when I saw the accident. |

*Future* **(Futur)**

| | |
|---|---|
| 13. **Il dit qu'il le fera.** | He says that he will do it. |
| 14. **Choisira-t-il le cadeau quand il sera de retour?** | Will he choose the gift when he gets back? |
| 15. **Si sa lettre arrive aujourd'hui, j'y répondrai immédiatement.** | If his letter arrives today, I'll answer it immediately. |

*Conditional* **(Conditionnel)**

| | |
|---|---|
| 16. **A-t-il dit qu'il le ferait?** | Did he say that he would do it? |
| 17. **Je ne savais pas si elle arriverait à l'heure.** | I didn't know whether she would arrive on time. |
| 18. **Si vos amis étudiaient tous les jours, ils n'auraient pas de difficulté.** | If your friends studied every day, they would not have any difficulty. |

## Compound Tenses

*Past Indefinite* **(Passé Composé)**

| | |
|---|---|
| 19. **Elle a déjà lu ce livre.** | She has already read that book. |

| | |
|---|---|
| 20. **Je les ai vus très souvent.** | I have seen them very often. |
| 21. **Il est entré sans frapper.** | He entered without knocking. |
| 22. **Nous n'avons pas compris cette explication.** | We didn't understand that explanation. |
| 23. **Pourquoi es-tu sorti hier soir?** | Why did you go out last night? |

*Pluperfect Indicative* **(Plus-que-parfait de l'Indicatif)**

| | |
|---|---|
| 24. **Je lui avais expliqué cela avant de le quitter.** | I had explained that to him before leaving him. |
| 25. **Votre sœur était déjà partie avant notre arrivée.** | Your sister had already left before our arrival. |
| 26. **Les aviez-vous connus avant leur visite?** | Had you known (met) them before their visit? |
| 27. **Si elle y avait été, je l'aurais vue.** | If she had been there, I would have seen her. |

*Future Perfect* **(Futur Antérieur)**

| | |
|---|---|
| 28. **Nous aurons étudié cela avant la fin du cours.** | We shall have studied that before the end of the course. |
| 29. **Aura-t-il reçu le message avant son retour?** | Will he have received the message before he returns? (his return) |
| 30. **Aussitôt que j'aurai fini ce livre, je vous le prêterai.** | As soon as I have finished this book, I'll lend it to you. |

*Past Conditional* **(Conditionnel Passé)**

| | |
|---|---|
| 31. **Je me demande s'il aurait accepté ce changement.** | I wonder whether he would have accepted that change. |
| 32. **Si vous aviez pris votre billet d'avance, vous n'auriez pas manqué le train.** | If you had bought your ticket in advance, you wouldn't have missed the train. |
| 33. **Ils seraient restés à l'hôtel s'ils n'avaient pas reçu le coup de téléphone.** | They would have stayed at the hotel if they had not received the telephone call. |

## NOTES

(a) Generally speaking, the use of the French verb tenses corresponds to that of English; but some difficulty springs from the fact that French does not have any "progressive" forms and has no auxiliary which corresponds to the English verb *do.* [ex. 2, 3, 6, 7, 12, 16, 17, 22, 23]

(b) The three most difficult tenses (present indicative, imperfect indicative, past indefinite) are considered in detail in Lesson 3. Here it is sufficient to notice the following:

(1) The French present indicative corresponds to three different forms of the present in English. [ex. 1-6]
(2) The French imperfect indicative corresponds to four different forms of the past in English. [ex. 7-12]
(3) The French past indefinite corresponds to the English present perfect, and to the simple past and emphatic past when they express a single unit of action. [ex. 19-23]

(c) Notice that in French the future and the future perfect correspond to the English present and present perfect, respectively, when used after the conjunctions **quand, lorsque, aussitôt que, dès que, tant que,** and **pendant que** when reference is to future time. [ex. 14, 30]

(d) Although *would* is used in English as the auxiliary of the conditional [ex. 16-18], it also has other meanings; therefore some English verbs in the *would*... form do not correspond to the conditional in French. [ex. 8] See also Les. 3, Note (a).

## EXERCISES

A. *For each of the English versions of the Pattern Sentences give the French equivalent. (Cover the left-hand column.)*

**B.** *Repeat these sentences, observing the relationship between the tense of the verb and the meaning of the modifying word, phrase, or clause.*

Je fais cela en ce moment.
Je faisais cela tous les jours.
Je faisais cela quand le message est arrivé.
J'ai fait cela hier soir.
Je ferai cela demain.
Je ferais cela si c'était permis.

*Following the patterns above, use the appropriate tense of each verb below according to the cue from the list on the right.*

J'écris cela ...
Vous écoutez cela ...
Tu lis cela ...
Nous buvons cela ...
Pierre étudie cela ...
Les élèves mangent cela ...

... en ce moment.
... tous les jours.
... quand le message est arrivé.
... hier soir.
... demain.
... si c'était permis.

**C.** *Change the French sample sentence to correspond to each English form.*

*Sample:* Je le vois. (I see it.)

I am seeing it.
I have seen it.
I saw it yesterday.
I used to see it often.
I will see it tomorrow.
I would see it . . .
I had seen it . . .
I will have seen it . . .
I would have seen it . . .

Variations:
(1) *Repeat, changing the subject pronoun to* vous, il, elle, nous, ils.
(2) *Repeat, changing the verb to* lire, trouver, entendre, faire.
(3) *Repeat, making sentences negative.*
(4) *Repeat, making sentences interrogative.*

*Sample:* J'y vais souvent. (I go there often.)

I am going there tomorrow.
I have gone there.
I went there yesterday.
I was going there . . .
I used to go there often.
I will go there tomorrow.
I would go there . . .
I had gone there . . .
I will have gone there . . .
I would have gone there . . .

Variations:
(1) *Repeat, changing the subject pronoun to* vous, il, elle, nous, ils.
(2) *Repeat, changing the verb to* retourner *and then* descendre (to stay [at a hotel]).
(3) *Repeat, making sentences negative.*
(4) *Repeat, making sentences interrogative.*

*Sample:* S'il travaille il gagnera l'argent. (If he works he will earn the money.)

If he worked he would earn the money.
If he had worked he would have earned the money.

Variation:
*Repeat, changing the subject pronouns to* vous, jc, cllc, nous, ils.

*Sample:* S'il part de bonne heure, il arrivera à temps. (If he leaves early, he will arrive in time.)

If he left early, he would arrive in time.
If he had left early, he would have arrived in time.

Variation:
*Repeat, changing the subject pronouns to* vous, je, elle, nous, ils.

D. *Answer in French with a complete sentence, including all details mentioned in the question. Pay close attention to the tenses of the verbs.*

1. Travaille-t-il tous les jours?
2. Est-ce que nous étudierons cela l'année prochaine?
3. Qui lui avait expliqué cela? (*answer:* Jean ... )
4. Y alliez-vous tous les soirs?
5. Vous aurait-il permis de le faire?
6. Les avait-on reçus avant cela?
7. Aviez-vous beaucoup d'amis à l'école?
8. Qui a répondu à la lettre? (*answer:* Jean ... )
9. Si elle reste ici, sera-t-elle contente?
10. Savait-elle que cela me plairait?
11. Avez-vous vu sa nouvelle voiture?
12. Les élèves comprenaient-ils toujours les explications?
13. Le feriez-vous si vous aviez l'argent?
14. Sont-ils sortis de bonne heure?
15. Etes-vous prêt à partir?
16. Est-ce que tu aurais réussi, si elle t'avait aidé?
17. Etais-tu avec ta famille?
18. Avons-nous assez de temps?
19. Auront-ils fini cela avant vendredi?
20. Viendra-t-il ici aussitôt qu'il arrivera?

E. *Read aloud, supplying the French for the verbs in parentheses.*

1. Nous *(would go)* avec vous si nous *(had)* assez de temps.
2. S'ils *(study)* bien la leçon, ils la *(will understand)* sans difficulté.
3. Leurs amis *(used to live)* dans cette vieille maison.
4. Vous *(found)* votre montre, n'est-ce pas?
5. Je le *(will see)* demain, je crois.
6. Elle *(will have finished)* tout ce travail avant midi.
7. Si je *(had left)* plus tôt, je *(would have arrived)* à l'heure.
8. Qui *(saw)* le film qui passe au Paramount?
9. Pendant que nous *(were traveling)* en Europe, le reste de la famille *(was)* à notre camp dans le Vermont.
10. Quand je *(see)* Françoise, je lui *(will tell)* ce que vous avez dit.

*Supplementary Written Exercises for Lesson 2 on pp. 102-103.*

# LESSON 3

## *Uses of the Present, Imperfect, and Past Indefinite*

### PATTERN SENTENCES

*Comparison of the Present* **(le Présent)** *and the Imperfect* **(l'Imparfait)**

| | |
|---|---|
| 1. **Je lis le journal tous les jours.** | I read the paper every day. |
| 2. **Je lisais le journal tous les jours avant de sortir.** | I used to (would) read the paper every day before going out. |
| 3. **Lisez-vous beaucoup de romans?** | Do you read many novels? |
| 4. **Lisiez-vous beaucoup de romans à cet âge?** | Did you read many novels at that age? |
| 5. **Elle ne lit pas assez.** | She doesn't read enough. |
| 6. **Elle ne lisait pas assez quand elle était à l'école.** | She didn't read enough when she was in school. |
| 7. **Il lit le journal en ce moment.** | He is reading the paper now. |
| 8. **Il lisait le journal quand je suis entré.** | He was reading the paper when I came in. |
| 9. **Il lit cette leçon depuis deux heures.** | He has been reading this lesson for two hours. |

| | |
|---|---|
| 10. **Il lisait cette leçon depuis deux heures quand enfin il a commencé à la comprendre.** | He had been reading this lesson for two hours when finally he began to understand it. |
| 11. **Les récits de ses voyages sont intéressants.** | The accounts of his travels are interesting. |
| 12. **Les récits de ses voyages étaient intéressants.** | The accounts of his travels were interesting. |
| 13. **Il ne fait pas si froid aujourd'hui.** | It is not so cold today. |
| 14. **Le vent doux murmurait dans les arbres.** | The gentle wind murmured in the trees. |

*Comparison of the Imperfect* **(l'Imparfait)** *and the Past Indefinite* **(le Passé Composé)**

| | |
|---|---|
| 15. **Nous voulions faire cela.** | We wanted to do that. |
| 16. **Nous avons décidé de faire cela.** | We decided to do that. |
| 17. **J'avais peur d'y aller.** | I was afraid to go there. |
| 18. **J'ai refusé d'y aller.** | I refused to go there. |
| 19. **Tout le monde savait qu'il pouvait le faire.** | Everybody knew that he could do it. |
| 20. **Il a pu le faire presque sans effort.** | He was able to do it (He succeeded in doing it) almost effortlessly. |
| 21. **Il lisait toujours sa leçon.** | He always read his lesson. |
| 22. **Il a lu la leçon avant de sortir.** | He read the lesson before he went out. |
| 23. **Les Grecs admiraient la beauté.** | The Greeks admired beauty. |
| 24. **Nous avons admiré surtout les peintures de la première salle.** | We admired especially the paintings in the first room. |
| 25. **J'étais avec lui quand il a téléphoné.** | I was with him when he telephoned. |
| 26. **Je regardais le groupe de touristes quand tout à coup j'ai reconnu votre cousin.** | I was looking at the group of tourists when suddenly I recognized your cousin. |
| 27. **Où alliez-vous quand je vous ai vu?** | Where were you going when I saw you? |
| 28. **Où êtes-vous allé hier soir?** | Where did you go last night? |
| 29. **Ils vivaient en paix avec les sauvages.** | They lived in peace with the savages. |

| | |
|---|---|
| 30. **S'il y pensait assez longtemps, il trouverait une solution.** | If he thought about it long enough, he would find a solution. |
| 31. **Ils ont fondé les premières colonies du nouveau monde.** | They founded the first colonies in the new world. |
| 32. **J'ai vu plusieurs voitures comme celle-là.** | I have seen several cars like that one. |
| 33. **Elle a dégà passé tous ses examens.** | She has already taken her exams. |

*Imperfect* **(l'Imparfait)** *Used to Propose an Action*

| | |
|---|---|
| 34. **Si nous y allions ensemble!** | Suppose we go there together. |
| 35. **Si elle revenait à deux heures!** | Suppose she comes back (Have her come back) at two o'clock. |

## NOTES

(a) In French the present indicative and the imperfect indicative express similar concepts, such as:

(1) actions which are customary or habitual [ex. 1-6]
(2) ideas that are purely descriptive [ex. 11-14]
(3) expressions corresponding to the English progressive forms [ex. 7-10]

| | |
|---|---|
| He is reading . . .<br>He has been reading . . . | **Il lit ...** |
| He was reading . . .<br>He had been reading . . . | **Il lisait ...** |

Notice the use of **depuis** to express *for* in sentences of the type represented by Pattern Sentences 9 and 10. The corresponding interrogative form is:

| | |
|---|---|
| **Depuis quand faites-vous cela?** | How long have you been doing that? |

(b) To distinguish between the imperfect and the past indefinite, remember these characteristics illustrated by the sentences above:

(1) The imperfect tells how things were, what was going on, what used to happen. Where it expresses action, the speaker is viewing the action *in progress,* not as a completed unit. It gives the background. It is used to express the condition in a conditional sentence. [ex. 30] Its emphasis is *descriptive.*

(2) The past indefinite tells specific things that happened. It expresses an action as a completed unit; the time limit is expressed or implied by the context. It is also used, like the English present perfect, to express a past action which is viewed in relationship to the present. [ex. 32, 33] Its emphasis is *narrative.*

(c) The imperfect introduced by **si** is used to propose an action. [ex. 34, 35]

## EXERCISES

**A.** *For each of the English versions of the Pattern Sentences give the French equivalent. (Cover the left-hand column.)*

**B.** *Repeat each sentence, changing the verb to the imperfect.*

*Examples:* Je ne sais pas cela. – Je ne savais pas cela.
Ils arrivent toujours de bonne heure. – Ils arrivaient toujours de bonne heure.

1. Elle s'appelle Jeanne.
2. Il fait beau.
3. Nous sommes contents d'être de retour.
4. Sa sœur n'aime pas les mathématiques.
5. Il est onze heures du soir.
6. Ils veulent vous plaire.
7. J'y vais le mercredi.
8. Il n'étudie pas assez.
9. A quelle heure te lèves-tu le matin?
10. Vous les recevez souvent, n'est-ce pas?

C. *Answer these questions in the affirmative, using complete sentences.*

1. Avez-vous fini votre lettre?
2. Etait-il à la maison quand vous avez téléphoné?
3. Est-elle ici depuis longtemps?
4. Etait-elle ici depuis longtemps avant votre arrivée?
5. Votre ami allait-il à cette école-ci?
6. M. Duval a-t-il décidé d'acheter la voiture?
7. Connaissez-vous la maison où nous habitions?
8. Avais-tu peur quand tu étais perdu dans le désert?
9. Avez-vous trouvé le stylo dans le tiroir?
10. Savait-il ce qu'elles voulaient?

*Repeat the above, giving answers in the negative.*

D. *Repeat each of the following sentences with each of the endings given. Use the present, the imperfect, or the past indefinite of the verb, as required to correspond to the ending.*

Je fais le devoir ...
Nous écoutons ce programme ...
Il écrit une lettre ...
Allez-vous au café ...?
Ils lisent le journal ...
Ma sœur met le couvert ...
Ces garçons sortent ...

... en ce moment.
... quand le téléphone a sonné.
... hier soir.
... tous les soirs autrefois.

E. *Give the French for the following:*

He is buying the book. He was buying the book. He has bought the book.

They fill the glasses. They used to fill the glasses. They have filled the glasses.

Do you always answer (*répondre à*) his letters? Did you always answer his letters? Have you always answered his letters?

The students are eating lunch (*prendre le déjeuner*). The students were eating lunch. The students have eaten lunch.

I live in Paris. I used to live in Paris. I have never lived in Paris.

She doesn't receive many letters. She didn't use to receive many letters. She hasn't received many letters.

I am not listening to the television. I was not listening to the television. I have never listened to the television.

**F.** *Give the French for the following:*

I studied that lesson yesterday.
I studied when I had the time.

He went to Paris yesterday.
He went to Paris when he had the time.

Did you take the examinations last week?
Did you take the examinations in the spring every year?

They arrived last week.
They arrived in the spring every year.

We lived in New York three years.
We lived in New York when I was little.

**G.** *Express each of the following sentences using* depuis *instead of* il y a *or* il y avait. *Make the necessary changes in word order as in the examples below.*

*Examples:* Il y a deux heures que je l'attends. *(Change to)* Je l'attends depuis deux heures. (I have been waiting for him for two hours.)

Il y avait deux heures que je les attendais quand le train est arrivé. *(Change to)* Je les attendais depuis deux heures quand le train est arrivé. (I had been waiting for them for two hours when the train arrived.)

Il y a quelques mois que nous habitons à Bordeaux.
Il y a longtemps qu'il travaille dans ce magasin.
Il y a vingt minutes que je les cherche.
Il y a plus de trois ans qu'elle étudie le français.
Il y a plusieurs années que je la connais.
Il y avait trois semaines que nous habitions à Paris quand vous êtes venu.

Il y avait longtemps qu'il travaillait dans ce magasin quand il a reçu cette offre.

Il y avait vingt minutes que je les cherchais quand mon frère a dit qu'il les avait.

**H.** *In the following narration, change the verbs to appropriate past tenses.*

Il est quatre heures et demie de l'après-midi. Il y a dans la chambre cinq ou six garçons qui lisent le journal ou écoutent la radio. Ils ont l'air tout à fait content. Mais, au milieu de ce contentement indolent, on entend tout à coup des pas lourds dans le couloir. C'est M. Durand qui vient voir si le travail continue comme d'habitude. On se lève vite. Ceux qui lisent cachent les journaux. On ferme la radio, et tout le monde se met à étudier. M. Durand frappe à la porte, puis sans attendre, il l'ouvre.

—Ca va, mes enfants? demande-t-il.

—Oui, monsieur, répondent-ils tous ensemble.

Ensuite, leur donnant un de ses sourires machinaux, il ferme la porte et s'en va.

**I.** *Complete each sentence using the imperfect or the past indefinite of the verb indicated, as appropriate.*

1. (habiter) Nous ________ cette maison quand j'étais petit.
2. (vouloir) Je ________ les connaître un peu mieux.
3. (expliquer) Le professeur ________ tout cela hier.
4. (arriver) Pierre ________ toujours le premier.
5. (entendre) Vous ________ ce qu'il m'a dit ce matin.
6. (voir) Mes amis ________ ce film quand ils étaient à Paris.
7. (partir) Je ________ le treize septembre.
8. (être) Tous les élèves ________ dans la salle de classe.
9. (connaître) Tu ________ tous les professeurs, n'est-ce pas?
10. (aller) Nous y ________ l'été dernier.
11. (avoir) Louise ________ froid pendant tout le voyage.
12. (sortir) A cet âge-là, vous ________ tous les soirs, n'est-ce pas?

*Supplementary Written Exercises for Lesson 3 are on p. 103.*

# LESSON 4

## *Personal Pronouns*

| FUNCTION | 1ST PERSON | | 2ND PERSON | | 3RD PERSON | | | |
|---|---|---|---|---|---|---|---|---|
| | SING. | PLUR. | SING. FAM. | SING. POL., PLUR. FAM. AND POL. | SING. | | PLUR. | |
| | | | | | *m.* | *f.* | *m.* | *f.* |
| SUBJECT | **je** | **nous** | **tu** | **vous** | **il** | **elle** | **ils** | **elles** |
| DIRECT OBJ. | **me** | **nous** | **te** | **vous** | **le** | **la** | **les** | |
| IND. OBJ. | **me** | **nous** | **te** | **vous** | **lui** | | **leur** | |
| REFLEXIVE | **me** | **nous** | **te** | **vous** | **se** | | **se** | |
| EMPHATIC* | **moi** | **nous** | **toi** | **vous** | **lui** | **elle** | **eux** | **elles** |

## PATTERN SENTENCES

### *First and Second Person, Direct and Indirect Objects*

1. **Il m'a choisi pour le poste.** — He chose me for the position.
2. **Il m'a donné le poste.** — He gave me the position. (He gave the position to me.)

* Pronouns here called "emphatic" are also called "disjunctive," "prepositional," or "without-verb." See pp. 128-129 for detailed explanation.

| | |
|---|---|
| 3. **T'a-t-il choisi pour le poste?** | Did he choose you for the position? |
| 4. **T'a-t-il donné le poste?** | Did he give you the position? |
| 5. **Il nous a choisis pour les postes.** | He chose us for the positions. |
| 6. **Il nous a donné les postes.** | He gave us the positions. |
| 7. **Il ne vous a pas choisi pour le poste.** | He didn't choose you for the position. |
| 8. **Il ne vous a pas donné le poste.** | He didn't give you the position. |
| 9. **Appelez-moi à dix heures.** | Call me at ten o'clock. |
| 10. **Donnez-moi ce livre, s'il vous plaît.** | Give me that book, please. |
| 11. **Ne m'appelez pas avant dix heures.** | Don't call me before ten o'clock. |
| 12. **Ne me donnez pas ce livre-là.** | Don't give me that book. |
| 13. **Lave-toi avant de t'habiller.** | Wash before you get dressed. |
| 14. **Ne t'habille pas avant de te laver.** | Don't get dressed before you wash. |
| 15. **Lave-toi bien les mains.** | Wash your hands well. |

*Third Person Direct Objects*

| | |
|---|---|
| 16. **Je le vois souvent.** | I see him (it) often. |
| 17. **Je la vois souvent.** | I see her (it) often. |
| 18. **Je les ai vus hier soir.** | I saw them last night. |

*Third Person Indirect Objects*

| | |
|---|---|
| 19. **Je lui ai montré la chambre.** | I showed him the room. (I showed the room to him.) |
| 20. **Je lui ai montré la chambre.** | I showed her the room. |
| 21. **Je lui ai montré la chambre, à elle.** | I showed her the room. *(emphatic pronoun added for clarity)* |
| 22. **Je ne leur ai pas montré la chambre.** | I didn't show them the room. |

*Third Person Direct Object with Indirect Object of First or Second Person*

| | |
|---|---|
| 23. **Mon père me le donnera.** | My father will give it (*m.*) to me. |
| 24. **Mon père me la donnera.** | My father will give it (*f.*) to me. |

| | |
|---|---|
| 25. **Mon père me les donnera.** | My father will give them to me. |
| 26. **Ton père te le donnera.** | Your father will give it to you. |
| 27. **Ton père te la donnera.** | Your father will give it to you. |
| 28. **Est-ce que ton père te les donnera?** | Will your father give them to you? |
| 29. **Nos parents nous le donneront.** | Our parents will give it to us. |
| 30. **Nos parents nous la donneront-ils?** | Will our parents give it to us? |
| 31. **Nos parents nous les donneront.** | Our parents will give them to us. |
| 32. **Vos parents vous le donneront.** | Your parents will give it to you. |
| 33. **Vos parents ne vous la donneront pas.** | Your parents will not give it to you. |
| 34. **Vos parents vous les donneront.** | Your parents will give them to you. |
| 35. **Montrez-le-moi.** | Show it to me. |
| 36. **Ne me le montrez pas.** | Don't show it to me. |
| 37. **Montrez-les-nous.** | Show them to us. |
| 38. **Ne nous les montrez pas.** | Don't show them to us. |

*Two Pronoun Objects both of Third Person*

| | |
|---|---|
| 39. **Mon père le lui donnera.** | My father will give it to him (her). |
| 40. **Votre père la lui donnera.** | Your father will give it to him. |
| 41. **Son père les lui donnera.** | His father will give them to him. |
| 42. **Son père les lui donnera.** | Her father will give them to her. |
| 43. **Nos parents le leur donneront.** | Our parents will give it to them. |
| 44. **Vos parents la leur donneront.** | Your parents will give it to them. |
| 45. **Leurs parents les leur donneront.** | Their parents will give them to them. |
| 46. **Montrez-la-lui.** | Show it (*f.*) to him (her). |
| 47. **Ne la lui montrez pas.** | Don't show it to him. |
| 48. **Montrons-les-lui.** | Let's show them to him. |
| 49. **Ne les lui montrons pas.** | Let's not show them to him. |
| 50. **Montrez-le-leur.** | Show it to them. |
| 51. **Ne le leur montrez pas.** | Don't show it to them. |
| 52. **Montrez-les-leur.** | Show them to them. |
| 53. **Ne les leur montrez pas.** | Don't show them to them. |

*Third Person Indirect Objects with Direct Object of First or Second Person*

| | |
|---|---|
| 54. **Je me suis présenté à lui.** | I introduced myself to him. |
| 55. **Je me suis présenté à elle.** | I introduced myself to her. |
| 56. **Il m'a présenté à eux.** | He introduced me to them (*m. or mixed*). |
| 57. **Je te présenterai à elles.** | I'll introduce you to them (*f.*). |
| 58. **Qui vous a présentés à lui?** | Who introduced you to him? |
| 59. **Nous nous sommes présentés à eux.** | We introduced ourselves to them. |

*Objects of Prepositions*

| | |
|---|---|
| 60. **Venez-vous avec moi ce matin?** | Are you coming with me this morning? |
| 61. **Oui, je viens avec vous.** | Yes, I am coming with you. |
| 62. **Alors, mon petit, après le déjeuner je vais m'occuper de toi.** | Well then, my child, after lunch I'm going to attend to you. |
| 63. **Voulez-vous aller chez elle ou chez lui?** | Do you want to go to her house or his house? |
| 64. **Il a fait tout cela pour nous.** | He did all that for us. |
| 65. **Etes-vous revenu sans eux?** | Did you come back without them? |
| 66. **Qui sont ces gens derrière elles?** | Who are those people behind them (*f.*)? |

*Compound Subjects and Objects*

| | |
|---|---|
| 67. **Vous et moi pourrons faire cela.** | You and I will be able to do that. |
| 68. **J'y suis allé avec Jean et lui.** | I went there with John and him. |
| 69. **J'ai vu lui et elle hier soir.** | I saw him and her last night. |
| 70. **Où les avez-vous vus, lui et elle?** | Where did you see him and her? |

*Predicate Pronouns with* **c'est**

| | |
|---|---|
| 71. **Je ne sais pas si c'était vous ou lui.** | I don't know whether it was you or he. |
| 72. **C'est moi qui dois le faire.** | It is I who must do it. (I am the one who must do it.) |

73. **Ce n'est pas nous qui avons écrit cette lettre; ce sont eux qui l'ont écrite.** It isn't we who wrote that letter; it's they who wrote it. (We're not the ones who wrote that letter; they're the ones who wrote it.)

*Third Person Object, Reflexive*

74. **Elle s'est levée très tard ce matin.** She got up very late this morning.
75. **Ils se sont expliqué leurs problèmes.** They explained their problems to each other.
76. **Ce jeune homme s'est présenté à nous.** This young man introduced himself to us.

## NOTES

(a) From the table it is apparent that the personal pronoun objects present real variations only in the third person.

(1) The French for *we* or *us* is always **nous.**

(2) The French for *you* is always **vous** (except for the familiar singular: **tu, te, toi** [see p. 126]).

(3) **Me** and **te** are used only as objects directly *before the verb.* **Moi** and **toi** are used in all other cases,* that is, in any emphatic position. [ex. 9, 10, 13, 15, 35, 60, 62, 67, 72]

(b) Note that when a direct object *precedes* the verb in a compound tense, the past participle agrees with the object in gender and number. [ex. 1, 5, 7, 18, 54-56, 58, 59, 70, 73, 74, 76] This affects the pronunciation only when **-e** or **-es** is added to a previously silent final consonant. [ex. 73]

(c) As indirect object **lui** means either *to him* or *to her.* [ex. 19, 20, 39-42, 46-49] In cases where the context would not make the reference clear, the preposition **à** and a disjunctive pronoun are added. [ex. 21]

*Except when followed by **en** or **y** in the affirmative imperative. (**Donnez-m'en!** *Give me some!* **Va-t'en!** *Go away!*)

(d) After prepositions [ex. 60-66], in compound subjects and objects [ex. 67-70], or in positions separated from the verb [ex. 21, 54-66] only emphatic (disjunctive) pronouns are used. See also pp. 128-129.

(e) When the direct object of the verb is **se** or a pronoun of the first or second person, the indirect object is expressed by an emphatic pronoun after **à**. [ex. 54-59, 76]

(f) The reflexive **se** does not change for gender or number, and may be either direct or indirect object. [ex. 74-76]

(g) In the other persons (first and second) the reflexive objects are the same as the other object forms. [ex. 13-15, 54, 55, 59, 62]

For *details* on the position of pronoun objects see pp. 127-128.

## EXERCISES

For the mastery of French pronoun objects, the goal of the English-speaking student must be the achievement of automatic response. Therefore a great many manipulative drills are included in this lesson. It is recommended that such practice be repeated throughout the course until control of the patterns is firmly established.

**A.** *For each of the English versions of the Pattern Sentences give the French equivalent. (Cover the left-hand column.)*

**B.** *Repeat each sentence, changing the verb to the negative.*

*Examples:* Il te connaît. – Il ne te connaît pas.
Ma mère lui parle. – Ma mère ne lui parle pas.
Je les ai achetés. – Je ne les ai pas achetés.
L'avez-vous compris? – Ne l'avez-vous pas compris?

1. Je le vois souvent.
2. Vous leur écriviez.
3. Elle me choisit.
4. Ils nous punissent.

5. Tu lui as expliqué cela.
6. Nous les avons finis.
7. Est-ce que tu l'as appris?
8. Je leur ai montré la chambre.
9. Il vous a envoyé la lettre.
10. Leur a-t-il dit cela?

**C.** *Repeat each sentence, changing the verb to the past indefinite.*

*Examples:* Je le vois. – Je l'ai vu.
Elle ne me comprend pas. – Elle ne m'a pas compris.
Où les achète-t-il? – Où les a-t-il achetés?
Qui lui dit cela? – Qui lui a dit cela?

1. Nous l'apprenons.
2. Elle me voit.
3. Vous les mettez sur la table.
4. Tu ne lui parles pas.
5. Je ne leur réponds pas.
6. M. Dumont nous invite à la fête.
7. Les lisez-vous?
8. Le comprennent-ils?
9. Qui te dit cela?
10. Pourquoi la croyons-nous?

**D.** *Repeat each sentence, replacing the noun direct object by a pronoun.*

*Examples:* Je connais ce garçon. – Je le connais.
Ils ont vendu la pendule. – Ils l'ont vendue.
Tu ne choisis pas ces livres. – Tu ne les choisis pas.
Achetons-nous les articles? – Les achetons-nous?

1. Elle comprend la leçon.
2. Vous voyez le magasin.
3. Tu connais mon ami.
4. Nous cherchons les souliers.
5. Je répète la phrase.
6. Ils achètent les livres.
7. Vous avez vendu la voiture.
8. J'ai étudié les leçons.

9. Elles ont visité le village.
10. Il a choisi les cadeaux.
11. Nous ne comprenons pas la leçon.
12. Elle n'a pas vu ce magasin.
13. Je n'ai pas écrit les lettres.
14. Vois-tu cet homme?
15. Connaissez-vous cette femme?
16. Ont-ils vendu ces articles?

E. *Answer in the affirmative, replacing the noun direct object by a pronoun.*

*Examples:* Connaît-il cette jeune fille? – Oui, monsieur, il la connaît.
Ont-ils compris le problème? – Oui, monsieur, ils l'ont compris.
Est-ce que j'ai invité ces gens-là? – Oui, monsieur, vous les avez invités.

1. Comprend-il le problème?
2. Voyez-vous cette maison-là?
3. Ecrivent-elles les lettres?
4. Prends-tu l'autobus?
5. Conduisez-vous la voiture?
6. Ont-ils reçu le cadeau?
7. Avez-vous vu la photo?
8. A-t-elle invité ses amis?
9. As-tu vendu le chapeau?
10. Est-ce que je connais ces gens?

*Repeat the exercise, answering in the negative.*

F. *Repeat each sentence, replacing the noun indirect object by a pronoun.*

*Examples:* Vous parlez au directeur. – Vous lui parlez.
J'ai écrit à mes amis. – Je leur ai écrit.
As-tu donné cela à Jean? – Lui as-tu donné cela?
On n'a pas lu la lettre aux étudiants. – On ne leur a pas lu la lettre.

1. Je parle souvent à Pierre.
2. Vous écrivez à votre mère.
3. Ils disent cela aux élèves.
4. Nous donnons cela à M. Dupont.
5. On montre la chambre aux étudiants.
6. Explique-t-on cela aux parents?
7. Tu as dit cela à ma sœur.
8. J'ai montré cela à vos enfants.
9. Avez-vous parlé de cela au professeur?
10. A-t-elle expliqué cela à ses amies?
11. Nous ne lisons pas cela aux enfants.
12. Je n'ai jamais écrit à mon frère.

**G.** *Answer in the affirmative, replacing the noun indirect object by a pronoun.*

*Examples:* Montre-t-il la chambre aux touristes? – Oui, monsieur, il leur montre la chambre.
Avez-vous donné cela à votre père? – Oui, monsieur, je lui ai donné cela.
Est-ce que j'ai dit cela aux autres élèves? – Oui, monsieur, vous leur avez dit cela.

1. Parle-t-il souvent à Marie?
2. Ecrivez-vous à M. Durand?
3. Disent-ils cela à leurs enfants?
4. Lit-elle cela aux autres étudiantes?
5. As-tu montré le livre à ton ami?
6. Avons-nous écrit à Mme Martin?
7. Est-ce que j'ai expliqué cela aux élèves?
8. A-t-on donné cela au général?

*Repeat the exercise, answering in the negative.*

**H.** *Read each group aloud at a normal rate. Then re-read, making the pronoun substitutions indicated at the right.*

Je le lui ai donné. *2nd time – change* le *to* la

Je le lui avais donné. *3rd time – change* le *to* les
Je le lui donnerai. *4th time – change* lui *to* leur
*5th time – change* le *to* les *and* lui *to* leur

Je ne le lui ai pas donné. *Make the same changes as above.*
Je ne le lui avais pas donné.
Je ne le lui donnerai pas.

| | |
|---|---|
| Qui vous l'a donné? | vous *to* nous |
| Qui vous l'avait donné? | vous *to* me |
| Qui vous le donnera? | le *to* la |
| Qui vous l'avait donné? | le *to* les |

| | |
|---|---|
| Elle ne me l'a pas donné. | me *to* nous |
| Elle ne me l'avait pas donné. | me *to* vous |
| Elle ne me le donnera pas. | le *to* la |
| | le *to* les |

| | |
|---|---|
| Donnez-le-moi. | le *to* la |
| Ne me le donnez pas. | le *to* les |
| | moi (me) *to* nous |
| | le *to* les *and* moi (me) *to* nous |

I. *Following the pattern of the example, supply the missing pronoun objects.*

*Example:* Où est-il? Montrez-*le*-moi. *Le* voici. *(One student may give the first two parts and another student the third.)*

Où est-elle? Montrez- __________ -moi. __________ voici.
Où sont-ils? Montrez- __________ -moi. __________ voici.
Où sont-elles? Montrez- __________ -moi. __________ voici.
Où est la maison? Montrez- __________ -moi. __________ voilà.
Où sont les livres? Montrez- __________ -moi. __________ voilà.
Où êtes-vous? Je ne __________ vois pas. __________ voici.
Où es-tu? Je ne __________ vois pas. __________ voici.
Où est ton frère? Je ne __________ vois pas. __________ voilà.
Où est ta sœur? Je ne __________ vois pas. __________ voilà.
Où sont vos amis? Je ne __________ vois pas. __________ voilà.

J. *Repeat each sentence, replacing the noun direct object by a pronoun.*

*Examples:* Il nous montre le magasin. – Il nous le montre.
Je lui lis ces histoires. – Je les lui lis.
Qui vous a dit ces nouvelles? – Qui vous les a dites?
Nous leur avons écrit la lettre. – Nous la leur avons écrite.

1. Je te donne ce livre-là.
2. Elle me montre les photos.
3. On nous dit cette nouvelle.
4. Il vous envoie ces livres.
5. Tu m'as écrit cette lettre.
6. Il t'a expliqué le problème.
7. Qui m'a donné ces cadeaux?
8. Je vous ai lu les nouvelles.
9. Vous nous avez montré la maison.
10. On lui promet le poste.
11. Je leur explique la leçon.
12. Vous lui avez donné ces livres.
13. Nous leur avons montré les cadeaux.
14. Elle lui a écrit la lettre.

*(In which cases above is the spelling of the verb affected? The pronunciation?)*

K. *Repeat each sentence, replacing the noun indirect object by a pronoun.*

*Examples:* Il le montre au général. – Il le lui montre.
Je les lis aux enfants. – Je les leur lis.
Nous l'avons écrite à nos parents. – Nous la leur avons écrite.

1. Je l'explique à Pierre.
2. Elle les montre aux autres élèves.
3. Nous la donnons à nos enfants.
4. Vous le dites à la jeune fille.
5. Il l'a écrite à son frère.
6. Tu les as lues à ces étudiants.

7. Ils les ont envoyés à leur mère.
8. Nous l'avons montré à ces gens-là.

**L.** *Use the words listed, in turn, to complete the question. In the two-part answer use only pronouns, as in the example.*

*Example:* Est-il allé chez Françoise? Non, il n'est pas allé chez elle. Il est allé chez vous.

| | | |
|---|---|---|
| Est-il allé chez ________? | Jean<br>lui<br>nous<br>eux<br>elle<br>votre oncle<br>moi<br>vous<br>elles<br>Marie<br>les Dupont | Non, il n'est pas allé chez ________. Il est allé chez ________. |

*(This exercise may be varied by changing the subject* [êtes-vous allé, sont-ils allés, *etc.*]*.)*

**M.** *Use the words listed, in turn, to complete the question. In answering use only pronouns.*

| | | |
|---|---|---|
| Est-ce que Martine est avec ________? | Paul<br>Louise<br>vous<br>ses frères<br>toi<br>Paul et Jean<br>Marie et Jeanne<br>ses parents<br>Jean et vous | Non, elle n'est pas avec ________. |

*(This exercise may also be varied by changing the question to* Voyage-t-il, Parliez-vous, *etc.)*

N. *Answer each question in the affirmative, using complete sentences and substituting pronouns for the italicized words. Repeat, giving negative answers.*

1. A-t-il acheté *la voiture?* 2. Avez-vous vu *Jacques et son frère?* 3. Aiment-ils *ce pays sauvage?* 4. A-t-on annoncé *les nouveaux cours?* 5. Est-ce que j'ai mis *mon livre* sur le piano? 6. Votre sœur a-t-elle écrit *à sa tante?* 7. Voulez-vous parler *au directeur?* 8. Vont-ils envoyer cela *à leurs parents?* 9. Vous a-t-on raconté *cette histoire incroyable?* 10. Nous ont-ils livré *les paquets* ce matin? 11. Lui avez-vous dit *la bonne nouvelle?* 12. A-t-il montré *sa bicyclette à son cousin?* 13. Ont-ils donné *l'argent aux enfants?* 14. Enverrez-vous *les revues à Jean et moi?* 15. Vous a-t-il expliqué *cette leçon?*

O. *Read aloud, then re-read, changing the italicized nouns to pronouns.*

1. J'écrirai *les lettres* dès que j'arriverai à Londres. 2. Qui a perdu *cette montre d'or?* 3. Vous verrez *la pièce amusante* si vous allez au théâtre. 4. Avez-vous pris *les billets?* 5. Elle a déjà expliqué cela *aux enfants.* 6. Il n'avait pas encore reçu *les cadeaux.* 7. Qui les a envoyés *à M. Durand?* 8. On vous rendra *le stylo* après la classe. 9. Elle va montrer *la lettre à sa mère.* 10. Mon père a vendu *son bateau à Jean et Marie.*

*Supplementary Written Exercises for Lesson 4 are on p. 103.*

# LESSON 5

## *Demonstrative Adjectives and Pronouns*

| | ADJECTIVES | | PRONOUNS | |
|---|---|---|---|---|
| MASC. SING. | **ce, cet** | this, that | **celui** | this (one), that (one), the one |
| FEM. SING. | **cette** | | **celle** | |
| MASC. PLUR. | **ces** | these, those | **ceux** | these, those, the ones |
| FEM. PLUR. | **ces** | | **celles** | |
| NEUTER | | | **ceci** this **cela (ça)** that | |

## PATTERN SENTENCES

*Demonstrative Adjectives*

1. **Il fait beau ce matin.** — The weather is nice this morning.
2. **Il fait chaud cet après-midi.** — It's warm this afternoon.
3. **Cette femme est la concierge.** — This woman is the concierge.

| | |
|---|---|
| 4. **Connaissez-vous cette église?** | Do you know that church? |
| 5. **Ces livres sont très lourds.** | These books are very heavy. |
| 6. **Qui a acheté ces oranges?** | Who bought those oranges? |
| 7. **Je n'aime pas ce livre-ci.** | I don't like this book. |
| 8. **Cet enfant-là ne comprend pas du tout.** | That child doesn't understand at all. |
| 9. **Cette voiture-ci est-elle plus longue que cette voiture-là?** | Is this car longer than that car? |
| 10. **Je crois que ces hommes-ci travaillent mieux que ces hommes-là.** | I believe that these men work better than those men. |

**Ce** *used as Subject of* **être**

| | |
|---|---|
| 11. **C'est lui qui l'a envoyé.** | He's the one who sent it. (It is he who sent it.) |
| 12. **C'est nous qu'ils ont vus.** | We're the ones they saw. (It is we whom they saw.) |
| 13. **Ce sont elles qui l'ont dit.** | They're the ones who said so. (It is they who said it.) |
| 14. **Ah! C'est toi, mon vieux!** | Ah! It's you, old chap! (old man, pal, fellow, etc.) |
| 15. **Qui est cet homme? C'est le nouveau professeur.** | Who is that man? He's the new teacher. |
| 16. **Est-ce Marie qui vient d'entrer? Oui, c'est Marie.** | Is it Mary who just came in? Yes, it's Mary. |
| 17. **Ce sont mes amis Paul et Jean.** | They are my friends Paul and John. |
| 18. **Voulez-vous bien le faire? Ce ne sera pas difficile.** | Will you do it? It won't be hard. |
| 19. **Il doit offrir de les aider. C'est le moins qu'il peut faire.** | He ought to offer to help them. It's the least he can do. |
| 20. **Je ne comprends pas exactement tout ce qu'il dit, mais c'est intéressant.** | I don't understand exactly all that he is saying, but it is interesting. |

*Demonstrative Pronouns*

| | |
|---|---|
| 21. **J'ai lu son premier livre et aussi celui qu'il a écrit après son exil.** | I have read his first book and also the one he wrote after his exile. |

22. **Il n'était pas sûr si c'était la voiture de Jean ou celle de son frère.** He wasn't sure whether it was John's car or his brother's.
23. **J'aime beaucoup la plupart des films français, mais je n'aime pas ceux de cette compagnie-là.** I like most French movies very much, but I don't like those of that company. (I don't like that company's.)
24. **Ces peintures-ci me semblent meilleures que celles que nous avons vues hier.** These paintings seem better to me than those we saw yesterday.
25. **Voici les deux stylos. Celui-ci coûte beaucoup plus que celui-là.** Here are the two pens. This one costs a lot more than that one.
26. **Cette leçon-ci est plus difficile que celle-là.** This lesson is more difficult than that one.
27. **Ma mère m'a donné toutes ces cravates. Aimez-vous celle-ci?** My mother gave me all these ties. Do you like this one?
28. **Nous avons étudié plusieurs romans du 19$^{e}$ siècle et d'autres du 20$^{e}$ siècle. J'ai trouvé ceux-ci moins intéressants que ceux-là.** We studied several novels of the 19th century and others of the 20th century. I found the latter less interesting than the former.

*The Neuter (Indefinite) Demonstratives*

29. **Ecoutez bien ceci; c'est très important.** Listen carefully to this; it's very important.
30. **Merci bien, je ne savais pas cela (ça).** Thank you, I didn't know that.
31. **Qu'est-ce que c'est que cela (ça)?** What's that?
32. **Ça? C'est la plume de ma tante!** That? That's my aunt's pen!
33. **Cela ne leur plaît pas.** They don't like that. (That doesn't please them.)

## NOTES

(a) With the demonstrative adjectives, **-ci** is added for *this, these,* and **-là** for *that, those,* when required for emphasis, clarity, or comparison. [ex. 7-10, 23, 24, 26]

(b) Notice the following cases where **ce** (rather than **il, elle, ils, elles**) is used as the subject of **être.**

(1) Always when **être** is followed by a predicate pronoun. [ex. 11-14]
(2) Generally when **être** is followed by a predicate noun. [ex. 15-17, 22, 32] See also pp. 130-132.
(3) When referring to a previously mentioned action or idea. [ex. 18-20, 29]

(c) The form of the demonstrative pronoun **(celui, celle, ceux,** or **celles)** is in agreement with the preceding noun for which it stands (the "antecedent"). [ex. 21-28]

(d) **Celui, celle, ceux, celles** are never used without a modifier–either a dependent clause [ex. 21, 24], a phrase [ex. 22, 23], or the particles **-ci** and **-là.** [ex. 25-28]

(e) The demonstrative pronoun with **-ci** may mean *the latter* and with **-là,** *the former.* [ex. 28]

(f) Since French has no possessive form for nouns, the demonstrative pronoun with the preposition **de** and its object expresses this concept. [ex. 22, 23]

(g) The neuter pronouns **ceci** and **cela (ça)** are not used when there is a specific antecedent (which would determine gender and number); they are normally used to stand for a whole idea or action, or for an object which the speaker has not yet identified by a name. **Ça,** the shortened form of **cela,** is not used in formal language. [ex. 29-33]

## EXERCISES

**A.** *For each of the English versions of the Pattern Sentences give the French equivalent. (Cover the left-hand column.)*

**B.** *Read aloud the sample sentence, then substitute in turn each of the nouns below for* livre, *making any other changes entailed by the substitution.*

*Sample:* Ce livre-ci est celui que vous cherchez.

| | | | |
|---|---|---|---|
| la maison | la voiture | l'article *(m.)* | le disque |
| le journal | l'hôtel *(m.)* | la femme | l'ami |
| l'homme | le magasin | la jeune fille | l'amie |
| l'île *(f.)* | la revue | la boutique | la rue |

*Repeat, using the plural of each noun.*

**C.** *Repeat the following question and answer, substituting in turn each of the nouns listed below for* pays, *making any other changes entailed by the substitution.*

*Question:* Aimez-vous ce pays-ci?
*Answer:* Non, je préfère celui que nous avons visité la semaine dernière.

| | | | |
|---|---|---|---|
| le parc | la région | le musée | l'endroit *(m.)* |
| la ville | le quartier | l'église *(f.)* | le monument |
| l'école *(f.)* | le village | le château | la boutique |

*Repeat, using the plural of each noun.*

**D.** *Do as in exercise* **C** *above, substituting the nouns listed for the italicized noun in the question.*

(1) Parlez-vous de ce *pays*-ci? Non, je parle de celui-là.

| | | |
|---|---|---|
| la chambre | l'avenue *(f.)* | le bureau |
| l'hôtel *(m.)* | le salon | la bouteille |

(2) Pensez-vous à ce *bâtiment-ci?* Non, je pense à celui de notre ville.

| | | |
|---|---|---|
| la gare | la place | le pont |
| le marché | le théâtre | l'immeuble *(m.)* |

(3) Avez-vous votre *livre?* Non, mais j'ai celui de Maurice.

| | | |
|---|---|---|
| la voiture | le cahier | le vélo |
| l'appareil *(m.)* | la grammaire | la valise |

*Repeat, changing the nouns to the plural. In* (3) *change the answer to* Non, mais nous avons ________ des Dupont.

E. *Read aloud, using* ce, ceci, *or* cela (ça) *in the blank.*

1. Je vais y aller à pied. ________ est le moyen le plus rapide.
2. Qui vient d'entrer? ________ est mon camarade René.
3. Est-ce vous qu'on a demandé? Non, ________ n'est pas moi.
4. Voulez-vous m'aider? Je ne comprends pas ________ .
5. Ecoutez. Avez-vous jamais entendu ________ ?
6. Vous êtes-vous bien amusé hier soir? Oui, ________ a été épatant.
7. ________ sont toujours Jean et Françoise qui ne veulent jamais rien faire.
8. Vous allez passer les vacances à la montagne? ________ sera très agréable.
9. Qui vous a dit ________ ?
10. Voyez-vous cette voiture? ________ est la Renault de mon oncle.
11. Qu'est-ce que c'est que ________ ?
12. ________ est une carte de France.

*Supplementary Written Exercises for Lesson 5 are on pp. 103-104.*

# LESSON 6

## *Relative and Interrogative Pronouns*

The relative and interrogative pronouns are grouped together because part of the difficulty that they offer is in distinguishing, where necessary, the two uses. Studying and practicing them together makes possible a clearer understanding and a surer command.

Compare the following table of the most common forms of the two.

| | RELATIVE | INTERROGATIVE |
|---|---|---|
| | *who, whom (that)* | *who? whom?* |
| SUBJECT | **qui** | **qui?** |
| OBJECT | **que** | **qui?** |
| OBJ. OF PREP. | **qui** | **qui?** |
| | *which, that* | *what?* |
| SUBJECT | **qui** | **qu'est-ce qui?** |
| OBJECT | **que** | **que, qu'est-ce que?** |
| OBJ. OF PREP. | **lequel**, etc. | **quoi?** |

Where the preposition involved is **de**, the special relative pronoun **dont** is generally used instead of **de qui** or **duquel**, etc.

## PATTERN SENTENCES

*Subject of Verb*

| | |
|---|---|
| 1. **Qui a apporté ce paquet?** | Who brought this parcel? |
| 2. **Je n'ai pas vu l'homme qui l'a apporté.** | I didn't see the man who brought it. |
| 3. **Qui sont ces gens?** | Who are these people? |
| 4. **Ce sont les visiteurs qui viennent d'arriver.** | They are the visitors who have just arrived. |
| 5. **Qu'est-ce qui cause ces accidents?** | What causes those accidents? |
| 6. **Avez-vous trouvé des livres qui expliquent cela?** | Have you found any books which explain that? |
| 7. **Qu'est-ce qui t'inquiète?** | What worries you? |
| 8. **Je n'ai pas vu le camion qui l'a apporté.** | I didn't see the truck that brought it. |

*Object of Verb*

| | |
|---|---|
| 9. **Qui a-t-on interrogé?** | Whom did they question? |
| 10. **On a interrogé la femme que la bonne a signalée.** | They questioned the woman (whom) the maid pointed out. |
| 11. **Qui Robert cherche-t-il?** | For whom is Robert looking? (Whom is Robert seeking?) |
| 12. **Il cherche les jeunes filles qu'il a vues hier.** | He is looking for the girls (whom) he saw yesterday. |
| 13. **Qu'avez-vous apporté?** | What did you bring? |
| 14. **Voici les paquets que j'ai apportés.** | Here are the parcels (that) I brought. |
| 15. **Qu'est-ce qu'il a mentionné?** | What did he mention? |
| 16. **Où est le livre qu'il a mentionné?** | Where is the book (which) he mentioned? |

*Object of Preposition*

| | |
|---|---|
| 17. **Avec qui avez-vous fait ce voyage?** | With whom did you take that trip? |
| 18. **Je vais vous présenter l'ami avec qui j'ai fait le voyage.** | I am going to introduce to you the friend with whom I took the trip. |
| 19. **Pour qui a-t-il acheté cela?** | For whom did he buy that? |
| 20. **Vous connaissez bien la personne pour qui il a acheté cela.** | You are well acquainted with the person for whom he bought that. |
| 21. **Avec quoi ont-ils fait cette expérience?** | With what did they do that experiment? |
| 22. **Je lui ai montré la machine avec laquelle ils ont fait ces expériences.** | I showed him the machine with which they did those experiments. |
| 23. **Sur quoi a-t-il basé ses soupçons?** | Upon what did he base his suspicions? |
| 24. **Voici les renseignements sur lesquels il a basé ses soupçons.** | Here is the information upon which he based his suspicions. |
| 25. **A quoi pensait-elle tout à l'heure?** | What was she thinking about a little while ago? |
| 26. **Celui-ci n'est pas le plan auquel elle pensait.** | This (one) is not the plan of which she was thinking. |
| 27. **De qui parliez-vous tout à l'heure?** | Of whom were you speaking a little while ago? |
| 28. **Marie est-elle la jeune fille dont vous parliez?** | Is Mary the girl of whom you were speaking? |
| 29. **A qui est cette voiture?** | Whose car is this? |
| 30. **On a trouvé le monsieur dont la voiture a été démolie.** | They found the gentleman whose car was wrecked. |
| 31. **De quoi avez-vous besoin?** | What do you need? |
| 32. **Voilà justement le chapeau dont j'ai besoin.** | There is just the hat (that) I need. |
| 33. **Voyez-vous cette grange à côté de laquelle se trouve le tracteur rouge?** | Do you see that barn with the red tractor beside it? |

## NOTES

(a) Only **lequel** varies in gender and number for agreement with its antecedent. In the masculine singular and in the plural it combines with the prepositions **à** and **de**. [ex. 22, 24, 26, 33]

| | | | |
|---|---|---|---|
| *m.s.* | **lequel** | **auquel** | **duquel** |
| *f.s.* | **laquelle** | **à laquelle** | **de laquelle** |
| *m.pl.* | **lesquels** | **auxquels** | **desquels** |
| *f.pl.* | **lesquelles** | **auxquelles** | **desquelles** |

(b) The relative pronoun may not be omitted in French, whereas in English the object forms *whom, that,* and *which* are often omitted. [ex. 10, 12, 14, 16, 32]

(c) Notice in Pattern Sentence 29 the use of **à** with the verb **être** to denote ownership. [See also Les. 9: 15-18.]

(d) The English *whose,* as a relative, is translated into French by **dont** [ex. 30] ; but the student will have a better understanding of the variations of word order with **dont** if he remembers that **dont** retains its basic meaning: *of whom, of which.*

| | |
|---|---|
| **Voici le garçon dont vous avez lu la composition.** | Here is the boy whose composition you read.<br>Here is the boy *of whom* you read the composition. |

Note also that **dont** is not used with compound prepositions ending in **de (à côté de, auprès de**, etc.). [ex. 33]

(e) Notice that the interrogatives **que** and **qu'est-ce que** differ only in the word order of the question. With **que** the subject and verb are inverted. [ex. 13, 15]

(f) Notice that the translation of *who* in all cases may be **qui.**

See also pp. 132-134.

## EXERCISES

A. *For each of the English versions of the Pattern Sentences give the French equivalent. (Cover the left-hand column.)*

B. *Combine the two sentences using* qui *to introduce the subordinate clause.*

*Examples:* Il connaissait la personne. Cette personne a dit cela.
Il connaissait la personne qui a dit cela.
Nous désirons les chambres. Ces chambres donnent sur le lac.
Nous désirons les chambres qui donnent sur le lac.

1. J'ai rencontré l'homme. Cet homme a gagné le prix.
2. Vous verrez les jeunes filles. Ces jeunes filles habitent ici.
3. Elles ont invité les garçons. Ces garçons sont arrivés ce matin.
4. Nous admirons la femme. Cette femme a écrit ces articles.
5. Voici le livre. Ce livre explique tout cela.
6. Qui a vu l'accident? Cet accident a causé les dommages.
7. As-tu acheté la peinture? Cette peinture était dans la devanture.
8. On n'achète pas les choses. Ces choses coûtent trop cher.

C. *Combine the two sentences using* que *to introduce the subordinate clause.*

*Examples:* Je n'aime pas la robe. Elle porte cette robe.
Je n'aime pas la robe qu'elle porte.
Il a écrit aux gens. Marie connaît ces gens.
Il a écrit aux gens que Marie connaît.

1. Elles admirent l'acteur. Les critiques ont choisi cet acteur.
2. Ce ne sont pas les élèves. Nous avons vu ces élèves.
3. J'ai parlé avec le médecin. Vous avez recommandé ce médecin.
4. Ils avaient oublié la femme. Pierre voulait inviter cette femme.
5. Nous finirons les lettres. Ils attendent ces lettres.
6. Tu conduis la voiture. Ta sœur a acheté cette voiture.
7. Elle comprend le problème. Son père lui a expliqué ce problème.
8. Vous avez reçu le cadeau. Il a envoyé ce cadeau.

D. *Form an appropriate relative clause introduced by* dont *from each of the sentences below. Begin your sentence with* C'est le ... , C'est la ... , Ce sont les ... , *as in the following three examples.*

*Examples:* Nous parlions de cette question. – C'est la question dont nous parlions.
Ils ont besoin de ce stylo. – C'est le stylo dont ils ont besoin.
Vous étiez fier de ces élèves l'année dernière. – Ce sont les élèves dont vous étiez fier l'année dernière.

1. Vous souffrez de cette maladie.
2. Ils attendent tout de ce gouvernement.
3. Nous profitons de ce commerce.
4. Il semblait content de cette photo.
5. Je me lassais autrefois de ces études.
6. Elle s'ennuyait autrefois de ces sports.
7. Tu t'occupes de ces préparatifs.
8. On se moquait de leurs menaces.
9. Vous aurez besoin de ces renseignements.
10. Ils ont pris congé de leur ami.

E. *Combine the following pairs of sentences, using the appropriate relative pronoun to replace the italicized words.*

*Examples:* Voici mon cousin Jean. *Jean* nous a envoyé ce cadeau.
Voici mon cousin Jean qui nous a envoyé ce cadeau.
Voici l'élève. Vous cherchiez *cet élève.*
Voici l'élève que vous cherchiez.
Voici l'élève. Vous parliez de *cet élève* tout à l'heure.
Voici l'élève dont vous parliez tout à l'heure.

J'ai vu mon oncle Jules. *L'oncle Jules* demeure à New York.
J'ai vu la personne. Elle a décrit *cette personne.*
J'ai vu la personne. Elle a parlé à *cette personne.*

Où est le train? *Ce train* part à onze heures.
Où est le train? Vous m'avez recommandé *ce train.*
Où est le train? On a parlé de *ce train* dans l'article.

Voilà les journaux. Votre père a apporté *ces journaux.*
Voilà les journaux. *Ces journaux* racontent tous les événements.
Voilà le journal. J'ai vu l'article dans *ce journal.*

Ils n'ont pas acheté la voiture. Vous êtes venu à Paris dans *cette voiture.*
Ils n'ont pas acheté la voiture. Ils ont examiné *cette voiture* hier.
Ils n'ont pas acheté la voiture. *Cette voiture* était dans l'exposition.

Nous avons rencontré les femmes. *Ces femmes* étaient au café hier soir.
Nous avons rencontré les femmes. Albert parlait avec *ces femmes* au café.
Nous avons rencontré les femmes. Nous avions vu *ces femmes* au café.

Avez-vous étudié la leçon? Nous avons *cette leçon* pour demain.
Avez-vous étudié la leçon? Le professeur parlera de *cette leçon* demain.
Avez-vous étudié la leçon? *Cette leçon* explique ce principe-là.

Je connais bien ce garçon. *Ce garçon* vient de descendre à notre hôtel.
Je connais bien ce garçon. On a trouvé *ce garçon* dans le parc.
Je connais bien ce garçon. La mère de *ce garçon* vient d'entrer.

Il a perdu le stylo. Le général Dumont a signé le traité avec *ce stylo.*
Il a perdu le stylo. Vous lui aviez donné *ce stylo.*
Il a perdu le stylo. *Ce stylo* était dans sa poche.

C'est la même jeune fille. Robert a vu *cette jeune fille* au bal.
C'est la même jeune fille. *Cette jeune fille* est dans notre classe.
C'est la même jeune fille. Hélène a passé quinze jours chez *cette jeune fille.*

Cet homme-là est le grand avocat. Vous avez entendu beaucoup d'éloges de *cet avocat.*
Cet homme-là est le grand avocat. On a nommé *cet avocat* ministre de la justice.

Cet homme-là est le grand avocat. *Cet avocat* a prononcé le discours principal.

Il m'a montré la solution du problème. Je pensais à *ce problème.*
Il m'a montré la solution du problème. Le professeur nous avait posé *ce problème.*
Il m'a montré la solution du problème. *Ce problème* nous inquiétait.

**F.** *Use* qui, qu'est-ce qui, que, *or* qu'est-ce que, *as appropriate, to introduce each question.*

1. ________ a dit cela?
2. ________ vous donnera l'argent?
3. ________ leur fait croire cela?
4. ________ fait tourner le monde?
5. ________ a-t-on choisi pour le poste?
6. ________ va-t-elle inviter au bal?
7. ________ avez-vous fait?
8. ________ nous avons commandé?
9. ________ a-t-il dit?
10. ________ ils ont acheté?
11. ________ vous apprenez dans cette classe?
12. ________ lui a-t-il promis?

**G.** *Use* qui *or* quoi, *as appropriate, to complete each question.*

1. A ________ a-t-elle envoyé la lettre?
2. De ________ avons-nous besoin pour les réparations?
3. Sur ________ allez-vous poser cette lourde statue?
4. Avec ________ ont-ils fait le voyage?
5. De ________ s'agit-il?
6. De ________ faut-il prendre congé avant de partir?
7. A ________ pensent les jeunes gens au printemps?
8. Sur ________ comptez-vous pour vous aider?
9. Avec ________ faut-il mêler le vin?
10. A ________ as-tu révélé notre secret?

**H.** *Make up a question for which each of the following sentences might be a direct answer. Use an interrogative pronoun in place of the italicized words.*

*Examples: Charles* m'a envoyé cette photo. – Qui vous a envoyé cette photo?
Je cherche *une bonne bicyclette.* – Que cherchez-vous?
Il a commandé cela pour *sa sœur.* – Pour qui a-t-il commandé cela?
*L'auberge* se trouve au pied de la montagne. – Qu'est-ce qui se trouve au pied de la montagne?

1. *Mon oncle* m'a donné cette montre.
2. Mon oncle m'a donné *cette montre.*
3. *Le docteur Bertin* a dit qu'elle est très malade.
4. Le docteur Bertin a dit *qu'elle est très malade.*
5. *Maurice* va faire ce voyage avec les Dupont.
6. Maurice va faire ce voyage avec *les Dupont.*
7. *Sa température* indique qu'il va mieux.
8. On va informer *son père* de l'accident.
9. On va informer son père de *l'accident.*
10. Je désire *un peu plus de temps.*
11. J'ai acheté ce cadeau pour *Louise.*
12. Ils ont choisi *le lieutenant Arras* pour le poste.
13. *M. Durand* est le propriétaire de cette boutique.
14. Nous avons acheté *une nouvelle voiture.*
15. Elles ont parlé des *problèmes économiques.*
16. Il va écrire une composition sur *les causes des crises politiques.*
17. Il faut donner cet argent à *M. Duval.*
18. *La nouvelle machine* rend possible cette immense production.
19. *La maladie du roi* a causé ce retard.
20. Ma sœur habite chez *des amis de mon père.*
21. Pierre a fait cela avec *les outils que vous lui avez donnés.*
22. Ce livre est à *moi.*

I. *Read aloud, using* qui, que, *or* dont *to fill the blanks.*

1. ________ vous a dit cela? 2. Je ne connais pas l'homme ________ lui a dit cela. 3. C'est un homme ________ nous avons vu au théâtre. 4. A ________ l'avez-vous raconté? 5. Je ne sais pas à ________ je l'ai raconté. 6. Chez ________ sont-ils allés? 7. De ________ parliez-vous tout à l'heure? 8. Je désire voir l'agent de police ________ vous parliez. 9. Pour ________ a-t-il

acheté ce stylo? 10. Je ne connais pas la personne pour ________ il l'a acheté. 11. Connaissez-vous l'artiste ________ la peinture a gagné le prix? 12. Avec ________ êtes-vous allé à l'exposition? 13. ________ l'agent de police a-t-il arrêté? 14. On a mentionné plusieurs personnes ________ il a arrêtées. 15. Voilà la jeune fille ________ on a admiré la robe.

J. *Express the French for* what, which, *or* of which *in the following sentences.*

1. Voici la lettre ________ mon père m'a envoyée. 2. De ________ parle-t-il dans cette lettre? 3. C'est la même lettre dans ________ il a mentionné l'accident. 4. ________ a-t-il dit? 5. ________ a causé cet accident? 6. Parlez-vous de l'accident ________ a eu lieu la semaine dernière? 7. Avec ________ a-t-on réparé la voiture? 8. Voici quelques outils avec ________ on a fait les réparations. 9. Je connais très bien l'endroit ________ il a parlé. 10. ________ désirez-vous à présent? 11. ________ votre ami a vu dans la rue? 12. Je crois que c'était un chapeau ________ il a vu. 13. On nous a posé des questions ________ étaient assez difficiles. 14. ________ vous a impressionné le plus? 15. Voilà la machine ________ vous aurez besoin pour ce travail. 16. ________ le professeur vous a demandé de faire?

*Supplementary Written Exercises for Lesson 6 are on p. 104.*

# LESSON 7

## *Special Relatives and Interrogatives*

### PATTERN SENTENCES

*The Relative Pronoun* **où**

| | |
|---|---|
| 1. **Je me rappelle le jour où votre frère est arrivé.** | I remember the day when your brother arrived. |
| 2. **Vous n'étiez pas là au moment où l'accident est arrivé.** | You weren't there at the time when the accident happened. |
| 3. **Voici une boutique où vous trouverez d'excellents articles.** | Here is a shop where (in which) you will find some excellent articles. |
| 4. **Je leur ai montré la table où je l'avais mis.** | I showed them the table on which (where) I had put it. |

*Relative Pronouns Which Include Their Own Antecedent*

| | |
|---|---|
| 5. **On essaie de découvrir ce qui a causé l'accident.** | They are trying to discover what caused the accident. |
| 6. **Je vais vous dire ce que l'agent de police a dit.** | I am going to tell you what the policeman said. |

| | |
|---|---|
| 7. **Nous leur avons donné ce dont ils avaient besoin.** | We gave them what they needed. |
| 8. **Tout ce qui brille n'est pas or.** | All that glitters is not gold. |
| 9. **J'ai déjà dépensé tout ce que mon père m'a donné.** | I have already spent all that my father gave me. |
| 10. **Elle nous a révélé tout ce dont elle avait peur.** | She revealed to us everything (that) she was afraid of. |

*The Interrogative Adjective*

| | |
|---|---|
| 11. **Quel titre a-t-il donné à son livre?** | What title did he give his book? |
| 12. **Quel est le titre de son livre?** | What is the title of his book? |
| 13. **Quelle explication a-t-on trouvée?** | What explanation have they found? |
| 14. **Quelle est l'explication de ce phénomène?** | What is the explanation of this phenomenon? |
| 15. **Quels romans avez-vous choisis?** | What (which) novels did you choose? |
| 16. **Quels sont les romans que vous avez choisis?** | Which are the novels that you selected? |
| 17. **Quelles nations vont participer à ce programme?** | What (which) nations are going to participate in this program? |
| 18. **Quelles sont les nations qui vont participer à ce programme?** | Which are the nations that are going to participate in this program? |

*What (kind of thing) is . . .*

| | |
|---|---|
| 19. **Qu'est-ce que c'est qu'un roman?** | What is a novel? |
| 20. **Qu'est-ce que c'est qu'une nation?** | What is a nation? |
| 21. **Qu'est-ce que c'est que la philosophie?** | What is philosophy? |
| 22. **Qu'est-ce que c'est?** | What is it? |
| 23. **Qu'est-ce que tout cela?** | What is all that? |

*The Interrogative Pronoun* **lequel**

| | |
|---|---|
| 24. **Laquelle de ces nations est la plus forte?** | Which (one) of these nations is the strongest? |
| 25. **Lequel de ces titres préférez-vous?** | Which (one) of these titles do you prefer? |
| 26. **Désirez-vous cette photo? Laquelle?** | Do you want this picture? Which one? |
| 27. **Voici tous les romans que nous avons lus. Lesquels préférez-vous?** | Here are all the novels that we have read. Which ones do you prefer? |
| 28. **A laquelle de mes sœurs voulez-vous parler?** | To which (one) of my sisters do you wish to speak? |
| 29. **Duquel de ces chevaux parlez-vous?** | Which (one) of these horses are you talking about? |
| 30. **Avant de vous décider, auxquels de ces projets avez-vous pensé?** | Before making up your mind, which (ones) of these plans did you think about? |

## NOTES

(a) **Où** is used as a relative adverbial pronoun when the antecedent is a noun of time or place. [ex. 1-4] With nouns of time, **où** *(when)* is used almost exclusively; but with nouns of place to express *where, in which,* etc., the regular prepositional forms **(dans lequel, sur laquelle,** etc.) are frequently used.

(b) The distinctions between **ce qui, ce que,** and **ce dont** (meaning *what* or *that which*) are the same as for the simple relatives **qui** *(subj.),* **que** *(obj.),* and **dont (de +** *obj.*). The relative after **tout** always takes one of these compound forms **(tout ce qui,** etc. *all that, everything that).* [ex. 5-10]

(c) *What* or *which* as an adjective is rendered by **quel. Quel** has four forms to agree in gender and number with the noun to which it refers. [ex. 11-18] To understand the adjectival nature of **quel** used with **être**, it may be useful to imagine the noun which is understood:

**Quel (titre) est le titre de son livre?**
**Quelle (explication) est l'explication de ce phénomène?** etc.

(d) When the question *What is . . . ? (What are . . . ?)* requests the definition or explanation of the thing concerned, the formula **Qu'est-ce que c'est que ... ?** is used. This formula is occasionally shortened to **Qu'est-ce que ... ?** [ex. 19-23]

(e) *Which one? (which?* as a pronoun) is rendered by the proper form of **lequel.** [ex. 24-30]

## EXERCISES

**A.** *For each of the English versions of the Pattern Sentences give the French equivalent. (Cover the left-hand column.)*

**B.** *For each question, give an answer beginning* Oui, et ... , *in which you express another idea based on that of the question.*

*Examples:* Vous rappelez-vous le jour où votre frère est arrivé?
Oui, et je me rappelle aussi le jour où il est parti.
Avez-vous trouvé la boutique où l'on vend ces gants?
Oui, et j'ai trouvé aussi une boutique où l'on vend d'excellents chapeaux.

Etiez-vous à la maison la nuit où son grand-père est mort?
A-t-elle mentionné le soir où elle a perdu son soulier au cinéma?
Ont-ils parlé de l'année où le professeur Dupont a fait son voyage?
Etiez-vous avec lui au moment où il a reçu la lettre?
Avez-vous visité la ville où j'habite?
As-tu cherché dans le tiroir où je mets les mouchoirs?
Connaissez-vous la rue où la police a trouvé la voiture?

*Repeat the questions above. Give an answer beginning* Non, mais ... , *in which you express an alternate idea, using the same form as in the question.*

*Examples:* Vous rappelez-vous le jour où votre frère est arrivé?
Non, mais je me rappelle le jour où il est allé chez le médecin.

Avez-vous trouvé la boutique où l'on vend ces gants?
Non, mais j'ai trouvé un café où la bière est excellente.

C. *Repeat each sentence, replacing the noun antecedent by* ce.

*Examples:* On fait la chose qu'on veut. – On fait ce qu'on veut.
On donne le pourboire qu'on veut. – On donne ce qu'on veut.
On mange le mets qu'on veut. – On mange ce qu'on veut.

1. On écrit l'article qu'on veut.
2. On achète la voiture qu'on veut.
3. On prend les fruits qu'on veut.
4. On lit les romans qu'on veut.
5. On boit la boisson qu'on veut.
6. On choisit le cadeau qu'on veut.
7. On paie le prix qu'on veut.
8. On étudie les matières qu'on veut.

D. *Repeat each sentence, omitting the noun antecedent and using* ce qui, ce que, *or* ce dont.

*Examples:* Qui peut expliquer la réaction qui a causé l'accident? – Qui peut expliquer ce qui a causé l'accident?
Elle sait la réponse que j'attends. – Elle sait ce que j'attends.
Je ne comprends pas les problèmes dont il parle. – Je ne comprends pas ce dont il parle.

1. Voici l'article qui vous a donné cette impression.
2. J'ai trouvé le livre qui explique cela.
3. Ta mère n'aime pas les vêtements que tu portes.
4. Il n'acceptera pas les compositions que nous écrivons.
5. Voilà la question dont nous parlions.
6. Vous avez le stylo dont j'ai besoin.
7. Nous n'achetons pas les choses qui coûtent trop cher.
8. Je n'ai pas reçu les lettres qu'elle a envoyées.

9. Elle comprend le problème que vous avez expliqué.
10. On ne sait pas les détails dont elle s'occupe.
11. Tu as vu les objets qui étaient sur la table.
12. Vous ne mentionnez jamais les exploits dont vous êtes si fier.

E. *Read aloud, using* ce qui, ce que, *or* ce dont *to fill the blanks.*

1. Je ne sais pas __________ le fait courir.
2. Savez-vous __________ ces gens désirent?
3. Il n'a pas compris __________ l'agent de police parlait.
4. Je vais vous dire __________ m'a frappé.
5. Son père lui donne tout __________ il a besoin.
6. On nous a expliqué __________ était dans le petite boîte.
7. Le professeur voulait savoir __________ les élèves avaient fait.
8. Ma mère n'a jamais dit __________ elle voulait de nous
9. Je voudrais bien savoir __________ était arrivé au petit chien.
10. Avez-vous découvert __________ ils étaient si fiers?
11. Votre oncle vous dira __________ ces garçons ont demandé.
12. Il ne va pas croire __________ j'ai appris.
13. Voilà tout __________ est nécessaire pour ce projet.
14. On nous a répété tout __________ ils se plaignaient.
15. Faites __________ vous voulez.

F. *Compose questions beginning with the appropriate forms of* quel, *for which the statements below would be answers.*

*Examples:* Nous avons la septième leçon pour aujourd'hui. – Quelle leçon avons-nous pour aujourd'hui?
Les élèves qui étudient bien l'apprennent vite. – Quels élèves l'apprennent vite?
New York est la plus grande ville des Etats-Unis. – Quelle est la plus grande ville des Etats-Unis?
La physique est la science qui traite de cela. – Quelle est la science qui traite de cela?

1. J'ai perdu mon livre de français.
2. Elle préfère cette photo-ci.
3. Nous avons choisi les marchandises de la compagnie DuPont.
4. Les élèves qui ont gagné le prix sont Marie et Joseph.
5. Le problème le plus difficile est le premier.

6. La nouvelle usine a produit ces marchandises.
7. Paris est la capitale de la France.
8. Leur plus grand désir c'est de s'évader.
9. Sa meilleure qualité c'est son intelligence.
10. Les états de Californie et de New York produisent les meilleurs vins.
11. Le titre de son article est ≪Paradoxe≫.
12. J'ai visité la France, la Belgique et la Suisse.

G. *Read aloud the following questions, supplying* qu'est-ce que c'est que *or a form of* quel.

1. ________ un continent?
2. ________ continent a le plus grand nombre d'habitants?
3. ________ est le continent dont vous parlez?
4. A ________ hôtel êtes-vous descendu?
5. ________ sont les poèmes les plus populaires?
6. ________ un poème épique?
7. ________ poèmes de Musset sont les mieux connus?
8. ________ femme avait une sœur nommée Marthe?
9. ________ une femme de chambre?
10. ________ est la femme qui a gagné le prix?
11. Dans ________ villes trouve-t-on les meilleurs musées?
12. ________ animaux habitent cette région?
13. A ________ station faut-il descendre?
14. De ________ outils avez-vous besoin?
15. ________ le patriotisme?

H. *Read aloud the statement and the question, using each noun, in turn, in the statement and the proper form of* lequel *in the question. In the questions, use the plural for items that generally come in pairs and the singular for the others.*

(1) Voici les { stylos *(m.)* / souliers *(m.)* / photos *(f.)* / livres *(m.)* / lunettes *(f.)* / chaussettes *(f.)* / cravates *(f.)* / gants *(m.)* / chemises *(f.)* } que j'ai { achetés. / achetées. } ________ préférez-vous?

(2) Il y a deux { médecins / avocats / masseuses / ingénieurs / concierges / infirmières / commerçants } dans ce bâtiment. A ______ voulez-vous parler?

*Repeat (2) using the question:* De ______ parlez-vous?
*Repeat (2) using the question:* Pour ______ travaillez-vous?

*Supplementary Written Exercises for Lesson 7 are on p. 104.*

# LESSON 8

## *Subjunctive*

### PATTERN SENTENCES

*After Verbs of Volition*

| | |
|---|---|
| 1. **Je veux qu'il comprenne mon idée.** | I want him to understand my idea. |
| 2. **On préfère que les femmes aillent les premières.** | They prefer that the women go first. |
| 3. **A-t-il demandé que vous sachiez cela avant lundi?** | Did he ask that you know that before Monday? |
| 4. **Nous désirions qu'elle vienne avec son frère.** | We wanted her to come with her brother. |
| 5. **On a défendu que cela se fasse à l'école.** | It was forbidden that that be done in school. |
| 6. **Aimez-vous mieux que je revienne plus tard?** | Do you prefer that I come back later? |

*After Expressions of Emotion*

| | |
|---|---|
| 7. **Je crains qu'il ne comprenne pas votre projet.** | I am afraid that he will not understand your plan. |
| 8. **Elle s'étonne que vous ayez si vite fini votre travail.** | She is surprised that you finished your work so fast. |
| 9. **Avez-vous peur qu'il veuille le voir?** | Are you afraid that he will want to see it? |
| 10. **Je regrette qu'ils ne puissent pas venir.** | I'm sorry that they cannot come. |
| 11. **Etes-vous content que votre fils ait réussi aux examens?** | Are you glad that your son passed the exams? |
| 12. **Nous avons honte que cela soit arrivé dans notre pays.** | We are ashamed that that happened in our country. |

*After Expressions of Doubt, Denial, Uncertainty*

| | |
|---|---|
| 13. **Nous doutons qu'elle finisse avant cinq heures.** | We doubt that she will finish before five o'clock. |
| 14. **Je ne crois pas que ça soit vrai.** | I don't believe that that is true. |
| 15. **Le gouvernement nie que les faits soient ainsi.** | The government denies that those are the facts (that the facts are thus). |
| 16. **Ils ne sont pas certains qu'elle puisse aller.** | They aren't sure that she can go. |
| 17. **Je ne suis pas sûr que vous ayez bien compris.** | I am not sure that you understood well. |

*After Impersonal Expressions*

| | |
|---|---|
| 18. **Il faut que tout le monde le sache.** | Everyone must know it. (It is necessary that everyone know it.) |
| 19. **Il est bon que vous vous reposiez un peu.** | It is good for you to rest a little. |
| 20. **Il est juste qu'il soit puni.** | It is just that he be punished. |
| 21. **Il est peu probable que je les voie.** | It is improbable that I will see them. |
| 22. **C'est dommage que nous n'ayons pas assez d'argent.** | It is too bad that we don't have enough money. |

*Modifying Indefinite Antecedent*

| | |
|---|---|
| 23. **Elle cherche un médecin qui lui dise qu'elle a quelque chose de grave.** | She is looking for a doctor who will tell her that she has something serious. |
| 24. **Nous essayons de trouver quelqu'un qui le comprenne.** | We are trying to find someone who understands it. |
| 25. **Connaissez-vous un pays où l'on soit absolument libre?** | Do you know a country where one is absolutely free? |

*Modifying Negative Antecedent*

| | |
|---|---|
| 26. **Il n'y a personne qui veuille que cela se passe.** | There is no one who wants that to happen. |
| 27. **Je n'ai rien vu qui puisse l'égaler.** | I have seen nothing which can equal it. |
| 28. **Il n'y a pas d'avion qui aille si vite.** | There isn't any plane that goes so fast. |

*Modifying Superlative Antecedent*

| | |
|---|---|
| 29. **C'est la meilleure place que je puisse vous offrir.** | It's the best seat that I can offer you. |
| 30. **Vous êtes la seule personne qui soit capable de le faire.** | You are the only person who is capable of doing it. |

*Introduced by* **bien que** *and* **quoique**

| | |
|---|---|
| 31. **Bien que nous ayons fait tout notre possible, elle n'est pas contente.** | Although we have done all we can, she is not satisfied. |
| 32. **Quoiqu'elle le dise mille fois, je ne le croirai pas.** | Although she may say so a thousand times, I won't believe it. |

*Introduced by* **à moins que** *and* **pourvu que**

| | |
|---|---|
| 33. **A moins qu'il veuille demander pardon, je refuse de le voir.** | Unless he will ask (my) pardon, I refuse to see him. |
| 34. **Pourvu qu'il me demande pardon, je veux bien le voir.** | Provided that he asks my pardon, I am willing to see him. |

*Introduced by* **pour que** *and* **afin que**

| | |
|---|---|
| 35. **Je vais le répéter pour que vous le compreniez.** | I am going to repeat it so that you may understand it. |
| 36. **Va-t-il nous prêter l'argent afin que nous finissions le projet?** | Is he going to lend us the money in order that we may finish the project? |

*Introduced by* **avant que** *and* **jusqu'à ce que**

| | |
|---|---|
| 37. **Nous devons faire cela avant qu'elle parte.** | We are supposed to do that before she leaves. |
| 38. **Continuez à faire cela jusqu'à ce que vous soyez fatigué.** | Continue doing that until you are tired. |

*Introduced by* **sans que** *and* **de peur que**

| | |
|---|---|
| 39. **Il faut le faire sans qu'il te voie.** | You must do it without his seeing you. |
| 40. **Je l'ai fait de peur qu'il me punisse.** | I did it for fear that he might punish me. |

*No Change of Subject – No Subjunctive*

| | |
|---|---|
| 41. **Je voudrais comprendre votre idée.** | I would like to understand your idea. |
| 42. **N'avez-vous pas peur de tomber?** | Aren't you afraid you will fall? |
| 43. **Je ne suis pas sûr de bien comprendre.** | I am not sure that I understand well. |
| 44. **Il faut le faire tout de suite.** | It must be done immediately. |
| 45. **J'ai emprunté de l'argent afin de finir le projet.** | I borrowed some money in order to finish the project. |

*Comparison of Present and Past Subjunctive*

| | |
|---|---|
| 46. **Je suis heureux qu'ils viennent ce soir.** | I am glad that they are coming this evening. |
| 47. **Je suis heureux qu'ils soient venus hier.** | I am glad that they came yesterday. |
| 48. **J'étais heureux qu'ils viennent sans retard.** | I was glad that they were coming without delay. |

| | |
|---|---|
| 49. **J'étais heureux qu'ils soient venus avant la nuit.** | I was glad that they had come before dark (before night). |
| 50. **Nous cherchons une secrétaire qui connaisse la ville.** | We are looking for a secretary who knows the city. |
| 51. **Nous cherchons une secrétaire qui ait étudié le russe.** | We are looking for a secretary who has studied Russian. |
| 52. **Nous cherchions une secrétaire qui connaisse la ville.** | We were looking for a secretary who was acquainted with the city. |

## NOTES

(a) Remember that, practically speaking, the subjunctive is limited to subordinate clauses.

(b) Notice that, where the subjunctive is used, there is always some element preceding which indicates an *attitude* toward the subordinate statement. The subordinate clause which takes the subjunctive may state a fact, but, if so, it is a fact viewed subjectively. [ex. 8, 11, 12, 22, 31, 47] More often it expresses something which is not a statement of fact.

(c) Subordinate clauses may be classified in three categories:

(1) Noun clauses [ex. 1-22, 46-49]
(2) Adjective Clauses [ex. 23-30, 50-52]
(3) Adverb clauses [ex. 31-40]

(d) If the subordinate clause is a noun clause, the factor which governs whether or not the subjunctive is used is the idea expressed in the principal clause. The following ideas take the subjunctive:

(1) Volition [ex. 1-6]
(2) Emotion [ex. 7-12, 46-49]
(3) Doubt, denial, uncertainty [ex. 13-17]
(4) Opinions in impersonal form [ex. 18-22]

(e) The use of the subjunctive in an adjective clause depends upon the word modified (that is, the antecedent of the relative pronoun). If the person or thing referred to is vague, unidentified, non-existent, or presented as unique or superlative, the modifying clause takes the subjunctive. [ex. 23-30, 50-52]

(f) Adverbial clauses take the subjunctive if they are introduced by certain adverbial conjunctions. Those listed in the Pattern Sentences are the most commonly used. [ex. 31-40]

(g) With noun clauses, if no new subject is expressed for the dependent verb, an infinitive is used in French. Compare the following examples: 41 and 1, 42 and 9, 43 and 17, 44 and 18. This happens with adverb clauses only if a corresponding preposition may be substituted for the conjunction. (See pp. 159-160.) [ex. 36 and 45]

(h) In colloquial French, the subjunctive has only two tenses: the present and the past. The past subjunctive is used when the dependent verb expresses an action already completed at the time referred to by the main clause. Otherwise, the present subjunctive is used. [ex. 8, 11, 12, 17, 31, 46-52]

See also pp. 155-161 .

## EXERCISES

A. *For each of the English versions of the Pattern Sentences give the French equivalent. (Cover the left-hand column.)*

B. *Read each sentence aloud; then repeat it, changing* je, *the subject of the dependent verb, successively to* tu, nous, vous, elles, *and* l'enfant. *Make the other changes entailed by the change of subject.*

1. Désire-t-il que j'aille au bureau?
2. Il ne veut pas que je prenne la voiture.
3. Il s'étonne que je sois si malade.
4. Il est content que je veuille l'aider.
5. Il a peur que j'aie trop de travail.
6. Il doute que je puisse le faire.
7. Il ne croit pas que je réponde franchement.
8. Il faut que je comprenne le problème.

9. Il est bon que je sache tout ce qui se passe.
10. Il est possible que je sois un peu en retard.
11. Quoique je l'aie invité à rester, il est parti.
12. Dites-lui de ne pas sortir avant que je finisse le travail.

C. *Supply a short clause, using the subjunctive, to complete each of the following sentences. The list of phrases to the right is intended to suggest possible ideas, but you need not confine yourself to this list. Remember that the dependent clause must have a different subject.*

| | |
|---|---|
| 1. Je veux que ... | répondre à ma question |
| 2. Je préfère que ... | aller à New York |
| 3. Je désire que ... | finir si vite |
| 4. Je regrette que ... | aller si lentement |
| 5. Je m'étonne que ... | pouvoir le faire |
| 6. J'ai peur que ... | comprendre son plan |
| 7. Je doute que ... | manquer le train |
| 8. Je ne suis pas sûr que ... | venir avec nous |
| 9. Je nie que ... | être responsable de cela |
| 10. Je ne connais personne qui ... | savoir la cause de cela |

*Repeat the exercise above, changing* je, *in turn, to* nous, elle, ils.
*Repeat the exercise (except 8 & 10) in the interrogative with the subject* vous (Voulez-vous que ... etc.).

D. *Convert each of the sentences to a subordinate clause introduced by an appropriate one of the four introductory clauses listed to the left.*

Le professeur veut que ...
Elle a peur que ...
On ne pense pas que ...
Est-il possible que ... ?

1. Pierre le recevra tout de suite.
2. Ils croiront tout cela.
3. Tu reviendras dans une heure.
4. M. DuPont le sait déjà.
5. Tous les élèves seront absents.
6. Je ne réussirai pas aux examens.
7. Tout le monde sera content.
8. Nous y allons en même temps.
9. Cela prendra trop de travail.
10. Vous ne comprendrez pas.
11. Les autres ont les mêmes privilèges.
12. Vous pourrez le faire.

**E.** *Read aloud, choosing the proper beginning to correspond to each of the dependent clauses.*

Connaissez-vous un pays ...
Connaissez-vous le pays ...

... où tous les habitants soient riches?
... où il n'y ait aucune forme de gouvernement?
... où ses parents habitaient?
... où les écoles soient parfaites?
... où cet accident est arrivé?
... où nos amis sont allés?
... où tout le monde soit content?
... où il n'y ait pas d'impôts?
... où Jean Martin a étudié?
... où se trouve le mont Blanc?

**F.** *Introduce the dependent clause by* pourvu que *instead of* si *and reverse the order of the two clauses.*

*Examples:* Si vous venez ici, je vous aiderai. – Je vous aiderai pourvu que vous veniez ici.
Si elle le finit à temps, on vous l'enverra. – On vous l'enverra pourvu qu'elle le finisse à temps.

1. Si je reçois l'argent, je pourrai les acheter.
2. Si tu vends la maison, nous pourrons partir.
3. S'il le veut, on lui donnera le poste.
4. Si nous faisons le travail, nous gagnerons l'argent.
5. Si elle y va, vous la verrez.
6. Si les autres peuvent sortir ce soir, nous irons au bal.
7. Si vous conduisez, on nous prêtera la voiture.
8. Si on le lit lentement, vous comprendrez bien.

**G.** *Read each sentence aloud using the present subjunctive or the past subjunctive, as appropriate.*

1. Etes-vous content que je {revienne / sois revenu} demain?
2. Nous ne sommes pas sûrs qu'il {aille / soit allé} avec eux hier.

3. Je regrette qu'elle ne les {voie pas / ait pas vus} hier soir.
4. C'est dommage que nous les {quittions / ayons quittés} lundi prochain.
5. Je ne crois pas que tu {fasses / aies fait} cela la semaine dernière.
6. Elle n'est pas certaine que vous {croyiez / ayez cru} d'abord ce qu'elle a dit.
7. Il est peu probable qu'ils {puissent / aient pu} les acheter dimanche passé.
8. Elle a peur qu'il {vende / ait vendu} la voiture la semaine prochaine.

H. *Answer* "Non" *and indicate that the person mentioned will do the action himself.*

*Examples:* Voulez-vous que les autres fassent cela? – Non, je veux le faire moi-même.
Préfère-t-elle que nous les écrivions? – Non, elle préfère les écrire elle-même.
Aimerait-il que Marie conduise? – Non, il aimerait conduire lui-même.

1. Aimes-tu mieux que Pierre les achète?
2. Voulez-vous que je le fasse?
3. Veulent-ils que tu le prépares?
4. Préfère-t-il que Jean le finisse?
5. Désire-t-elle que je les choisisse?
6. Aimeriez-vous que Marie la lise?
7. Veux-tu que nous les aidions?
8. Veulent-elles que vous l'invitiez?

I. *Read aloud, using the subjunctive, the indicative, or the infinitive of the verb in parentheses.*

1. Nous voulons que vous *(attendre)* le taxi. 2. Avez-vous peur qu'il *(venir)* trop tard? 3. Il a dit que le taxi *(être)* là. 4. Je ne suis

pas sûr qu'ils *(être)* capables de cela. 5. Il est bon que nous les *(choisir)* un autre jour. 6. Il n'y a aucun autre jour qui leur *(convenir)*. 7. Je le ferai à moins qu'il nous *(écrire)* avant mardi. 8. Tout le monde est content de *(rester)* à la maison. 9. Ils ne croient pas que vous *(pouvoir)* le faire. 10. Il est peu probable que nous le *(finir)* demain. 11. Mon père désire que nous *(aller)* tous ensemble. 12. Préférez-vous que je *(revenir)* plus tard? 13. Je m'étonne que tant de gens *(vouloir)* y aller. 14. Il faut que vous *(être)* de retour de bonne heure. 15. Nous ne sommes pas certains que vous *(avoir)* raison. 16. J'ai promis de *(répondre)* tout de suite. 17. Quoi qu'il *(faire)*, il n'arrive jamais à comprendre. 18. Elle est partie sans que nous le *(savoir)*. 19. Il n'est pas juste que les autres *(faire)* tout le travail. 20. Il n'y a personne qui *(comprendre)* tous les problèmes. 21. Elle est heureuse que vous *(apprendre)* si vite le français. 22. Je vais me retirer pour que vous *(pouvoir)* dormir.

*Supplementary Written Exercises for Lesson 8 are on p. 105.*

# LESSON 9

## *Possessive Adjectives and Pronouns*

### Possessive Adjectives

| | SING. | | PLUR. |
|---|---|---|---|
| | *Masc.* | *Fem.* | |
| my | **mon** | **ma (mon)** | **mes** |
| your | **ton** | **ta (ton)** | **tes** |
| his / her / its | **son** | **sa (son)** | **ses** |
| our | **notre** | **notre** | **nos** |
| your | **votre** | **votre** | **vos** |
| their | **leur** | **leur** | **leurs** |

### Possessive Pronouns

| | SING. | | PLUR. | |
|---|---|---|---|---|
| | *Masc.* | *Fem.* | *Masc.* | *Fem.* |
| mine | **le mien** | **la mienne** | **les miens** | **les miennes** |
| yours | **le tien** | **la tienne** | **les tiens** | **les tiennes** |
| his / hers / . . . | **le sien** | **la sienne** | **les siens** | **les siennes** |
| ours | **le nôtre** | **la nôtre** | **les nôtres** | **les nôtres** |
| yours | **le vôtre** | **la vôtre** | **les vôtres** | **les vôtres** |
| theirs | **le leur** | **la leur** | **les leurs** | **les leurs** |

## PATTERN SENTENCES

*Possessive Adjectives and Pronouns*

| | |
|---|---|
| 1. **Allez chercher mon complet, ma chemise et mes souliers, s'il vous plaît.** | Go get my suit, shirt, and shoes, please. |
| 2. **Leur oncle est le directeur de notre école.** | Their uncle is the headmaster of our school. |
| 3. **Ton amie va raconter son histoire.** | Your (girl) friend is going to tell her story. |
| 4. **Mon bureau est plus proche que le sien.** | My office is closer than his (hers). |
| 5. **Cette voiture-ci coûte plus cher que la vôtre.** | This car costs more than yours. |
| 6. **Voici toutes les valises. Lesquelles désire-t-il – les miennes ou les vôtres?** | Here are all the suitcases. Which ones does he want – mine or yours? |
| 7. **Parle-t-elle de vos enfants ou des nôtres?** | Is she talking about your children or ours? |
| 8. **Les élèves ont pris leur place.** | The pupils took their seats. |

*Definite Article for Possessive*

| | |
|---|---|
| 9. **Je vais me laver les mains.** | I'm going to wash my hands. |
| 9a. **Je vais lui laver les mains.** | I'm going to wash his (her) hands. |
| 10. **Elle s'est coupé le doigt.** | She cut her finger. |
| 10a. **Elle m'a coupé le doigt.** | She cut my finger. |
| 11. **La voilà dans le grand fauteuil, les yeux fermés, étreignant dans les bras sa vieille poupée.** | There she is in the big armchair, with her eyes closed, clasping her old doll in her arms. |
| 12. **J'ai mal à la tête.** | My head aches. |
| 13. **L'explosion a blessé le soldat au visage, aux bras et aux pieds.** | The explosion wounded the soldier in the (his) face, arms, and feet. |
| 14. **Tous les élèves ont levé la main droite.** | All the pupils raised their right hands. |

*Possession Expressed with* **être à**

| | |
|---|---|
| 15. **A qui est ce stylo?** | Whose pen is this? |
| 16. **Il est à moi.** | It is mine. |
| 17. **Ce portefeuille est à vous, monsieur, n'est-ce pas?** | This wallet is yours, sir, isn't it? |
| 18. **A qui sont ces gants? Ils sont à M. Duval.** | Whose gloves are these? They are Mr. Duval's. |

*Possessive of Nouns*

| | |
|---|---|
| 19. **La maison de M. Dupont est à côté de la mienne.** | Mr. Dupont's house is next to mine. |
| 20. **La voiture de votre cousin et celle de mon père sont de la même marque.** | Your cousin's car and my father's are (of) the same make. |
| 21. **Vos amis et ceux de Robert vont faire le voyage en avion.** | Your friends and Robert's are going to make the trip by plane. |

## NOTES

(a) Possessive adjectives and pronouns agree in gender and number with the nouns they modify or replace. [ex. 1-8, 19-21]

(b) The possessive adjectives are generally repeated in French before each noun modified. [ex. 1]

(c) The alternate feminine singular forms of the possessive adjective (**mon, ton, son**) are used before feminine singular nouns which begin with a vowel or a mute **h**. [ex. 3]

(d) The possessive adjective is seldom used in French with parts of the body when the ownership is obvious. In such cases the definite article is commonly used. [ex. 9-14] Where an action upon some part of the body is expressed, the personal reference (ownership) is generally expressed by an indirect object. [ex. 9-10a] See also Les. 1.

(e) Simple statements of ownership (*This book is mine. They are Mary's, etc.*) are usually expressed by **être à** with a noun or pronoun object. [ex. 15-18]

(f) Since French nouns have no possessive form, possession is expressed by the preposition **de.** When the possessed noun is omitted, a demonstrative pronoun must replace it in French. [ex. 19-21]

(g) Notice in Pattern Sentences 8 and 14 that a "distributive singular" is used in French where the corresponding English requires a plural noun. Where the subject of the verb is plural but each person *has* (or *uses,* or *washes,* or *takes,* etc.) only one item, the object in French generally is expressed in the singular.

## EXERCISES

**A.** *For each of the English versions of the Pattern Sentences give the French equivalent. (Cover the left-hand column.)*

**B.** *Repeat these examples:*

J'ai une machine. – C'est ma machine.
Robert a un disque. – C'est son disque.
Ils ont des idées. – Ce sont leurs idées.

*Continue responding to each sentence by a statement beginning with* C'est *or* Ce sont *and using the possessive adjective which corresponds to the subject.*

J'ai un stylo.
Marie a un cahier.
Nous avons un garage.
Tu as une femme.
Ils ont une maison.
Vous avez une photo.
Vos amis ont un téléviseur.

Tu as une orange.
Louise a une automobile.
Pierre a une voiture.
Mes parents ont des meubles.
Vous avez des amis.
J'ai des livres.
Nous avons des peintures.

C. *Repeat the following sentences, substituting the correct forms of the possessive adjectives in parentheses for those in the sentence.*

Ton chapeau, ta cravate et tes chaussettes sont de la même couleur. *(mon, son, votre)*
Votre hôpital, votre église, votre bibliothèque et vos écoles sont très modernes. *(notre, leur)*
Mon amie Louise, mon oncle, ma tante et mes petits cousins vont bientôt arriver. *(ton, son, notre, votre, leur)*

D. *Repeat aloud supplying the possessive pronouns. In each case, use successively all the possessive pronouns which are appropriate in that particular sentence. (For example, in sentence 1, omit* le mien *and* le nôtre *as not appropriate.)*

1. Voici mon livre de francais. Où est ________ ?
2. Voici ta nouvelle bicyclette. Où est ________ ?
3. Voici notre nouvelle voiture. Où est ________ ?
4. Voilà ses parents. Où sont ________ ?
5. Voilà leurs sœurs. Où sont ________ ?
6. Voilà votre cahier. Où est ________ ?

E. *Repeat the following sentence aloud rapidly, changing the subject successively to* tu, il, elle, nous, vous, ils, elles.

Je vais me laver la figure.

*This may be repeated several times by changing* la figure *to* les mains, etc., *and by changing the tense of the verb* (Je me suis lavé la figure, etc.). *How does the meaning change if* me *is changed to* te? lui? vous? leur? (Je vais te laver la figure, etc.)

F. *Practice the following questions and answers, supplying names* (Jean, Marie, etc.) *or pronouns for the blanks, and substituting other nouns for those italicized. In answering, the student must use different names or pronouns from those in the two preceding answers. Make any changes in agreement entailed by the noun changes.*

*Question:* A qui est ce *stylo?*
*Answer:* Il est à ________ .
*Question:* Ce *chapeau* est-il à ________ ?
*Answer:* Non, il n'est pas à ________ ; il est à ________ .

G. *Say the following in French:*

| | |
|---|---|
| John's house | the teacher's house |
| Mary's house | the doctor's house |
| his uncle's house | Mr. Dupont's house |
| my father's house | Mrs. Duval's house |

*Repeat, changing* la maison *to* le stylo, les amis, la chambre.

*Repeat, adding in each case . . .* and mine. *(example:* la maison de Jean et la mienne) *Continue variations, adding* and yours, and hers, and ours.

*Repeat, making pairs in which a demonstrative pronoun is substituted for the noun in the second part. (example:* la maison de Jean et celle de son oncle*)*

*Supplementary Written Exercises for Lesson 9 are on p. 105.*

# LESSON 10

## *Passive Voice, Adverbial Pronouns* y *and* en, *Partitive Pronoun* en

## PATTERN SENTENCES

### Passive Voice

*Regular Passive with* **être**

| | |
|---|---|
| 1. **Ce travail est fait par des ouvriers très habiles.** | This work is done by very skillful workmen. |
| 2. **Son dernier ouvrage a été achevé par un de ses élèves.** | His last work was completed by one of his pupils. |
| 3. **Tous les bâtiments avaient été détruits par l'orage.** | All the buildings had been destroyed by the storm. |
| 4. **La jeune héroïne sera décorée par le roi.** | The young heroine will be decorated by the king. |
| 5. **Il était admiré de tous ses confrères.** | He was admired by all his colleagues. |

*Substitutes for Passive Voice*

| | |
|---|---|
| 6. **On avait déjà établi certains faits essentiels.** | Certain basic facts had already been established. |
| 7. **On nous a servi un repas délicieux.** | We were served a delicious meal. |
| 8. **On le fera avant la fin de la semaine.** | It will be done before the end of the week. |
| 9. **On l'admirait beaucoup.** | He was very much admired. |
| 10. **Ces fleurs se voient partout.** | These flowers are seen everywhere. |
| 11. **Cela se comprend facilement.** | That is easily understood. |
| 12. **Les tours du château se voyaient de loin.** | The towers of the castle were seen (were visible) from a distance. |
| 13. **Tout à coup la porte s'est ouverte.** | Suddenly the door was opened (the door opened). |
| 14. **Cela ne se fait pas dans le beau monde.** | That isn't done in polite society. |

## Adverbial Pronouns *y* and *en*

**Y** *related to* **à, en, sur, dans,** *etc.;* **en** *related to* **de**

| | |
|---|---|
| 15. **Je croyais que vous étiez à New York. – Non, mais je compte y aller demain.** | I thought you were in New York. – No, but I expect to go there tomorrow. |
| 16. **En France il fait très beau au mois de mai. Quand j'y étais j'ai vu de magnifiques jardins.** | In France it is very beautiful in May. When I was there I saw some magnificent gardens. |
| 17. **Pensez-vous souvent à ce beau voyage? – Oui, nous y pensons souvent.** | Do you often think about that fine trip? – Yes, we think about it often. |
| 17a. **Pensez-vous souvent à notre ami Charles? – Oui, nous pensons souvent à lui.** | Do you often think about our friend Charles? – Yes, we often think of him. |
| 18. **Je l'ai laissé sur le bureau, mais il n'y est plus.** | I left it on the desk, but it is no longer there. |

19. **Avez-vous mis les paquets dans ma voiture? – Oui, monsieur, vous les y trouverez.** Did you put the packages in my car? – Yes sir, you will find them there.
20. **Ma femme se souvient de cela; mais moi, je ne m'en souviens pas.** My wife remembers that, but I don't remember it.
21. **Etes-vous fiers de leurs accomplissements? – Oui, nous en sommes fiers.** Are you proud of their accomplishments? – Yes, we are proud of them.
22. **Que pensez-vous de son discours? – Oh, ce que j'en pense n'est pas important.** What do you think of his speech? – Oh, what I think about it is not important.

22a. **Que pensez-vous de Charles Dupont? – Oh, ce que je pense de lui n'est pas important.** What do you think of Charles Dupont? – Oh, what I think about him isn't important.

23. **Ont-ils besoin de ceci? – Non, ils n'en ont pas besoin.** Do they need this? – No, they don't need it.
24. **Le bébé a-t-il peur de cette poupée? – Oui, il en a peur.** Is the baby afraid of that doll? – Yes, he's afraid of it.

## Partitive Pronoun *en*

25. **Voulez-vous du gâteau? – Non, merci, nous en avons.** Do you want some cake? – No, thank you, we have some.
26. **Elle n'a pas acheté de croissants parce qu'elle en avait déjà.** She didn't buy any croissants because she already had some.
27. **Voilà des lettres pour moi. En avez-vous reçu aussi?** There are some letters for me. Did you receive some too?
28. **Vous avez plusieurs numéros de cette revue scientifique, n'est-ce pas? – Oui, mais je n'en ai pas de récents.** You have several numbers of that scientific magazine, haven't you? – Yes, but I don't have any recent ones.
29. **J'ai dit à la vendeuse que je cherchais un chapeau, et elle m'en a montré plusieurs.** I told the salesgirl that I was looking for a hat, and she showed me several.
30. **Avez-vous vu les nouvelles Simcas? En voilà deux de l'autre côté de la rue.** Have you seen the new Simcas? There are two on the other side of the street.

| | |
|---|---|
| 31. **La plupart des médecins sont très capables, mais j'en ai vu aussi d'inhabiles.** | Most doctors are very capable, but I have also seen some incompetent ones. |
| 32. **Quelles pâtisseries appétissantes! Je vais en acheter quelques-unes.** | What tempting pastries! I'm going to buy some (a few). |
| 33. **Vous aimez ces fleurs? On en trouve beaucoup chez moi.** | You like those flowers? One finds many (of them) where I come from. |

## NOTES

(a) The passive voice is formed in French as it is in English – that is, the appropriate form of the verb **être** *(to be)* plus the past participle. [ex. 1-5] Notice that in these five examples the agent is expressed ( ... **par des ouvriers** ... , ... **par un de ses élèves** ... ,etc.).

(b) When no agent is expressed, the passive voice is rarely used in French. Ideas frequently expressed in English in passive form are expressed in French by the indefinite pronoun **on** as subject of an active verb [ex. 6-9] or by a reflexive verb [ex. 10-14]. Of these two, the **on** construction is more commonly used and more widely applicable. For example, the **on** construction could have been used to express the ideas in Pattern Sentences 10 to 14, but the reverse is not true – that is, the reflexive form would not be appropriate for the ideas in Pattern Sentences 7 to 9. The limitations on the use of the reflexive form cannot be reduced to simple, practical guide lines for intermediate students; therefore the student is advised to cultivate principally the **on** construction in his active practice at this stage, while observing and analyzing the reflexive usage as he hears it or reads it.

(c) The adverbial pronoun **y** stands for the prepositions **à, dans, en, sur** (and others expressing location or direction toward) plus their objects. [ex. 15-19]

(d) The adverbial pronoun **en** stands for the preposition **de** plus its object. [ex. 20-24]

(e) **En** is also the partitive pronoun used as object of a verb. It is equivalent to the English *some* or *any* not followed by a noun, or to *of it, of them.* [ex. 25-33] Note the use of **de** before the adjective modifying **en**. [ex. 28]

(f) Note that **en** is required with the verb in French whenever the complement of the verb is an expression of quantity not accompanied by a noun. This includes **quelques-uns,** the emphatic pronoun form corresponding to the English *some, a few.* [ex. 29, 30, 32, 33]

(g) The adverbial pronouns **y** and **en** are not used to stand for persons. [ex. 17a, 22a] The partitive pronoun **en** may stand for persons. [ex. 31]

## EXERCISES

**A.** *For each of the English versions of the Pattern Sentences give the French equivalent. (Cover the left-hand column.)*

**B.** *Give the equivalent* on *construction for each of the sentences below expressed in passive form.*

*Examples:* Ce garage a été construit en 1950. – On a construit ce garage en 1950.
Tous ces articles seront vendus demain. – On vendra tous ces articles demain.

1. Le contrat a été signé hier.
2. Les voitures ont été réparées la semaine dernière.
3. Le travail sera fini demain.
4. Les nouvelles seront annoncées demain soir.
5. Cela a été écrit en 1800.
6. Ces choses ont été trouvées avant cela.
7. Quelque chose de nouveau sera découvert.
8. Les nouvelles idées seront acceptées plus tard.

**C.** *Answer the following questions in the negative, following closely the construction used in the question.*

1. Sait-on jamais ce que ces gens vont faire?

2. Dit-on que la situation est stable à présent?
3. Trouve-t-on ces articles dans les grands magasins?
4. Sert-on des cocktails dans les cafés?
5. Fait-on cela dans votre pays?
6. Parle-t-on français en Angleterre?
7. Comprend-on bien tout ce que cela veut dire?
8. Est-ce qu'on lui a dit de rentrer avant onze heures?
9. Est-ce que cela se voit partout en France?
10. Est-ce que cela se fait comme ça?

D. *Examine the examples given below. Then give the French for the following sentences, using* (a) *or* (b) *as a model.*

(a) Ce pont a été construit par les Romains. *This bridge was built by the Romans.*
(b) On a fait élargir les chemins. *The roads were widened.*

1. This song is heard everywhere.
2. That is easily understood.
3. Many young people were invited.
4. That building was constructed by Mr. Durand.
5. The work was finished by another man.
6. French is spoken in Quebec.
7. The work was quickly finished.
8. The visitors will be welcomed *(accueillis)* by the *préfet.*
9. That newspaper is read in every home.
10. I was informed of the accident.

E. *Repeat each sentence substituting* y *for the prepositional phrase.*

*Examples:* Elles sont arrivées à l'église en même temps. – Elles y sont arrivées en même temps.
Vous les mettez toujours dans ce tiroir. – Vous les y mettez toujours.
A-t-il répondu à ta lettre? – Y a-t-il répondu?

1. Je vais à New York.
2. Ils habitent au Canada.
3. Vous arriverez en France demain.
4. Vos gants étaient sur la table.

5. Le stylo n'était pas dans sa poche.
6. Ces élèves ne sont pas à l'école.
7. Est-elle à la maison?
8. Avez-vous pensé à ce problème?
9. J'ai mis la bague dans cette boîte.
10. Cela est arrivé devant l'hôpital.
11. Il s'intéresse à notre projet.
12. Pierre nous rejoindra au café.
13. On les vend en Amérique du Sud.
14. Tu l'as trouvé au salon.

**F.** *Repeat each sentence substituting* en *for* de *plus the noun.*

*Examples:* Tout le monde parle de cette affaire. – Tout le monde en parle.
Je me souviens de l'occasion. – Je m'en souviens.
Ont-ils des idées utiles? – En ont-ils?
Tu as vu beaucoup de monuments. – Tu en as vu beaucoup.

1. Il parle toujours de cette aventure.
2. Nous avons besoin de ces papiers.
3. Elle n'est pas contente de leurs promesses.
4. J'ai eu de la difficulté.
5. Tu prendras des frites, n'est-ce pas?
6. Ils se rendent compte de la situation.
7. Que pensez-vous de mon idée?
8. Voulez-vous du vin?
9. Il a mangé un peu de viande.
10. Ils ont bu trop de bière.

**G.** *Give a simple answer to each question, using* y *or* en *to replace the italicized words.*

1. Quand êtes-vous allé *en Angleterre?*
2. Est-ce que Jeanne était *à l'école* ce matin?
3. Combien *de livres* avez-vous achetés?
4. A-t-elle parlé *de cet article?*
5. Pensez-vous *aux vacances prochaines?*
6. Combien *d'élèves* y a-t-il dans la classe?

7. Comptez-vous aller *à Paris* cet été?
8. Est-ce que la lettre était *dans le tiroir?*
9. Avez-vous besoin *de ma voiture?*
10. Est-ce que votre mère a acheté *des souliers?*
11. Les élèves ont-ils peur *des examens?*
12. Ont-ils beaucoup *d'argent?*
13. Avez-vous trouvé la lettre *sur la table?*
14. Est-ce que tu t'intéresses *aux mathématiques?*

*Supplementary Written Exercises for Lesson 10 are on p. 105.*

# LESSON 11

## *The Prepositions* en *and* à

### PATTERN SENTENCES

*Preposition* **en** *with Present Participle*

| | |
|---|---|
| 1. **En descendant du taxi, elle a aperçu son père.** | (Upon) getting out of the taxi, she caught sight of her father. |
| 2. **En questionnant cet homme, j'ai appris qu'il venait d'arriver.** | (Upon) questioning that man, I learned that he had just arrived. |
| 3. **On peut le faire en travaillant jour et nuit.** | One can do it by working day and night. |
| 4. **Je l'ai remarqué en me lavant la figure.** | I noticed it while washing my face. |
| 5. **Il me regardait en souriant.** | He was looking at me (and) smiling. |

*Preposition* **en** *with Feminine Geographical Names and Masculine Singular Names Beginning with a Vowel*

| | |
|---|---|
| 6. **On trouve ces plantes en Afrique mais pas en Europe.** | These plants are found in Africa but not in Europe. |

7. **Allez-vous en Italie ou en Allemagne cet été?** Are you going to Italy or Germany this summer?
8. **Il a voyagé partout en France, mais surtout en Champagne et en Alsace.** He has traveled everywhere in France, but especially in Champagne and Alsace.
9. **Mes parents habitaient autrefois en Pennsylvanie, mais ils sont actuellement en Californie.** My parents lived formerly in Pennsylvania, but now they are in California.
10. **Après quelques jours en Israël, ils sont passés en Irak et ensuite en Iran.** After a few days in Israel, they went on to Iraq and then to Iran.
11. **On ne trouve pas le même climat en Equateur qu'en Uruguay.** One doesn't find the same climate in Ecuador as in Uruguay.
12. **La ville d'Arras se trouve en Artois, pas en Anjou.** The city of Arras is located in Artois, not in Anjou.

### *Other Uses of* en

13. **Nous pouvons le faire en dix minutes.** We can do it in ten minutes.
14. **Y allez-vous en été ou en hiver?** Do you go there in (the) summer or winter?
15. **Je suis né en 1912.** I was born in 1912.
16. **Nous y allons en voiture (en taxi, en autobus, en chemin de fer, en bateau, en avion).** We are going there by car (by taxi, by bus, by railroad, by boat, by plane).
17. **Ces gens-là s'habillent en pull-over et en blue-jean même pour aller à l'église.** Those people dress in pull-overs and blue jeans even to go to church.

### *Preposition* à *with Geographical Names*

18. **Pendant qu'il était au Canada, il est allé à Québec, à Montréal et à Toronto.** While he was in Canada, he went to Quebec, Montreal, and Toronto.
19. **En Espagne et au Portugal on trouve d'excellents vins.** In Spain and Portugal one finds excellent wines.
20. **A la fin de notre visite aux Etats-Unis, nous nous sommes réunis à New York.** At the end of our visit to the United States, we met in New York.

*Preposition* **à** *Joining Noun or Adjective to Infinitive*

|  |  |
|---|---|
| 21. **Avez-vous du travail à faire?** | Do you have any (some) work to do? |
| 22. **J'ai une lettre à écrire.** | I have a letter to write. |
| 23. **Voici une maison à louer.** | Here is a house for rent (to be rented). |
| 24. **Voilà quelque chose d'intéressant à voir!** | There's something interesting to see! |
| 25. **Ce livre est difficile à lire.** | This book is hard to read. |
| 26. **Ce qu'il a fait c'est impossible à comprendre.** | What he did is impossible to understand. |

*Other Uses of* **à**

|  |  |
|---|---|
| 27. **Ils passent la journée à monter à cheval ou à vélo, ou à jouer au tennis, et le soir à jouer aux cartes.** | They spend the day riding horseback or on bikes, or playing tennis, and the evening playing cards. |
| 28. **Ma maison est à deux pas d'ici.** | My house is a very short distance from here (two steps from here). |
| 29. **Le bateau était à cent mètres du rivage.** | The boat was a hundred meters from the shore. |
| 30. **Versailles est à vingt-trois kilomètres de Paris.** | Versailles is twenty-three kilometers from Paris. |
| 31. **la salle à manger** | the dining room |
| **la chambre à coucher** | the bedroom |
| **une machine à écrire** | a typewriter |
| **une machine à laver** | a washing machine |
| **un fer à repasser** | an iron (for pressing clothes, etc.) |
| **un panier à papier** | a wastepaper basket |
| **une tasse à café** | a coffee cup |
| **une brosse à dents** | a toothbrush |
| 32. **un avion à deux moteurs** | a bi-motored plane |
| **un stylo à cartouche** | a cartridge pen |
| **des cigarettes à bout filtrant** | filter-tipped cigarettes |
| **une jeune fille à l'air modeste** | a modest-mannered girl |
| **la dame aux camélias** | the lady with the camelias |
| **l'homme au nez aquilin** | the man with the aquiline nose |

| | |
|---|---|
| **l'avenue aux larges trottoirs** | the avenue with the wide sidewalks |

## NOTES

(a) **En** is the only French preposition which may take a present participle (gerund) as complement. In this use, it may be translated *upon, by, while,* or with no preposition at all in the English version. [ex. 1-5] Remember that other prepositions take the infinitive (**sans dire** *without saying).*

(b) The preposition **en** expresses both *to* and *in* before the name of a large geographical unit (continent, country, province, state) if the name is feminine [ex. 6-9] or if it is masculine singular and begins with a vowel [ex. 10-12]. Feminine names are those ending in mute **-e** (notable exceptions: **le Mexique, le Cambodge).** Those with other endings are masculine (with rare exceptions).

(c) When **en** translates *in* before expressions of time, it generally has the connotation of *during* or *within.* [ex. 13-15] Compare this with **dans** in the following sentence: **Je serai de retour dans une demi-heure.** *I shall be back in (at the end of) half an hour.*

(d) **En** is generally used in phrases expressing means of transportation. [ex. 16] However, when speaking of things which one does not get *into,* the preposition **à** is commonly used: **à cheval, à bicyclette, à pied,** etc.

(e) With masculine names of countries (except those in [b] above), **à** is used to express *in* or *to.* [ex. 18-20] The definite article is not omitted with masculine names of countries; it combines with **à** to form **au** or **aux.**

(f) With the names of states of the United States which do not have a French form which is feminine and ends in mute **-e (la Californie, la Virginie, la Louisiane,** etc.), *in* is generally expressed by **dans le** or by **dans l'état de**: **dans le Kansas** *in Kansas,* **dans l'état de Montana** *in (the state of) Montana.*

(g) When geographical place names are modified, *in* is usually expressed by **dans** (plus the definite article) and *to* by **à** (plus the definite article): **dans**

**l'ancienne Grèce** *in ancient Greece,* **à l'Angleterre de Shakespeare** *to Shakespeare's England.*

(h) With names of cities **à** is used to express *in, to,* or *at.* [ex. 18, 20] Names of cities do not take the article unless it is part of the name **(le Havre – au Havre).**

(i) Notice the relationship *(. . . to be done, . . . to be written)* which is expressed by **à** when it joins a noun or an adjective to an infinitive. [ex. 21-26] In other cases, **de** is generally used between a noun or adjective and an infinitive: **Je suis content de rester à la maison.** *I am happy to stay home.*

(j) Notice the use of **à** in expressions referring to sports and games: **monter à cheval, jouer au tennis, jouer aux cartes.** [ex. 27]

(k) Notice the use of **à** to express distance from something. [ex. 28-30]

(l) Notice the use of **à** in phrases indicating use or special characteristics. [ex. 31, 32]

(m) Notice that **en** characteristically is *not* followed by the definite article.

(n) Other hints on prepositional problems are found in the end vocabulary under the appropriate word listing **(penser à ... , passer du temps à ... ,** etc.).

## EXERCISES

**A.** *For each of the English versions of the Pattern Sentences give the French equivalent. (Cover the left-hand column.)*

**B.** *Rephrase the following sentences using* en *and the present participle, as in the example:*

*Example:* Quand on parle on apprend à parler.
En parlant on apprend à parler.

Quand on lit on apprend à lire.
Quand on chante on apprend à chanter.
Quand on pose des questions on apprend les faits.
Quand il écoutait les disques, il apprenait les leçons.
Quand elle est descendue du taxi, elle a vu son ami.
Quand ils sont sortis, c'était Jean qui allait le premier.
Quand on passe par Nîmes, on peut les voir.
Quand on se couche de bonne heure, on dort très bien.
Quand je me lève de bonne heure, je travaille mieux.
Quand nous nous lavons ainsi, nous ne courons pas de risque.
Pendant que je cherchais dans le garage, j'ai trouvé ceci.
Pendant que j'examinais ce livre, j'ai remarqué cela.

C. *Read aloud, using* en, à, au, *or* aux *in the blanks as required.*

1. Beaucoup d'Américains voyagent ________ Europe chaque été. 2. Allez-vous ________ France l'été prochain? 3. Nous allons passer quinze jours ________ Paris et huit jours ________ Rome. 4. Avez-vous de proches parents qui habitent ________ Italie? 5. Non, actuellement tous mes parents habitent ________ Etats-Unis ou ________ Amérique du Sud. 6. On trouve toutes sortes de climat ________ Afrique. 7. Le Président est allé ________ Brésil et ________ Argentine. 8. Cet acteur est né ________ Normandie, mais il a passé la plus grande partie de sa vie ________ Californie. 9. Comptez-vous aller ________ Genève ou ________ Lausanne? 10. ________ Danemark on commence l'étude des langues dans l'école élémentaire. 11. Cette compagnie a des succursales ________ Japon et ________ Israël. 12. Quand va-t-il ________ Uruguay?

D. *Repeat the following sentence substituting, in order, each of the nouns listed in place of* du travail *and each of the infinitives (as appropriate in meaning) in place of* faire. *(Retain* faire *if appropriate.)*

J'ai *du travail* à *faire.*

| | |
|---|---|
| des livres | dépenser |
| une lettre | écrire |
| une leçon | étudier |
| deux examens difficiles | passer |
| un coup de téléphone | laver |

| | |
|---|---|
| de l'argent | lire |
| un article | réparer |
| du linge | vendre |
| une machine | |
| une vieille maison | |

*Repeat the above, making the verb negative.* (Je n'ai pas de travail ... )
*Repeat, using different subjects.* (Il a du travail ... )
*Repeat, changing to interrogative.* (Avez-vous du travail ... ? ) *These questions may be answered in the negative with an extended answer.* (Non, mais j'ai un repas à préparer, etc.)

E. *Make combinations of a noun from the left column and a phrase from the right column, according to meaning.*

*Example:* le roi à la barbe blanche *the king with the white beard*

| | |
|---|---|
| une voiture | aux yeux bleus |
| la jeune fille | à deux étages |
| le chien | à la belle voix |
| une maison | à deux battants |
| l'oiseau | à quatre places |
| la porte | à l'air savant |
| le professeur | aux larges trottoirs |
| l'élève | aux longues oreilles |
| l'avenue | au bec jaune |
| le garçon | à l'air stupide |
| la chanteuse | aux grands pieds |

*This may be varied by making complete sentences.* (Le roi à la barbe blanche est Edouard VII.)

*Supplementary Written Exercises for Lesson 11 are on p. 106.*

# LESSON 12

## Connaître *and* Savoir; Venir de *& Infinitive; The Causal* faire; *Comparison of* quitter, sortir, partir

### PATTERN SENTENCES

#### *Distinction between* **connaître** *and* **savoir**

| | |
|---|---|
| 1. **Je ne connais pas ces gens-là.** | I don't know those people. |
| 2. **Savez-vous où ils habitent?** | Do you know where they live? |
| 3. **Notre guide connaissait bien tous les endroits les plus pittoresques.** | Our guide was well acquainted with all the most picturesque places. |
| 4. **Il ne savait pas très bien l'anglais.** | He didn't know English very well. |
| 5. **Connaissez-vous cette chanson?** | Do you know that song? |
| 6. **Oui, mais je n'en sais pas le titre.** | Yes, but I don't know the title of it. |
| 7. **Il est jeune; il ne connaît pas encore le monde.** | He is young; he doesn't yet know the world. |
| 8. **Cela se peut, mais il sait que les amitiés sont importantes.** | That may be, but he knows that friendships are important. |

| | |
|---|---|
| 9. **Il y a certains monuments que l'on connaît de vue ou connaît de nom sans en savoir grand'-chose.** | There are certain historic buildings that people know by sight or by name without knowing much about them. |
| 10. **Après une année d'études, ils ne savent presque rien.** | After a year's study, they know almost nothing. |
| 11. **Savez-vous jouer du piano?** | Can you play the piano? |
| 12. **Je ne sais pas jouer aux échecs.** | I don't know how to play chess. |
| 13. **Je ne sais pas le faire sans aide.** | I can't do it without help. |

### Venir de + *Infinitive*

| | |
|---|---|
| 14. **Nous venons d'acheter un nouveau téléviseur.** | We have just bought a new television set. |
| 15. **Je viens de recevoir ce télégramme.** | I have just received this telegram. |
| 16. **Ils viennent d'annoncer la naissance du prince.** | They have just announced the birth of the prince. |
| 17. **L'arbitre venait d'arrêter le combat.** | The referee had just stopped the fight. |
| 18. **Vous veniez de vous marier à ce moment-là, n'est-ce pas?** | You had just gotten married at that time, hadn't you? |

### *The Causal* faire

| | |
|---|---|
| 19. **J'ai fait laver ma voiture.** | I had my car washed. |
| 19a. **Je l'ai fait laver.** | I had it washed. |
| 20. **Le professeur faisait lire les élèves.** | The teacher had (made) the pupils read. |
| 20a. **Il les faisait lire.** | He had them read. |
| 21. **Il leur faisait lire trois contes par semaine.** | He had them * read three stories a week. |

*Of course, the indirect object can also be used with its more common meanings (*to somebody, for somebody*); so that P.S. 21, for example, could also mean: *He had three stories read to them each week.* When one is dealing with isolated sentences (as in these grammatical examples), they may appear more ambiguous than they would be in real contextual use, where the situation or other indications outside the sentence itself generally make the meaning clear. See also P.S. 21a, 24a, 25 and Note (c).

| | |
|---|---|
| 21a. **Il les leur faisait lire chaque semaine.** | He had them read them each week. |
| 22. **Il faisait écrire une critique de chaque conte par chaque élève.** | He had a critique of each story written by each student. |
| 23. **On fait passer cet examen à tous les élèves.** | They make all students take that exam. |
| 24. **Elle m'a fait nettoyer ma chambre.** | She made me clean my room. |
| 24a. **Elle me l'a fait nettoyer.** | She made me clean it. (*or* She had it cleaned for me.) |
| 25. **Elle la lui a fait nettoyer.** | She had her (him) clean it. (*or* She had it cleaned for her [him].) |
| 26. **Elle a fait nettoyer ma chambre par la bonne.** | She had my room cleaned by the maid. |
| 26a. **Elle l'a fait nettoyer par elle.** | She had it cleaned by her. |
| 27. **Laissez-moi faire réparer votre montre.** | Let me have your watch repaired. |
| 28. **Je la ferai réparer par M. Béjart, qui est horloger.** | I'll have it repaired by Mr. Bejart, who is a watchmaker. |
| 29. **Qui a fait sortir cette femme?** | Who had (made) that woman leave? |
| 29a. **Qui l'a fait sortir?** | Who had her leave? |
| 30. **Il faut faire venir le médecin.** | We (you, they, etc.) must send for the doctor. |
| 31. **Le médecin l'a fait boire.** | The doctor had him (her) drink. |
| 32. **Il lui a fait boire beaucoup d'eau.** | He had him (her) drink a lot of water. |

*Comparison of* **quitter, sortir, partir**

| | |
|---|---|
| 33. **J'ai quitté le bureau à cinq heures.** | I left the office at five o'clock. |
| 34. **Les Durand nous ont quittés à Dijon.** | The Durands left us in Dijon. |
| 35. **Pierre et Paul ont dû se quitter à Rome.** | Peter and Paul had to separate in Rome. |
| 36. **Il ne l'a pas quittée des yeux pendant toute la soirée.** | He hasn't taken his eyes off her all evening. |

| | |
|---|---|
| 37. **Après cette année, je vais quitter l'enseignement.** | After this year, I'm going to give up teaching. |
| 38. **Ne quittez pas!** | Hold the phone! |
| 39. **Il est sorti du commissariat de police accompagné par un agent.** | He came out of the police station accompanied by a policeman. |
| 40. **Aucun élève ne peut sortir avant d'avoir fini le devoir.** | No pupil may leave before finishing the assigned exercise. |
| 41. **Ma femme et moi ne sortons pas beaucoup.** | My wife and I don't go out very much. |
| 42. **Il ne sera pas facile de sortir de cet embarras.** | It won't be easy to get out of this difficulty. |
| 43. **Il a sorti de sa poche un paquet de cigarettes.** | He took a pack of cigarettes out of his pocket. |
| 44. **Nous partirons de Londres pour rentrer aux Etats-Unis.** | We will leave from London to return to the United States. |
| 45. **Son père part pour le bureau toujours à neuf heures moins le quart.** | His father always leaves for the office at a quarter to nine. |
| 46. **Quand partez-vous pour Madrid?** | When are you leaving for Madrid? |
| 47. **Nous avons décidé de ne pas partir.** | We have decided not to go away. |
| 48. **A quelle heure part le train de Lyon?** | (At) what time does the Lyons train leave? |

## NOTES

(a) **Connaître** means *to know* in the sense of *be acquainted with* or *recognize.* **Savoir** means *to know* in the sense of *understand* or *possess knowledge.* **Savoir** (+ infinitive) means *to know how to (do something).* [ex. 1-13]

(b) The idiom **venir de** (+ infinitive) is used in only two tenses: the present *(has just . . . , have just . . .)* and the imperfect *(had just . . .).* [ex. 14-18]

(c) **Faire** followed by an infinitive means *to have (something) done.* In this construction, the dependent infinitive follows directly after the verb **faire.**

Any personal pronoun objects precede **faire** rather than the dependent infinitive (except in the affirmative imperative, where they follow directly after **faire**: **Faites-la chanter.** *Have her sing.* or *Have it sung.).*

Notice that the "doer" of the action is expressed as a direct object if the dependent infinitive is used intransitively (i.e. has no direct object). [ex. 20, 20a, 29-31]

But if the infinitive has a direct object, the "doer" is expressed as an indirect object [ex. 21, 21a, 23-25, 32] or as the object of the preposition **par** [ex. 22, 26, 26a, 28]. The **par** form is preferable where emphasis is desired or where the indirect object form would be ambiguous.

(d) Note that there is no agreement of the past participle of **faire** in this causal construction. [ex. 19a, 24a, 25, 26a, 29a, 31]

(e) **Quitter** is used only with an object; that is, it is always transitive. (In Pattern Sentence 38, the object *le téléphone* is understood.) **Quitter** takes the auxiliary **avoir** in compound tenses. [ex. 33-38]

(f) The intransitive verbs **sortir** *(to go out)* and **partir** *(to go away)* are conjugated with **être** in the compound tenses. The preposition **de** is used before the place left (**partir de New York** *leave New York,* **sortir de la chambre** *leave the room*). [ex. 39-42, 44-48]

(g) **Sortir** may also be used with an object *(to take . . . out).* With this transitive meaning, it takes the auxiliary **avoir**. [ex. 43]

## EXERCISES

**A.** *For each of the English versions of the Pattern Sentences give the French equivalent. (Cover the left-hand column.)*

**B.** *Read each sentence aloud, using the appropriate form of* savoir *or* connaître.

1. Je ne ________ pas cette région du pays. 2. Je ________ que ces gens-là sont des pêcheurs. 3. Il m'a demandé si je ________ où ils habitent. 4. Voici les Dupont. Les ________ -vous? 5. Je ________ ce tableau. C'est le *Bouquet de fleurs* de

Cézanne. 6. Tout le monde ________ ce célèbre café. 7. Mon père ne ________ pas encore que j'ai réussi aux examens. 8. Votre ami ________ très bien jouer de la guitare. 9. Oui, mais il ne ________ pas jouer au bridge. 10. C'est demain que nous aurons l'examen, et je ne ________ presque rien. 11. Tout le monde ________ que ce n'est pas vrai. 12. Mon frère ________ bien Londres et Paris.

C. *Choose the appropriate beginning for the question indicated.*

Savez-vous ...
Connaissez-vous ...

1. ... la date?
2. ... cette jeune fille?
3. ... où elle demeure?
4. ... cet endroit?
5. ... pourquoi il est célèbre?
6. ... quand il a été fondé?
7. ... quelle heure il est?
8. ... ce théâtre?
9. ... quel acteur joue ce rôle?
10. ... l'acteur qui joue ce rôle?
11. ... beaucoup de personnes dans la ville?
12. ... beaucoup sur ce sujet-là?
13. ... qu'ils sont malades?
14. ... nager?

D. *Use* venir de *to reword the following sentences, as in the example.*

*Example:* Il est arrivé ce matin. – Il vient d'arriver ce matin.

1. J'ai acheté une nouvelle voiture.
2. Nous avons vu votre ami Charles.
3. Ils sont sortis de la salle.
4. Elle a trouvé sa montre.
5. Qu'est-ce que vous avez fait?
6. Les garçons ont fini tout le travail.

*Repeat, using* venir de *in the imperfect and adding a second clause as in the following example:* Il venait d'arriver ce matin quand vous avez téléphoné.

**E.** *Following the pattern of the example, use each of the phrases below to answer the question.*

*Example:* Qu'est-ce qu'il vous fait faire?
Il nous fait manger tous les légumes.

Qu'est-ce qu'il vous fait faire?

... lire deux pièces par semaine.
... écrire beaucoup de compositions.
... réparer les dommages.
... écouter des disques français.
... assister à toutes ses conférences.
... laver sa voiture.

*Repeat, changing the question as follows and adjusting the answers accordingly:*

Qu'est-ce qu'il leur fait faire?
Qu'est-ce qu'il lui fait faire?
Qu'est-ce qu'il vous a fait faire?
Qu'est-ce qu'ils me feront faire?
Qu'est-ce qu'on nous fera faire?

**F.** *Repeat each sentence, changing any noun complements to pronouns.*

*Examples:* J'ai fait peindre le garage. – Je l'ai fait peindre.
Qui a fait courir les prisonniers? – Qui les a fait courir?
Elle fait manger sa soupe à Pierre. – Elle la lui fait manger.
Faites réparer la voiture par M. Durand. – Faites-la réparer par lui.

1. Nous faisons construire une nouvelle maison.
2. Elle a fait laver ses bas.
3. Faites sortir les élèves.

4. Qui fera venir le médecin?
5. J'ai fait apporter sa machine au mécanicien.
6. On fait payer ces droits à tous les voyageurs.
7. Vous ferez préparer le repas par Mme Savarin.
8. Ils ont fait détenir cette femme par les agents de police.
9. Est-ce que tu as fait envoyer le message?
10. On fera parler leurs amis.

G. *Use the appropriate form of* quitter, sortir, *or* partir.

1. On ne peut pas ________ de la salle pendant l'examen. 2. Tous les navires ________ de ce port. 3. Nous venons de ________ nos amis à l'entrée du métro. 4. Il ________ la maison hier soir sans rien dire. 5. Ils ________ demain pour la Grèce. 6. Je vais vous aider à ________ d'embarras. 7. Mon père ________ l'armée il y a cinq ans. 8. M. Fogg ________ toujours à la même heure pour aller au club. 9. Tous les autocars de cette compagnie ________ de la Place de l'Opéra. 10. Plusieurs gens ________ de l'hôtel en même temps. 11. Il n'est jamais chez lui. Il ________ tous les soirs. 12. Dites-lui de ne pas ________ son travail. Nous attendrons.

*Supplementary Written Exercises for Lesson 12 are on p. 106.*

# *Written Exercises for Lessons 1-12*

I. Definite, indefinite, and partitive articles. *Write in French:*

1. Did she buy some bread and wine? 2. She doesn't like wine; she prefers coffee. 3. We always have coffee for breakfast. 4. I wanted to buy some good pastries, but I didn't have any money. 5. What do you know about languages? 6. We used to speak German at home, and I have studied French and Spanish. 7. Is his father from Spain? 8. No, he is from Mexico, but he has spent a great deal of time in Spain, Portugal, and Italy. 9. I don't know Paris very well. Where is Friedland Avenue? 10. We are going to Washington, but we will spend a few days in New York also. 11. We don't have any classes on Saturdays. 12. Here is a chemistry book written in German. 13. Professor Rousseau is not Swiss; he is a Frenchman. 14. Have they done any research on poverty *(pauvreté f.)* and vice *(vice m.)*? 15. They didn't have the time in school last year. 16. Wash your hands quickly.

II. Verb tenses in the indicative. *Write in French:*

1. Are you finishing your work? 2. I don't understand that question. 3. She says that she has seen you often at school. 4. When

did they arrive? 5. He finished his work and went out. 6. We used to see them every day. 7. Were you finishing your work when I came in? 8. She was in the building when I left. 9. If we arrive on time, they will be there. 10. If they knew that, they wouldn't have any difficulty. 11. If I knew them, I would lend them the book. 12. If you had been there, you would have seen her. 13. He says that he will do it. 14. He said that he would do it. 15. As soon as you have finished this, we will return home.

III. Present, imperfect, and past indefinite. *Write in French:*

1. They always admire beautiful paintings. 2. They always admired beautiful paintings. 3. They have always admired beautiful paintings. 4. We are reading an interesting novel. 5. We were reading an interesting novel. 6. We have read many interesting novels. 7. Do you read this newspaper? 8. Did you always read that newspaper? 9. Did you read the newspaper last night? 10. I wanted to go there, but I decided to finish my lessons. 11. I was looking at the examination when your cousin came in. 12. She was with him when you telephoned. 13. He used to visit all the museums but he never looked at the paintings. 14. Who founded the first school in the new world? 15. If he read the newspapers, he would understand those things. 16. Suppose we write to them!

IV. Personal pronouns. *Write in French:*

1. I saw him yesterday and he gave me the position. 2. Did you introduce yourself to him? 3. Call me at eight o'clock. 4. Don't give her the letter; her father will give it to her. 5. Did he show them to you? 6. No, show them to me, please. 7. The teacher will give them to us. 8. Who gave them to him? 9. She told the story to us but she didn't tell it to them. 10. Was he talking about me? 11. I was with them at her house last night. 12. John showed it to me. 13. Who showed it to him? 14. Don't show it to her. 15. They washed and dressed as quickly as possible.

V. Demonstrative adjectives and pronouns. *Write in French:*

1. Is it warm this morning? 2. Who is that woman? 3. I know this boy, but I don't know that man. 4. Where did you buy these

oranges? 5. Those children don't understand at all. 6. Do you go to this school or that one? 7. This car and that one are French cars, aren't they? 8. He's the one who bought it. (It is he who bought it.) 9. Who are those children? They are my friends Paul and John. 10. We don't understand all that, but it is interesting. 11. This one is not his first book; it is the one he wrote in England. 12. It is not my brother's car; it is John's. 13. I have read the best novels of the 19th century and those of the 20th century. 14. What's that? 15. I don't know, but look at this. 16. We're the ones they saw in the restaurant.

VI. Relative and interrogative pronouns. *Write in French:*

1. Who is looking for me? 2. There is the boy who is looking for you. 3. What does he want? 4. Here is the letter that he mentioned. 5. To whom did she write that letter? 6. She wrote it to the girl with whom she lived in Marseilles. 7. With what did they finish the work? 8. I'm the one who finished the work you are talking about. (It is I who finished the work of which you are speaking.) 9. Whom did they invite to our house? 10. I don't know the people whom they invited. 11. What worries him? 12. I am going to explain to you the problem that worries him. 13. Did you see the car in which they were traveling? 14. This is not the car I was thinking about. 15. Are you the man whose truck was wrecked? 16. Whose hat is this?

VII. Special relatives and interrogatives. *Write in French:*

1. He doesn't remember the day when I met him in Grenoble. 2. We visited the house in which my father was born. 3. Here is what interested us. 4. I shall tell you all that we did during our visit. 5. Tell me what you need and I will give you what we have. 6. What train did they take? 7. Which of those trains is the best? 8. What is the explanation that they gave you for going to Biarritz? 9. Which of the hotels are you thinking about? 10. What is a *concierge*? 11. With which one of the two policemen were you talking? 12. Which ones of your friends did you meet? 13. Were they with you at the moment when the policemen arrived? 14. Which are the best pictures that you took? 15. What pictures are you talking about?

VIII. The subjunctive. *Write in French:*

1. I would like to explain my plan. 2. I want all the students to understand my explanation. 3. They are afraid that they will not pass the examination. 4. We are glad that they passed the examination. 5. Do you prefer that we rest a bit? 6. I don't believe that that is necessary. 7. She wants us to arrive before six o'clock, so that we can see them before they leave. 8. We must travel fast. 9. He is surprised that you are going with us. 10. I am not sure that he has enough money. 11. It's too bad that that happened. 12. He had borrowed the money in order to take this trip. 13. Although that student may finish the examination before the others, he may not leave until eleven o'clock. 14. I doubt that he has answered all the questions. 15. Do you know a school where there are no examinations?

IX. Possessive adjectives and pronouns. *Write in French:*

1. Whose suitcase is this? 2. His suitcase is in the car and mine is in the house. 3. He lost his shoes, socks, shirt, tie, and glasses *(lunettes f.).* 4. Is that new Simca yours? 5. Yes, it's mine. 6. Their car is much longer than ours. 7. Are our schools larger than theirs? 8. Did they wash their faces? 9. Does your head ache? 10. My friends and Paul's will arrive tomorrow. 11. Paul's friends are coming by plane. 12. His uncle is the headmaster of your school.

X. Passive voice; adverbial pronouns *y* and *en;* partitive pronoun *en. Write in French:*

1. These people were invited by my uncle. 2. We were in Nice when they arrived there. 3. Did you go there last summer also? 4. They were served delicious meals in that hotel. 5. They left *(laisser)* their suitcases there because they didn't need them for the trip. 6. They will be found before morning. 7. No one saw the accident, but everybody was talking about it. 8. That is easily understood. 9. I bought some newspapers, and I see that you have some too. 10. Yes, I bought several in order to see all the pictures. 11. Were a lot of pictures taken? 12. When the door opened, everybody stood up.

XI. The prepositions *en* and *à*. *Write in French:*

1. In 1961 he went to Europe with his family. 2. Upon arriving in Paris, they went immediately to their hotel. 3. We saw them while walking *(se promener)* in the *Bois de Boulogne.* 4. We were in England this morning and we shall be in Switzerland this afternoon. 5. I never travel by boat in the winter. 6. I have a lot of work to do, but I can finish it by working day and night. 7. I would prefer to go horseback riding or play tennis. 8. Is that language hard to understand? 9. Do you have something interesting to read? 10. While waiting for them I met Françoise. 11. She's the girl with the blond hair who was on the boat with you, isn't she? 12. She brought her typewriter but she forgot her iron. 13. I am going to buy a new toothbrush before going to Chartres. 14. Chartres is ninety-six kilometers from Paris, isn't it? 15. We are going to Canada to see some friends in Toronto. 16. Did that happen in Iraq or in Israel?

**XII.** *Savoir & connaître; venir de* + inf.; *faire* + inf.; *quitter, sortir, partir. Write in French:*

1. I have just received a telegram from my friend Monique. 2. Do you know her? She is the girl with the blond hair who lives in Chartres. 3. No, but I know that she is coming to the United States next year. 4. She left our school because they made her speak English. 5. Her sister has just got married. 6. They are leaving tomorrow morning. 7. If you are going out this afternoon, may I borrow *(emprunter)* your typewriter? 8. They are having a house built a short distance from here. 9. Did you know that? 10. They know English, French, and German very well. 11. Does he know this section of the country? 12. They had just arrived here when we met them.

# *Reference Materials*

# *Supplementary Notes on Grammar and Usage*

(Written exercises based upon these notes are found immediately after this section on pp. 165-179.)

## NOUNS

### *A. Gender*

All French nouns are either masculine or feminine – there are no neuter nouns in French.

Learning the definite or the indefinite article with the noun is an easy way to remember the gender.

**le livre** **la grammaire** **un hôtel** **une automobile**

Learning nouns in context, as in the Pattern Sentences, for example, helps to fix in mind both the gender and the meaning. Active practice is the only effective means to real mastery, but the following notes may be of some additional value.

1. The names of months, days, and languages are masculine.

| | | |
|---|---|---|
| **juillet dernier** | **le dimanche** | **le chinois** |
| **avril prochain** | **(le) mardi gras** | **l'ancien français** |

2. Most abstract nouns are feminine.

| | | | |
|---|---|---|---|
| **la justice** | **la vertu** | **la paix** | **la culture** |
| **l'amitié** | **la volonté** | **la peur** | **la certitude** |

However, there are numerous exceptions – especially words ending in **–isme.**

| | | |
|---|---|---|
| **le bonheur** | **le patriotisme** | **le nationalisme** |
| **le courage** | **le réalisme** | **l'existentialisme** |
| **l'amour** | **le nazisme** | **le socialisme** |

3. The following endings may be considered characteristically masculine (although there are a number of exceptions).

| **–age** | **–eau** | **–ment** | any consonant except **–n** | |
|---|---|---|---|---|
| **le langage** | **le bureau** | **le châtiment** | **le fer** | **le bras** |
| **le courage** | **le château** | **le testament** | **le ballet** | **le calcul** |

4. The following endings may be considered characteristically feminine (although there are exceptions).

| **–ion** | **–ure** | an ending pronounced [ɑ̃s] | |
|---|---|---|---|
| **la nation** | **la figure** | **la dance** | **la prudence** |
| **la passion** | **la peinture** | **les vacances** | **la défense** |

**–e** preceded by vowel or double consonant

| | | | |
|---|---|---|---|
| **la vue** | **la classe** | **la consonne** | **la bagarre** |
| **la vie** | **la famille** | **l'emplette** | **la canaille** |

(Among the exceptions to the last item above are a number of common nouns ending in **–amme: le télégramme**, **le programme,** etc.)

*B. Number*

Most French nouns add a silent **–s** to form the plural.

**les amis  les pianos  les églises  les rats  les fers  les saisons**

The following exceptions should be remembered.

1. If the singular ends in **–s, –x,** or **–z,** there is no change in the plural.

   **le bras – les bras  la voix – les voix  le nez – les nez**

2. If the singular ends in **–al,** this becomes **–aux** in the plural.

   **le cheval – les chevaux  le général – les généraux**

3. Most nouns ending in **–eau** and **–eu,** and many in **–ou,** form the plural by adding a silent **–x.**

   **le bateau – les bateaux  le feu – les feux  le bijou – les bijoux**

4. Special exceptions.

   **l'œil – les yeux  le bal – les bals**
   **le ciel – les cieux  le travail – les travaux**

## ARTICLES (Definite, Indefinite, Partitive)

*A. General Remarks*

The student should notice that, whereas in English nouns are frequently used with no article (or similar limiting modifier), such a thing is very uncommon in French. Generally speaking, an English noun with no limiting modifier will take either the partitive article or the definite article when translated into French. (See Les. 1.) However, the partitive article and the indefinite article are generally omitted after **en** and **sans (une montre en or, un pont en acier, sans argent, sans amis),** after many expressions which require the preposition **de (remplir d'eau, servir de guide, avoir besoin de renseigne-**

**ments)**, and in many phrases with the preposition **à (aller à pied, monter à cheval, un verre à vin, un panier à papier).**

The contrary is to be observed in the use of predicate nouns with a purely adjectival value. Here, English often uses an indefinite article whereas none is used in French (the word being treated as an adjective unless it is further qualified).

| | |
|---|---|
| **Son père est médecin.** | Her father is a doctor. |
| **Votre ami est-il catholique?** | Is your friend a Catholic? |
| **Cette chanteuse est Canadienne.** | That singer is a Canadian. |

*B. Remarks Supplementary to the Notes of Lesson 1*

1. Remember that the definite articles **le** and **les** (but not **la** or **l'**) combine with the prepositions **à** and **de**.

   | | |
   |---|---|
   | **à + le = au** | **de + le = du** |
   | **à + les = aux** | **de + les = des** |

2. The definite article is used when an adjective precedes a name.

   **la petite Yvette** little Yvette  **la belle Marlène** beautiful Marlene

3. The definite article is used between the price and the following expression of weight or measure.

   **mille francs la douzaine** a thousand francs a dozen
   **cent francs la bouteille** a hundred francs a bottle

4. Notice in the examples above that **un** is not used before **cent** and **mille**.

5. **De** usually replaces either the indefinite article or the partitive article before a noun which is the object of a negative verb or the complement of **il n'y a pas.**

   | | |
   |---|---|
   | **N'avez-vous pas de voiture?** | Don't you have a car? |
   | **Il n'a jamais d'argent.** | He never has any money. |
   | **Il n'y a pas de lait dans le verre.** | There is no milk in the glass. |

6. By exception, a few names of states and countries are used without the definite article.

| | |
|---|---|
| **Hawaii est un état; Israël et Cuba sont des pays.** | Hawaii is a state; Israel and Cuba are countries. |

7. The article (particularly the indefinite article) is sometimes omitted before nouns used in apposition.

| | |
|---|---|
| **C'est l'œuvre de Titien, peintre italien du 16$^{e}$ siècle.** | It's the work of Titian, an Italian painter of the 16th century. |
| **Il parle de Molière, auteur de** ***l'Avare.*** | He is speaking of Molière, the author of *l'Avare.* |

See also Les. 11 for use of article after the prepositions **en** and **à**.

## ADJECTIVES

### *A. General Remarks*

French adjectives offer difficulty to English-speaking students principally because of the necessity of developing the habit of observing the agreement in gender and number with the noun or pronoun modified. Obviously, this habit can be established only with practice – and in this category, written practice is the most effective.

### *B. Formation of the Feminine Singular*

Most adjectives add mute –**e** to the masculine singular to form the feminine singular.

| | |
|---|---|
| **un grand pays** | **une grande nation** |
| **le petit garçon** | **la petite fille** |
| **Ce livre est excellent.** | **Cette pièce est excellente.** |

Note that where this mute –**e** is added to a final silent consonant (as in the three examples above), the consonant becomes pronounced.

When the masculine singular already ends in mute –**e**, there is no change for the feminine.

| | |
|---|---|
| **un problème facile** | **une leçon facile** |
| **le pauvre homme** | **la pauvre femme** |
| **Son frère est riche.** | **Sa sœur est riche.** |

The following special cases should be remembered.

1. No French words end in unaccented –**e** + *single consonant* + *mute* –**e**. When the addition of the mute –**e** for the feminine would result in such an ending, either a grave accent is added to the –**e** preceding the consonant or the consonant is doubled.

| | |
|---|---|
| **cher, chère** | **actuel, actuelle** |
| **premier, première** | **ancien, ancienne** |
| **secret, secrète** | **muet, muette** |
| **inquiet, inquiète** | **net, nette** |

2. A final –**f** changes to –**v**, and a final –**x** changes to –**s** before a mute –**e**.

| | | |
|---|---|---|
| **bref, brève** | **neuf, neuve** | **heureux, heureuse** |
| **chétif, chétive** | **dangereux, dangereuse** | **paresseux, paresseuse** |

3. Three very common adjectives have a second masculine singular form which is used before words beginning with a vowel or mute **h**, and from which the feminine is derived.

| | | |
|---|---|---|
| **un beau jour** | **un bel enfant** | **une belle peinture** |
| **un nouveau livre** | **un nouvel air** | **une nouvelle voiture** |
| **un vieux musée** | **un vieil homme** | **une vieille actrice** |

4. Other special cases.

| | | |
|---|---|---|
| **bas, basse** | **blanc, blanche** | **fou (fol), folle** |
| **épais, épaisse** | **franc, franche** | **mou (mol), molle** |
| **gros, grosse** | **sec, sèche** | **bon, bonne** |
| **faux, fausse** | **grec, grecque** | **sot, sotte** |
| **roux, rousse** | **public, publique** | **favori, favorite** |

| | |
|---|---|
| **doux, douce** | **long, longue** |
| **frais, fraîche** | **gentil, gentille** |

*C. Formation of the Plurals*

All feminine plurals are formed by adding **–s** to the feminine singular.

The masculine plural forms of adjectives generally follow the spelling patterns noted on p. 111 above for the plural of nouns, with the following notable exceptions:

1. There are no common adjectives with a masculine singular ending in **–eu** except **bleu** *(blue)*, which adds **–s** for the masculine plural **(bleus).**
2. Adjectives with a masculine singular ending in **–ou** add **–s** for the masculine plural. **(fou – fous, mou – mous)**
3. A few adjectives with a masculine singular ending in **–al**, by exception, add **–s** for the masculine plural. **(final – finals, naval – navals, fatal – fatals)**

An adjective modifying two nouns of different genders is in the masculine plural.

*D. Adjective Phrases*

In English a word which is normally a noun may very frequently be pressed into service as an adjective.

| | |
|---|---|
| *a brick house* | *a coffee cup* |
| *some leather shoes* | *a wine glass* |

In French, such nouns remain nouns and must be joined by a preposition to the noun modified.

| | |
|---|---|
| **une maison de (en) briques** | **une tasse à café** |
| **des chaussures en cuir** | **un verre à vin** |

The prepositions **de** or **en** are used to express the material of which the object is made. The preposition **à** is generally used to indicate the use for which it is intended or a notable characteristic. [See Les. 11: 31, 32.]

### E. *Adjective Modifying* quelque chose *or* rien

When an adjective modifies **quelque chose** or **rien**, it is in the masculine singular and is joined by the preposition **de**.

| | |
|---|---|
| **quelque chose d'extraordinaire** | something extraordinary |
| **rien de nouveau** | nothing new |

### F. *The Adjective (and Indefinite Pronoun)* tout

Remember that the masculine plural form is irregular **(tous)** and that the definite article (or possessive or demonstrative adjective) is placed between **tout** and the noun.

| | |
|---|---|
| **J'ai déjà fait tout le travail** | I have already done all the work. |
| **Elle a perdu toute son influence.** | She has lost all her influence. |
| **Qui a acheté tous ces articles?** | Who bought all those articles? |
| **Ils fermeront toutes les écoles.** | They will close all the schools. |
| **Nous y allons tous les jours.** | We go there every day. |

Notice below the special meanings of the plural forms used with numbers.

| | |
|---|---|
| **Tous les deux ont répondu en même temps.** | Both of them answered at once. |
| **Je les ai invitées, toutes les cinq.** | I invited all five of them. |
| **On le fait tous les trois jours.** | That is done every three days. |
| **Il y a une photo après toutes les vingt pages.** | There is a picture after every twenty pages. |
| **Elle est absente tous les deux jours.** | She is absent every other day. |

The masculine singular **tout** is also used as an indefinite pronoun meaning *everything, all.*

| | |
|---|---|
| **Tout n'est pas perdu.** | Everything is not lost. |
| **Personne ne sait tout.** | No one knows everything. |
| **Elle a tout entendu.** | She heard everything. |

Notice above the position of **tout** between the auxiliary and the past participle when used as the object of a compound verb.

The plural forms also are used as pronouns similar to English *all.*

| | |
|---|---|
| **Tous** [tus] **sont partis en même temps.**<br>**Ils sont partis tous** [tus] **en même temps.** | All left at once (at the same time). |
| **Toutes sont parties en même temps.**<br>**Elles sont parties toutes en même temps.** | They all left at once (at the same time). |
| **Je les ai vus tous** [tus].<br>**Je les ai vues toutes.** | I saw them all.<br>I saw all of them. |

Note that when the masculine plural form **tous** is used as a pronoun, the final –s is pronounced. Practically speaking, one may say that the final –s is pronounced whenever **tous** is not followed by **les**, a possessive adjective, or a demonstrative adjective.

Notice in the following examples that **tous** as subject takes a plural verb form whereas **tout le monde** takes a singular.

| | |
|---|---|
| **Tous le disent. (Ils le disent tous.)** | (They) all say so. |
| **Tout le monde le dit.** | Everybody says so. |

(For **tout** used as an adverb see pp. 123-124.)

### *G. Position of Descriptive Adjectives*

There are no simple and absolute rules governing the position of descriptive adjectives in French. Therefore the only sure way to mastery is through hearing and reading as much good French as possible and imitating the usage observed. In the meanwhile, certain basic principles can be stated which will serve as reasonably accurate guides in most cases.

Most descriptive adjectives in French follow the nouns they modify. This is particularly true of the following types.

1. Adjectives of physical quality (color, shape, etc.)

   **une cravate bleue** a blue tie
   **la tour carrée** the square tower

2. Adjectives of nationality, religion, and similar categories

   **l'art égyptien** Egyptian art
   **un écrivain calviniste** a Calvinistic writer

3. Participles used as adjectives

   **un commerce ruiné** a ruined trade
   **la poupée dansante** the dancing doll

4. Long adjectives

   **une conversation fastidieuse** a dull conversation
   **une étude géologique** a geological study

5. Adjectives modified by adverbs

   **une histoire très longue** a very long story
   **des marchandises extrêmement chères** some very expensive goods

The following common adjectives generally precede the noun.

| | | | | |
|---|---|---|---|---|
| **beau** | **court** | **jeune** | **mauvais** | **petit** |
| **bon** | **grand** | **joli** | **méchant** | **vieux** |
| **cher** | **gros** | **long** | **nouveau** | **vilain** |

A few adjectives change in meaning according to their position before or after the noun.

**un ancien élève** a former pupil
**les mœurs anciennes** the ancient customs

**un brave garçon** a fine boy
**un homme brave** a brave man

**le dernier jour** the last day
**le mois dernier** last month

**la même ville** the same city
**la ville même** the very city, the city itself

**le pauvre roi** the poor king *(pity)*
**un jeune homme pauvre** a poor young man

**ma propre chambre** my own room
**des vêtements propres** clean clothes

**la seule fois** the only time
**son courage seul** his courage alone

### *H. Comparative and Superlative of Adjectives and Adverbs*

In comparative statements one expresses either superiority, inferiority, or equality. In French these relationships are expressed as follows:

| | |
|---|---|
| *superiority* | **plus** *(adj. or adv.)* **que** |
| *inferiority* | **moins** *(adj. or adv.)* **que** |
| *equality* | **aussi** *(adj. or adv.)* **que** |

| | |
|---|---|
| **Cette maison-ci est plus chère que celle-là.** | This house is more expensive than that one. |
| **Je vois les Martin moins fréquemment que les Dupont.** | I see the Martins less frequently than the Duponts. |
| **L'histoire est aussi intéressante que la littérature.** | History is as interesting as literature. |

In a negative statement, **si** may replace **aussi** above:

**Il n'est pas si grand que vous.** He is not as (so) tall as you.

There is no difference in French between the comparative and superlative forms.

| | |
|---|---|
| **Marie est la plus intelligente des deux.** | Mary is the more intelligent of the two. |
| **Jean est le plus intelligent de la classe.** | John is the most intelligent one in the class. |
| **C'est la meilleure des deux routes, mais ce n'est pas la meilleure route du pays.** | It's the better of the two roads, but it's not the best road in the country. |

Because of its meaning, the superlative always takes the definite article (or a possessive or other limiting adjective). When the adjective follows the noun in the superlative, the definite article is used twice.

| | |
|---|---|
| **C'est la pièce la plus amusante de l'année.** | It's the funniest play of the year. |

Notice that **de** is used in French after a superlative even though the English version may use *in*.

The adjective **bon** and the adverb **bien** have irregular forms for the comparative-superlative.

| | |
|---|---|
| **bon** good | **meilleur** better, best |
| **bien** well | **mieux** better, best |

## ADVERBS

### *A. Formation*

Many adverbs are formed by adding the suffix –**ment** to the feminine singular of the corresponding adjective. This derivation is like that of English adverbs ending in *–ly*.

| | |
|---|---|
| **gracieuse** gracious | **gracieusement** graciously |
| **sérieuse** serious | **sérieusement** seriously |
| **facile** easy | **facilement** easily |
| **pauvre** poor | **pauvrement** poorly |

The following special cases should be noted.

1. The adverbial ending **–ment** is added to the masculine singular if that form ends in a vowel.

| | |
|---|---|
| **joli** pretty | **joliment** prettily |
| **poli** polite | **poliment** politely |
| **vrai** true | **vraiment** truly |

But adjectives with two masculine singular forms add **–ment** to the feminine.

| | |
|---|---|
| **fou (fol) folle** crazy | **follement** madly |
| **beau (bel) belle** beautiful | **bellement** nicely |
| **nouveau (nouvel) nouvelle** new | **nouvellement** newly |

2. Most adjectives with the endings **–ant** and **–ent** change to **–amment** and **–emment** (pronounced alike: [amɑ̃] ).

| | |
|---|---|
| **constant** constant | **constamment** constantly |
| **prudent** prudent | **prudemment** prudently |

3. A number of adjectives change the mute **–e** of the feminine to **–é**.

| | |
|---|---|
| **énormément** enormously | **conformément** according, conformably |
| **profondément** profoundly | **communément** commonly |
| **aveuglément** blindly | **confusément** confusedly |

*B. Position*

There are no absolute rules for the placing of an adverb in respect to the verb it modifies, but the following remarks may serve as a guide to normal usage.

1. Adverbs generally follow immediately after the verb in simple tenses (or after the **pas** when negative, or after any pronoun joined to the verb by a hyphen).

| | |
|---|---|
| **Ce jeune homme danse bien.** | That young man dances well. |
| **Le voyez-vous souvent?** | Do you see him often? |

| | |
|---|---|
| **Donnez-le-moi vite.** | Give it to me quickly. |
| **On ne fait pas toujours la même chose.** | They don't always do the same thing. |

2. In compound tenses, long adverbs and adverbs of time and place **(hier, aujourd'hui, ici, là, partout)** generally follow the past participle.

| | |
|---|---|
| **Ils ont agi prudemment.** | They acted prudently. |
| **Je les ai vus hier.** | I saw them yesterday. |
| **L'avez-vous cherché partout?** | Did you look for it everywhere? |

If the verb has a *following* object as well as an adverbial modifier, the tendency is to place the shorter of the two before the longer.

| | |
|---|---|
| **Il a parlé franchement aux agents de police.** | He spoke frankly to the policemen. |
| **Elle a acheté cela aujourd'hui.** | She bought that today. |

3. Other short, common adverbs generally follow the auxiliary unit (i.e. the auxiliary, or the pronoun in inverted forms, or the **pas** in the negative) when used with compound tenses.

| | |
|---|---|
| **Elle a déjà fini toute la leçon.** | She has already finished the whole lesson. |
| **Avez-vous jamais vu un fleuve?** | Have you ever seen a river? |
| **Je n'ai pas encore lu ce livre.** | I haven't yet read that book. |

4. Do not place an adverb between the subject and the verb (unless it is distinctly parenthetical).

| | |
|---|---|
| **Il arrive toujours en retard.** | He always arrives late. |

### *C. Comparative and Superlative of Adverbs*

This is discussed along with adjectives on pp. 119-120.

### *D. Adverbs of Quantity (and Nouns of Quantity)*

The adverbs of quantity in French require the preposition **de** before a following noun. As in the case of most expressions requiring **de**, the partitive article is not expressed before these nouns. The common adverbs of quantity are:

| | | | |
|---|---|---|---|
| **beaucoup** | much, many, a great deal | **assez** | enough |
| **autant** | as much, as many | **moins** | less, fewer |
| **combien** | how much, how many | **peu** | little, few |
| **tant** | so much, so many | **plus** | more |
| **trop** | too much, too many | | |

| | |
|---|---|
| **Ce jeune homme a beaucoup d'amis.** | That young man has many friends. |
| **Combien de temps avons-nous?** | How much time do we have? |
| **Je ne désire pas tant d'argent.** | I do not desire so much money |
| **Elle a très peu de confiance.** | She has very little confidence. |

By exception, the adverb **bien**, when used with a noun as an expression of quantity, always takes the definite article.

| | |
|---|---|
| **Bien des jours, je ne sors pas du tout.** | Many days, I don't go out at all |

In French, *most* followed by a noun is expressed by **la plupart. La plupart** requires **de** + *the definite article* before the following noun.

| | |
|---|---|
| **La plupart des hommes ne sont pas ambitieux.** | Most men are not ambitious. |

Most nouns of quantity in French take **de** before a following noun, just as *of* is used in English.

| | |
|---|---|
| **J'ai commandé un bock de bière blonde.** | I ordered a glass of pale beer. |
| **Il n'a acheté qu'un kilo de sucre.** | He bought only one kilo of sugar. |

### *E. The Adverb* **tout**

**Tout** (meaning *wholly, completely, quite, very,* etc.) is used as an adverb to modify an adjective or another adverb. It differs from other adverbs in that its form is not entirely invariable. The feminine spellings **(toute, toutes)** are used when the adjective following is feminine and begins with a consonant or an aspirate **h**.

| | |
|---|---|
| **Paul est tout aimable.** | Paul is quite likable. |
| **Marie est tout aimable.** | Mary is quite likable. |
| **Ils étaient tout heureux.** | They were completely happy. |
| **Elles étaient tout heureuses.** | They were completely happy. |
| **Les garçons paraissent tout malheureux.** | The boys appear very unhappy. |
| **Les filles paraissent toutes malheureuses.** | The girls appear very unhappy. |
| **Ce jeune homme est tout confus.** | That young man is quite confused. |
| **Cette jeune fille est toute confuse.** | That young lady is quite confused. |
| **Mon père est tout honteux de cette erreur.** | My father is very ashamed of that error. |
| **Ma mère est toute honteuse de cette erreur.** | My mother is very ashamed of that error. |
| **Tout nouveau tout beau.** *(proverb)* | What is new has a special attraction. |
| **Je crois qu'elle habite tout près.** | I believe she lives quite nearby. |

Notice that the result of the spelling changes is that the adverb is always pronounced [tut] before any adjective modifying a feminine noun or pronoun.

**Tout** also occurs in many common fixed phrases such as:

**tout à fait** completely
**tout à coup** suddenly, all of a sudden
**tout à l'heure** a little while ago *(with verb in past)*, in a little while *(with verb in future)*
**tout au plus** at the most
**tout de suite** immediately
**tout d'un coup** all at once

# PERSONAL PRONOUNS

## *A. General Remarks*

The use of personal pronouns cannot be mastered by silent study alone. It is by hearing them in use and repeating them in sentences over and over again that mastery is attained. The following remarks will be useful only insofar as they help guide the student's active practice and help insure his retention by clarifying the patterns.

## *B. Kinds of Personal Pronouns*

The personal pronouns are generally classified according to their use under the following designations:

| | |
|---|---|
| conjunctive ("with-verb") pronouns | subject pronouns<br>direct object pronouns<br>indirect object pronouns<br>reflexive pronouns (direct or indirect object) |
| disjunctive ("without-verb") pronouns | prepositional pronouns<br>emphatic pronouns |

## *C. Meanings of the Personal Pronouns*

| *pronoun* | *subject* | *dir. obj.* | *indir. obj.* | *obj. of prep.* |
|---|---|---|---|---|
| **je** | I | | | |
| **me** | | me | (to) me | |
| **moi** | I | me | (to) me | me |
| **nous** | we | us | (to) us | us |
| **vous** | you | you | (to) you | you |
| **il** | he, it *(m.)* | | | |
| **elle** | she, it *(f.)* | | | her |
| **le** | | him, it *(m.)* | | |
| **la** | | her, it *(f.)* | | |
| **lui** | he | | (to) him, (to) her | him |
| **ils** | they *(m.)* | | | |

| *pronoun* | *subject* | *dir. obj.* | *indir. obj.* | *obj. of prep.* |
|---|---|---|---|---|
| **elles** | they *(f.)* | | | them *(f.)* |
| **les** | | them | | |
| **leur** | | | (to) them | |
| **eux** | they *(m.)* | | | them *(m.)* |
| **se** | | himself, herself, itself, themselves, each other | | |

**Me**, **moi**, **nous**, and **vous** may also be used reflexively, with the meanings *myself, ourselves, yourself, yourselves.*

In a few disjunctive uses, **lui**, **elle**, **eux**, and **elles** may be direct objects of the verb.

**Tu**, **te**, and **toi** are omitted from the list for the sake of simplicity. They have the same meanings as **vous** *(sing.)*. (See par. D below.)

### *D. The Familiar Singular Pronouns* **tu, te, toi**

The precise use of the (second-person singular) familiar pronouns **tu**, **te**, and **toi** varies somewhat according to the social milieu and other factors; but, generally speaking, these pronouns are used in addressing a person whom you normally call by his first name. When they are used, it is important to remember that:

1. **Tu**, **te**, and **toi** may not be used in addressing more than one person.
2. Where **tu**, **te**, or **toi** is used, all other references to the same person must be in corresponding familiar forms (verb forms, possessive adjectives, pronouns, etc.).

**Dis-moi, s'il te plaît, si tu as écrit à ta sœur, à ton frère et à tes parents.**

Where students are still wrestling with adjective agreements, verb forms, word order, choice of prepositions, etc., many teachers advise using **vous** exlusively, in order to eliminate one complication which they believe unnecessary at this stage of the student's progress.

### *E. Position of Conjunctive ("With-Verb") Pronoun Objects*

As abundantly illustrated in Lesson 4 (and numerous other examples throughout the book), personal pronoun objects are placed before the verb in French, except in an affirmative command.

Notice in the examples that when personal pronoun objects follow the verb in affirmative commands, they are joined by hyphens to the verb (and to each other if there are two).

The relative order for two pronoun objects which you have observed in the examples is:

| | | | | | |
|---|---|---|---|---|---|
| *Before* the verb: | **me**<br>**te**<br>**nous**<br>**vous**<br>**se** | preceding | **le**<br>**la**<br>**les** | preceding | **lui**<br>**leur** |
| *After* the verb: | *direct object* | preceding | *indirect object* | | |

Either before or after the verb, **y** and **en** follow all personal pronoun objects. [See Les. 10:19, 20, 29 and p. 150 note.] **Y** precedes **en** if the two are used together.

| | |
|---|---|
| **Vous avez un livre et il y en a deux sur le bureau.** | You have one book and there are two on the desk. |

In most cases where a pronoun object occurs with a principal verb and a dependent infinitive, the pronoun is the object of the infinitive and is placed between the principal verb and the infinitive.

| | |
|---|---|
| **Je vais le lui dire.** | I'm going to tell him (so). |
| **Voulez-vous les voir?** | Do you want to see them? |
| **Elle ne peut pas nous écrire.** | She can't write to us. |

But with the causal **faire** and verbs of perception (**voir**, **entendre**, **regarder**, etc.) used with dependent infinitives, the personal pronoun objects precede the principal verb.

| | |
|---|---|
| **Je vous le ferai nettoyer.** | I'll have it cleaned for you. |

| | |
|---|---|
| **Nous les regardions jouer.** | We used to watch them play. |
| **Qui les a entendu sortir?** | Who heard them leave? |

(Note that with verbs of perception, it is very rare that the pronoun could be construed as the object of the infinitive.)

### *F. Uses of Disjunctive (Emphatic) Pronouns*

The "disjunctive" pronouns are, as the name implies, the "without-verb" pronouns. That is, they are the only forms of the personal pronouns which are used outside the subject-object-verb unit. They are also called "emphatic" because the positions in which they are used involve a certain emphasis in normal intonation. This general statement, along with the examples and Notes of Lesson 4, constitutes a sufficient guide for all the common uses of the disjunctive pronouns.

Within the scope of the general statement above, the specific uses of the disjunctive (emphatic) pronouns may be classified as follows:

1. As objects of prepositions [See Les. 4:54-66.]
2. In compound subjects or objects [67-70]
3. As predicate pronouns after **être** [71-73]
4. Added to conjunctive pronouns for emphasis

| | |
|---|---|
| **Ce type m'a dit ça à moi!** | That fellow said that to *me!* |
| **Qui t'a demandé ton avis, toi?** | Who asked for *your* opinion? |
| **Je ne l'aime pas, lui.** | I don't like *him.* |
| **A elle – ça ne lui fait rien.** | To *her* that makes no difference. |
| **Nous ne céderons pas, nous!** | *We* won't give in! |
| **Ça vous va-t-il à vous?** | Is that O.K. with *you?* |
| **Eux – on les déteste.** | People detest *them.* |
| **Je leur avais expliqué tout cela à elles.** | I had explained all that to *them.* |

5. Added to conjunctive third person forms for greater clarity

| | |
|---|---|
| **Je lui ai dit à elle que vous étiez là.** | I told her that you were there. |

| | |
|---|---|
| **On l'a vu, lui, devant l'hôtel.** | He was seen in front of the hotel. |

6. When a pronoun subject is separated from its verb by intervening words

| | |
|---|---|
| **Toi seul comprends ma situation.** | You alone understand my situation. |
| **Lui, avant tout autre, doit le reconnaître.** | He, above all, should recognize it. |

7. When no verb is expressed (including use after **que** in comparisons)

| | |
|---|---|
| **Qui est là? – Moi, monsieur.** | Who is there? – I, sir. |
| **T'a-t-il aidé? Pas lui!** | Did he help you? – Not he! |
| **Nous ne sommes pas si riches qu'eux** | We are not so (as) rich as they. |
| **Je suis aussi grande qu'elle.** | I am as tall as she. |

8. With **-même** to mean *myself, yourself, etc.*

| | |
|---|---|
| **Je le ferai moi-même.** | I'll do it myself. |
| **Eux-mêmes, ils l'ont choisi.** | They themselves chose it. |
| **Ce type-là pense toujours à lui-même.** | That guy is always thinking about himself. |

But with reflexive verbs, the conjunctive reflexive pronoun has this meaning.

| | |
|---|---|
| **Je me suis blessé sans le savoir.** | I hurt myself without knowing it. |

The disjunctive form with **-même** is added to a reflexive only in rare cases. Emphasis is generally achieved in some other way.

| | |
|---|---|
| **Il s'est rasé (lui-même).** | He shaved himself. |
| **Il s'est rasé sans aide.** | He shaved himself without help. |
| **Il s'est rasé tout seul!** | He shaved all by himself! |

## THE DEMONSTRATIVE PRONOUN ce

The demonstrative **ce** is used as a pronoun only as subject of the verb **être.*** This occurs in sentences of the following types:

1. **Ce** is always the introductory subject when **être** is followed by a pronoun complement or by a name.

| | |
|---|---|
| **C'est moi.** | It is I. |
| **C'était nous.** | It was we. |
| **Ce sont eux.** | It is they. |
| **C'est le tien.** | It's yours. |
| **C'est celui de mon père.** | It's my father's. |
| **C'est cela (ça)!** | That's it! (That's right!) |
| **C'était Pierre.** | It was Peter. |
| **Ce sont Yvonne et Marie.** | It's Yvonne and Mary. |
| **Ce sera Mlle. Dupont.** | It's probably Miss Dupont. |
| **C'est le général Martin.** | It's General Martin. |

2. **Ce** is the subject when **être** is followed by a noun complement, except in completely unmodified statements of religion, nationality, profession, and related categories (where **il** or **elle** is used, as indicated on pp. 3 and 6).

| | |
|---|---|
| **C'est un pays.** | It's a country. |
| **C'est un pays d'Europe.** | It's a country of Europe. |
| **Ce sont des montagnes.** | They are mountains. |
| **Ce sont des montagnes élevées.** | They are high mountains. |
| **C'était un ingénieur qui a dit cela.** | It was an engineer who said that. |
| **Qui est là? – C'est le médecin.** | Who is there? – It's the doctor. |
| **Quelle est sa profession? – Il est médecin.** | What is his profession? – He's a doctor. |
| **Quels sont ces hommes vêtus de blanc? – Ce sont des médecins.** | Who are those men dressed in white? – They are doctors. |

* This includes a few cases in which the infinitive **être** may be preceded by **aller**, **devoir**, or **pouvoir**: **Allez-y! Ce doit (va) (peut) être facile!** *Go ahead! It should (is going to) (may) be easy!*

| | |
|---|---|
| **Elles sont bouddhistes.** | They are Buddhists. |
| **C'est un bouddhiste fanatique.** | He is a fanatical Buddhist. |
| **Elle était Autrichienne.** | She was an Austrian. |
| **C'est l'Autrichienne qui chante au café.** | She's the Austrian who sings in the cafe. |

3. Where the complement of **être** is an adjective, **ce** is used as subject to stand for a previously mentioned idea or action, or for an object not expressed as a specific noun (which would therefore have gender and number). Where reference is to a specific noun, the appropriate personal pronoun is used. When the predicate adjective is followed by an infinitive, the formula **C'est** *(adj.)* **à** *(infin.)* is used where the subject stands for something previously mentioned; the formula **Il est** *(adj.)* **de** *(infin.)* ... is used where the real subject follows the adjective.

| | |
|---|---|
| **C'est bon!** | That's good! |
| **Votre article? – Il est bon.** | Your article? – It's good. |
| **Sa voiture? – Elle est bonne.** | His car? – It's good. |
| **Rester au lit jusqu'à midi? C'est si bon!** | Staying in bed until noon? It's so good! |
| **C'est beau! Mais qu'est-ce que c'est?** | It's pretty! But what is it? |
| **Est-ce bon à manger?** | Is it good to eat? |
| **Il est bon de manger avec tempérance.** | It's good to eat temperately. (i.e. People should eat temperately.) |
| **C'est impossible!** | That's impossible! |
| **C'est impossible à croire.** | It's impossible to believe. |
| **Il est impossible de croire cela.** | It's impossible to believe that. |
| **C'est difficile!** | That's hard! |
| **C'est difficile à faire.** | It's hard to do. |
| **Il est difficile de faire cela.** | It's hard to do that. |

4. **Ce** is generally used as a redundant subject when the real subject of **être** is a clause or phrase.

| | |
|---|---|
| **Ce qu'il nous demande de faire, c'est dangereux.** | What he is asking us to do is dangerous. |

| | |
|---|---|
| **Prendre une telle décision sans y penser, c'est stupide!** | To make such a decision without thinking about it is stupid! |

*Special note:* In modern colloquial French usage, there is a tendency to use **c'est** in many cases where correct usage calls for **il est** or **elle est**.

## RELATIVE PRONOUNS

### *A. General Remarks*

A relative pronoun introduces an adjective clause and stands for the noun or pronoun modified by the clause.

As in the case of the personal pronouns and numerous other items, mastery is achieved principally by constant meaningful repetition of the patterns; but the following remarks may be of some additional value for those students who cannot easily "see the forest for the trees." These remarks are supplementary to the Notes of Lessons 6 and 7.

### *B. Non-prepositional Forms*

Notice that the two relatives **qui** and **que** suffice in all cases where the relative pronoun is not the object of a preposition. **Qui** is used as subject of the verb; **que** as object. [See Les. 6:2, 4, 6, 8, 10, 12, 14, 16.]

### *C. Common Prepositional Forms*

With most prepositions, **qui** is used if the antecedent is a person, and the proper form of **lequel** if it is a thing. [See 6:18, 20, 22, 24, 26, 33.]

### *D. Special Prepositional Forms (in addition to those in Lessons 6 and 7)*

1. **Lequel** is generally used instead of **qui** (for persons) as the object of a compound preposition or of one of the less common prepositions.

| | |
|---|---|
| **Avez-vous vu le jeune homme à côté duquel elle s'est assise?** | Did you see the young man beside whom she sat? |
| **Il parle souvent des gens parmi lesquels il habitait.** | He often speaks about the people among whom he used to live. |

2. Whereas **dont** is the relative pronoun usually used to replace **de** + *a noun,* the regular prepositional forms (**de qui, duquel,** etc.) may also be used.

| | |
|---|---|
| **Connaissez-vous le parti dont (duquel) il est le chef?** | Do you know the party of which he is the head? |

**Dont** is not used where (in the corresponding English) *whose* precedes a noun which is the object of a preposition.

| | |
|---|---|
| **Il est entré avec le garçon au père duquel il avait écrit.** | He entered with the boy to whose father he had written. |

3. **Quoi** is used as object of a preposition when reference is to an idea or an action rather than a specific noun.

| | |
|---|---|
| **Voilà à quoi je n'avais pas pensé!** | That's something I hadn't thought of! |

### *E. Other Remarks*

1. **Lequel** may be used instead of **qui** or **que** in order to add clarity to the reference.

| | |
|---|---|
| **Voici la sœur de M. Marot, laquelle vient de se marier.** | Here is Mr. Marot's sister, who just got married. |

2. When the relative pronouns **qui, que, dont,** and **quoi** are used with **ce** (**ce qui, ce que,** etc.), the demonstrative **ce** may be considered the antecedent.

| | |
|---|---|
| **Je vais vous expliquer ce qui m'inquiétait.** | I'm going to explain to you what worried me. |

| | |
|---|---|
| **Je vais vous expliquer le problème qui m'inquiétait.** | I'm going to explain to you the problem that worried me. |

## INTERROGATIVE PRONOUNS

The phrase **est-ce que (est-ce qui** when subject) is listed in Lesson 6 only with the subject and object forms of *what,* but it may be used with the other interrogative pronouns also. Compare the following examples to sentences 1, 9, 17, and 21 of Lesson 6.

| | |
|---|---|
| **Qui est-ce qui a apporté ce paquet?** | Who brought this parcel? |
| **Qui est-ce qu'on a interrogé?** | Whom did they question? |
| **Avec qui est-ce que vous avez fait ce voyage?** | With whom did you take that trip? |
| **Avec quoi est-ce qu'ils ont fait cette expérience?** | With what did they do that experiment? |

Since **est-ce que** contains an inverted subject and verb, the real subject and verb retain the declarative word order. These forms are omitted from the table and examples of Lesson 6 because they are less common and the student has little need to practice them actively.

## NEGATIVES

### *A. The Negative Particle* ne

The negative particle **ne** is required before any verb modified by a negative adverb or having a negative subject or complement (except in slang, where it is sometimes omitted).

| | |
|---|---|
| **Cet orateur ne finira jamais.** | That speaker will never finish. |
| **Personne ne les a vus.** | Nobody saw them. |
| **Elle n'a offert aucune explication.** | She offered no explanation. |

The negative particle is also required when the verb is followed by **que** meaning *only.*

| | |
|---|---|
| **Nous n'avons trouvé que problèmes.** | We found only problems. |

In reading, the student will encounter the use of **ne** called *pleonastic (redundant, unnecessary)* following certain expressions of fearing, preventing, doubting, etc. This **ne** is not translated into English, and the student has no need to use it actively in French.

| | |
|---|---|
| **Je crains qu'il ne vienne trop tard.** | I am afraid that he will come too late. |

### *B. Negative Words*

| | |
|---|---|
| **ne ... pas** | not *(general negation whose translations vary according to context)* |
| **ne ... point** | not *(same as* **ne ... pas,** *except emphatic and literary)* |
| **ne ... guère** | scarcely |
| **ne ... jamais** | never, not ever |
| **ne ... plus** | no longer, no more |
| **ne ... ni ... ni** | neither . . . nor |
| **ne ... personne** | no one, nobody, not anybody |
| **ne ... rien** | nothing, not anything |
| **ne ... aucun** | no . . . , not any . . . |
| **ne ... nul** | no . . . , not any . . . |

**Personne** and **rien,** being pronouns, may be used as subjects or objects of verbs or as objects of prepositions.

| | |
|---|---|
| **Personne ne veut le faire.** | Nobody wants to do it. |
| **Ils n'ont rien trouvé.** | They didn't find anything. |
| **Ne révélez à personne ce que je vous ai dit.** | Don't reveal to any one what I told you. |

**Aucun** and **nul,** being adjectives, agree in gender and number with the noun modified. **Nul** doubles the **–l** in the feminine **(nulle).** The use of **aucun** or **nul** in the plural is rather rare.

| | |
|---|---|
| **Il n'y a aucune raison pour ce retard.** | There is no reason for this delay. |
| **Nulle femme n'acceptera cette décision.** | No woman will accept this decision. |

*C. Position of Negative Words with Infinitives and Compound Tenses*

When used with an infinitive, **pas, point, jamais, plus,** and **rien** are placed with the **ne** before the verb.

| | |
|---|---|
| **Elle a promis de ne pas sortir.** | She promised not to go out. |
| **J'ai passé la journée à ne rien faire.** | I spent the day doing nothing. |

In compound tenses, all the negatives except **personne, aucun, nul,** and **ni ... ni** are generally placed before the past participle. **Personne** follows the past participle when used as complement of the verb. **Aucun, nul,** and **ni ... ni** stand before the words they modify or introduce.

| | |
|---|---|
| **Il n'est plus retourné à cette île.** | He didn't return any more to that island. |
| **Ils n'ont invité personne à la fête.** | They haven't invited any one to the celebration. |
| **Il n'a voulu ni rester ni partir.** | He didn't want either to stay or leave. |

## NUMBERS

*Cardinal Numbers*

| | | | |
|---|---|---|---|
| 1 | **un (une)** | 7 | **sept** |
| 2 | **deux** | 8 | **huit** |
| 3 | **trois** | 9 | **neuf** |
| 4 | **quatre** | 10 | **dix** |
| 5 | **cinq** | 11 | **onze** |
| 6 | **six** | 12 | **douze** |

| | |
|---|---|
| 13 | **treize** |
| 14 | **quatorze** |
| 15 | **quinze** |
| 16 | **seize** |
| 17 | **dix-sept** |
| 18 | **dix-huit** |
| 19 | **dix-neuf** |
| 20 | **vingt** |
| 21 | **vingt et un** |
| 22 | **vingt-deux** |
| 23 | **vingt-trois** |
| 30 | **trente** |
| 31 | **trente et un** |
| 32 | **trente-deux** |
| 40 | **quarante** |
| 50 | **cinquante** |
| 60 | **soixante** |
| 70 | **soixante-dix** |
| 71 | **soixante et onze** |
| 72 | **soixante-douze** |
| 79 | **soixante-dix-neuf** |
| 80 | **quatre-vingts** |
| 81 | **quatre-vingt-un** |
| 82 | **quatre-vingt-deux** |
| 90 | **quatre-vingt-dix** |
| 91 | **quatre-vingt-onze** |
| 99 | **quatre-vingt-dix-neuf** |
| 100 | **cent** |
| 101 | **cent un** |
| 102 | **cent deux** |
| 151 | **cent cinquante et un** |
| 200 | **deux cents** |
| 201 | **deux cent un** |
| 300 | **trois cents** |
| 380 | **trois cent quatre-vingts** |
| 1000 | **mille** |
| 1025 | **mille vingt-cinq** |
| 2000 | **deux mille** |
| 2500 | **deux mille cinq cents** |
| 100,000 | **cent mille** |
| 1,000,000 | **un million** |
| 2,000,000 | **deux millions** |
| 1/2 | **un demi, la moitié** |
| 1/3 | **un tiers** |
| 2/3 | **deux tiers** |
| 1/4 | **un quart** |
| 1/5 | **un cinquième** |
| 9/10 | **neuf dixièmes** |

### *A. Pronunciation*

The pronunciation of the numbers is best learned by imitation of a good model. These notes may aid in accurate imitation.

1. The numbers follow the usual principles of French pronunciation except that the final consonants of **cinq**, **six**, **sept**, **huit**, **neuf**, and **dix** are generally pronounced.
2. However, the final consonants of **cinq**, **six**, **huit**, and **dix** are not usually pronounced when followed by a noun or adjective beginning with a consonant, or when followed by **cent**, **mille**, **million**, etc.
3. The **–t** of **vingt** is pronounced in the numbers from 21 to 29 (but not in the **quatre-vingts** group).
4. The **–f** of **neuf** is pronounced **v** in **neuf ans** and **neuf heures**.

### *B. Spelling*

Larger numbers are no more commonly written out in French than in English; therefore the minor details of spelling which follow are of little practical importance. They are included for reference.

1. Notice that **mille** does not add –**s** for the plural.
2. **Mille** is generally spelled **mil** in dates.
3. **Cent** adds an –**s** for plural only when it terminates a number multiplying a noun **(deux cents pages).**
4. Notice that hyphens are not used in the numbers which include the conjunction **et**.

### *C. Other Notes*

1. The numbers from 1100 to 1900 may be expressed in either of two forms: **mille trois cent(s)** or **treize cent(s)**. In dates, the latter form is probably the more common **(1776: dix-sept cent soixante seize).**
2. Notice that **un** is not used before **cent** or **mille**. **Million** uses **un** and also requires **de** before a noun **(un million d'habitants).**

## *Ordinal Numbers*

Ordinal numbers (except **premier**) are formed by adding **–ième** to the cardinal numbers after dropping any final mute **–e**. For phonetic reasons, **–u** is added to the stem in **cinquième** and the **–f** changes to **–v** in forming **neuvième**.

**C'est la troisième fois qu'il l'a perdu.** It's the third time he has lost it.

In addition to **deuxième** for the second ordinal, there is also the form **second**. **Second** and **premier** are the only ordinals with separate feminine forms: **seconde**, **première**. When expressed as figures, the ordinals are indicated as follows: **1$^{er}$ (1$^{ère}$)**, **2$^{e}$**, **3$^{e}$**, **4$^{e}$**, etc.

With the exception of **premier**, the ordinals are not used (as they are in English) with the names of sovereigns.

**Elizabeth II (deux)** **Louis IX (neuf)** **Henri I$^{er}$ (premier)**

The ordinals are not used in dates, except the first day of the month.

**le onze novembre** | **le trente et un mai** | **le premier octobre**

*Approximate Numbers*

The suffix **–aine** may be added to the numbers **huit, dix, douze, vingt, trente, quarante, cinquante, soixante,** and **cent** to form a noun. Except for **une douzaine,** which means *a dozen,* these nouns express an approximate quantity.

| | |
|---|---|
| **Il a parlé avec une centaine de personnes.** | He spoke with about a hundred people. |

When this suffix is added, any final mute **e** is dropped and the **–x** of **dix** is changed to **–z (une dizaine de vélos** *about ten bikes).*

## TIME OF DAY

*A. The Hour*

| | |
|---|---|
| **Il est une heure.** | It is one o'clock. |
| **Il est cinq heures.** | It is five o'clock. |
| **Le train arrive à onze heures.** | The train arrives at eleven o'clock. |

*B. The Half-hour*

| | |
|---|---|
| **Il est trois heures et demie.** | It is three thirty. |
| **Elle est sortie avant six heures et demie.** | She went out before half past six. |

*C. After the Hour*

| | |
|---|---|
| **Il est une heure cinq.** | It is five (minutes) after one. |
| **Il est quatre heures et quart.** | It is quarter after four. |
| **L'avion est parti à dix heures vingt-deux.** | The plane left at ten twenty-two. |

*D. Before the Hour*

| | |
|---|---|
| **Il est sept heures moins treize.** | It is thirteen (minutes) of seven. |
| **Il est huit heures moins le quart.** | It is (a) quarter of eight. |

*E.* **Midi** *and* **minuit**

**Midi** *(midday, noon)* and **minuit** *(midnight)* are generally used in spoken French in preference to **douze heures** *(twelve o'clock).*

| | |
|---|---|
| **Il doit arriver à midi moins le quart.** | He should arrive at quarter of twelve. |
| **A minuit elle a dû quitter le bal.** | At midnight she had to leave the ball. |

*F. In written schedules, the French generally use the twenty-four hour system.*

| | | | | | |
|---|---|---|---|---|---|
| **0h 45** | 12:45 A.M. | **12h 20** | 12:20 P.M. | **13h 05** | 1:05 P.M. |
| **9h 12** | 9:12 A.M. | **17h 15** | 5:15 P.M. | **23h 59** | 11:59 P.M. |

*G. The Question "What time . . .?"*

| | |
|---|---|
| **Quelle heure est-il?** | What time is it? |
| **A quelle heure arrive le train?** | (At) what time does the train arrive? |

## SPECIAL USES OF devoir, faire, avoir

*A.* **Devoir** *with Dependent Infinitive*

The verb **devoir**, whose basic meaning is *to owe,* has various meanings according to its tense and the context when used with a dependent infinitive. The following sentences illustrate the most common of these meanings.

| | |
|---|---|
| **Vous devez faire cela tout de suite.** | You are to do that immediately.<br>You are supposed to do that immediately.<br>You have to do that immediately.<br>You must do that immediately. |
| **La lettre doit arriver ce matin.** | The letter should arrive this morning. |
| **C'est nous qui devions le faire.** | We are the ones who were to do it.<br>We are the ones who were supposed to do it. |
| **J'ai dû le faire sans le savoir.** | I must have done it without knowing. |
| **J'ai dû le faire malgré moi.** | I had to do it against my will (in spite of myself). |
| **On devrait faire son possible.** | One should (ought to) do what he can. |
| **Vous auriez dû le faire.** | You should have (ought to have) done it. |

*B. Common Idioms with* **faire**

Expressions referring to the weather

**faire beau (chaud, frais, froid, mauvais, du soleil, du vent, un temps agréable)** to be good (hot, cool, cold, bad, sunny, windy, pleasant) weather

| | |
|---|---|
| **Il fait froid mais il ne fait pas du vent.** | It is cold but it is not windy. |

Expressions referring to sports

**faire du sport (du ski, de la natation, du canotage,** etc.) to go in for sports, to engage in sports (skiing, swimming, boating, etc.)

| | |
|---|---|
| **Elle faisait du ski quand elle était jeune.** | She went in for skiing when she was young. |

Other expressions

**faire semblant de** + *inf.* to pretend to + *inf.*

| | |
|---|---|
| **Il fait toujours semblant d'être occupé.** | He always pretends to be busy. |
| **faire un voyage (une promenade)** | to take a trip (walk) |
| **Quand allez-vous faire ce voyage?** | When are you going to take that trip? |

(When phrases such as **à bicyclette, en auto, en bateau,** etc. are added to **promenade**, the English version becomes *ride* rather than *walk.* **Nous avons fait une promenade en bateau.** *We took a boat ride.)*

### *C. Common Idioms with* **avoir**

**avoir l'air** + *adj.* to look (seem, appear) + *adj.*

| | |
|---|---|
| **Il a l'air fatigué.** | He looks tired. |

(Although, grammatically, the adjective should agree with the noun **air**, the modern tendency is to make it agree with the subject. **Elle a l'air heureuse.** *She looks happy.)*

**avoir besoin de** to need, have need of

| | |
|---|---|
| **Ont-ils besoin d'argent?** | Do they need money? |

**avoir envie de** + *inf.* to feel like + *pr. part.*

| | |
|---|---|
| **Avez-vous envie de travailler?** | Do you feel like working? |

**avoir lieu** to take place

| | |
|---|---|
| **La réunion a eu lieu hier soir.** | The meeting was (took place) last night. |

**avoir mal à** to have (a) pain in, to ache

| | |
|---|---|
| **Qu'avez-vous? J'ai mal aux dents.** | What's the matter with you? I have a toothache. |
| **Il a mal à la jambe.** | His leg aches (hurts). |

**avoir ... ans** to be . . . years old

| | |
|---|---|
| **Quel âge avez-vous?** | How old are you? |
| **J'ai dix-neuf ans.** | I am nineteen (years old). |

**avoir raison (tort)** to be right (wrong)

| | |
|---|---|
| **Ils ont raison de faire cela.** | They are right to do (in doing) that. |

**avoir chaud (faim, froid, honte, peur, soif, sommeil)** to be warm (hungry, cold, ashamed, afraid, thirsty, sleepy)

| | |
|---|---|
| **Avez-vous faim?** | Are you hungry? |
| **Non, merci, mais j'ai très soif.** | No, thank you, but I am very thirsty. |

## SPELLING CHANGES IN THE CONJUGATION OF VERBS

1. In French, the letter –**i** changes to –**y** when it falls between two pronounced vowels. No change of sound is involved in this spelling change.

| | | |
|---|---|---|
| **croire**: | **je crois** | **nous croyons** |
| **fuir**: | **je fuis** | **vous fuyez** |
| **voir**: | **je vois** | **vous voyez** |
| **envoyer**: | **j'envoie** | **nous envoyons** |

(Since the –**er** verbs to which this applies have –**y** in the infinitive, the above mentioned change is generally thought of in reverse when applied to the first conjugation: –**y** changes to –**i** before mute –**e**.)

2. If the letter –**c** precedes –**e** in the infinitive, it changes to –**ç** before –**a**, –**o**, or –**u** in the various endings. This change retains the [s] sound of the –**c** in the infinitive.

| | | |
|---|---|---|
| **commencer:** | **nous commençons** | **je commençais** |
| **prononcer:** | **nous prononçons** | **je prononçais** |
| **recevoir:** | **je reçois** | **j'ai reçu** |
| **apercevoir:** | **j'aperçois** | **j'ai aperçu** |

3. Verbs whose infinitives end in –**ger** retain the –**e** before –**a** or –**o** in the endings. This change retains the "soft" sound of the –**g**.

| | | |
|---|---|---|
| **manger:** | **nous mangeons** | **je mangeais** |
| **voyager:** | **nous voyageons** | **je voyageais** |

4. Observe the following changes which occur when –**e** as the final stem vowel is followed by a single consonant (or two consonants which form one sound) and the mute endings –**e**, –**es**, –**ent** of the present indicative and the present subjunctive.

| | | | | |
|---|---|---|---|---|
| **mener:** | **je mène** | **tu mènes** | **il mène** | **ils mènent** |
| **répéter:** | **je répète** | **tu répètes** | **il répète** | **ils répètent** |
| **célébrer:** | **je célèbre** | **tu célèbres** | **il célèbre** | **ils célèbrent** |
| **appeler:** | **j'appelle** | **tu appelles** | **il appelle** | **ils appellent** |
| **jeter:** | **je jette** | **tu jettes** | **il jette** | **ils jettent** |

(1) Unaccented –**e** becomes –**è**.
(2) –**é** becomes –**è**.
(3) Most verbs ending in –**eler** or –**eter** (notable exception **acheter**) double the consonant instead of adding the grave accent to the –**e**.

The same changes occur before the mute –**e** in all six forms of the future and the conditional, except that –**é** remains unchanged.

**je mènerai, tu mèneras, il mènera, nous mènerons, vous mènerez, ils mèneront**
**j'appellerai, tu appelleras, il appellera, nous appellerons, vous appellerez, ils appelleront**
**je jetterais, tu jetterais, il jetterait, nous jetterions, vous jetteriez, ils jetteraient**

*but*

**je répéterai, tu répéteras, il répétera, nous répéterons, vous répéterez, ils répéteront**

## INFINITIVES AND PARTICIPLES

### *A. Present Infinitive*

1. The present infinitive is the form by which a verb is named.

| | |
|---|---|
| **Nous étudions les verbes** ***aller, partir,*** **et** ***descendre.*** | We are studying the verbs *to go, to leave,* and *to go down.* |

It is the form of the verb which, in English, follows the preposition *to.*

2. The most common uses of the infinitive are: (a) after a preposition, and (b) after a finite verb (or another infinitive).

| | |
|---|---|
| **Je les ai invités à venir demain.** | I invited them to come tomorrow. |
| **Vous avez promis de faire cela.** | You promised to do that. |
| **Elle est partie sans dire adieu.** | She left without saying good-by. |
| **Il veut sortir maintenant.** | He wants to go out now. |
| **Ils promettent de le faire travailler.** | They promise to make him work. |

It is important to remember that the infinitive is the only verb form that may follow a preposition (except the preposition **en**, which takes the present participle).

3. The infinitive is the only verb form that may be used as the subject of a verb, or as a predicate nominative.

| | |
|---|---|
| **Voir c'est croire.** | Seeing is believing. |

### *B. Past Infinitive*

The past infinitive is formed by the present infinitive of **avoir** or **être** and the past participle of the main verb. Its most common use is after the preposition **après**, where it is the only verb form that may be used.

| | |
|---|---|
| **Après avoir mangé il s'est endormi.** | After eating he went to sleep. |
| **Après être arrivé je me sentais fatigué.** | After arriving I felt tired. |

### *C. Present Participle*

1. The present participle of all verbs (except **avoir**, **être**, and **savoir**) may be formed by substituting the ending **–ant** for the **–ons** of the first person plural, present indicative.

| | | |
|---|---|---|
| **donner**: | **nous donnons** | **donnant** giving |
| **finir**: | **nous finissons** | **finissant** finishing |
| **vendre**: | **nous vendons** | **vendant** selling |
| **écrire**: | **nous écrivons** | **écrivant** writing |
| **voir**: | **nous voyons** | **voyant** seeing |

The present participles of **avoir**, **être**, and **savoir** are: **ayant** *having*, **étant** *being*, and **sachant** *knowing*.

2. The principal use of the present participle in French is in adverbial phrases. (See Les. 11.) It is used both with and without the preposition **en**. In most cases where the omission of the preposition **en** is permissible, the preposition *upon* would be appropriate in the corresponding English version. Where *by, while,* or *in* would be used in the corresponding English, the preposition **en** would normally be used in modern French.

| | |
|---|---|
| **(En) voyant le danger, il s'est arrêté.** | (Upon) seeing the danger, he stopped. |
| **(En) entrant dans la chambre, elle a poussé un cri.** | (Upon) entering the room, she screamed. |

**En prenant les billets d'avance, nous serons assurés de nos places.** (By) getting our tickets in advance, we shall be sure of our seats.

**En changeant de train, j'ai perdu ma valise.** (While) changing trains, I lost my suitcase.

**Les avez-vous rencontrés en passant par le village?** Did you meet them while passing through the village?

**En réfléchissant sur leur demande, nous nous sommes rendu compte de notre dépendance.** (In) thinking over their demand, we realized our dependence.

3. The present participle is also used as an adjective, in which case it agrees in gender and number with the noun.

**J'avais peur de sa main menaçante.** I was afraid of his menacing hand.

**La peinture s'intitule «la Poupée valsante».** This painting is called "The Waltzing Doll."

4. It is important to note the following two cases where the present participle is not used like the *–ing* form in English.

(a) to form progressive verb tenses (See Les. 3.)

| | |
|---|---|
| he is working | **il travaille** |
| they were sleeping | **ils dormaient** |
| you have been reading | **vous lisez** |
| I had been living | **j'habitais** |

(b) as object of a preposition (except **en**)

| | |
|---|---|
| without eating | **sans manger** |
| instead of going to bed | **au lieu de se coucher** |

### *D. Past Participle*

1. The past participle of a regular verb is formed by changing the infinitive ending –**er** to –**é**, –**ir** to –**i**, or –**re** to –**u**.

| | |
|---|---|
| **donner** | **donné** given |
| **finir** | **fini** finished |
| **vendre** | **vendu** sold |

2. All **–er** verbs have regular past participles, but those of irregular verbs of other conjugations must be memorized – preferably by learning the first person singular of the past indefinite. In this way you learn the past participle and the correct auxiliary **(avoir** or **être)** at the same time.
3. The past participle is used most commonly in forming the compound tenses.

| | |
|---|---|
| **j'ai reçu** | I have received |
| **nous avions étudié** | we had studied |
| **elle sera partie** | she will have left |
| **je me serais lavé** | I would have washed |

4. When used in the compound tenses, the past participle agrees in gender and number with:

**(a)** a preceding direct object (transitive verbs having the auxiliary **avoir;** reflexive verbs having the auxiliary **être).**

| | |
|---|---|
| **Je les ai vus au café.** | I saw them in the café. |
| **Est-ce Marie qu'il a invitée?** | Is it Mary that he invited? |
| **Elles se sont levées de bonne heure.** | They got up early. |

*(Note:* There is no agreement with **en** as a preceding direct object. **On lui a montré de bonnes pâtisseries et il en a acheté.** *They showed him some good pastries and he bought some.)*

(b) the subject of an intransitive verb whose auxiliary is **être.**

| | |
|---|---|
| **Elles sont allées en Europe.** | They went to Europe. |
| **Ma sœur est montée à sa chambre.** | My sister went up to her room. |
| **Ils ne sont rentrés qu'à minuit.** | They didn't come home until midnight. |

(*Note:* **Monter, descendre,** and **sortir** may sometimes be used transitively (that is, have on object) – in which case they are conjugated with the auxiliary **avoir** and follow (a) above: **C'est lui qui a monté les bagages et moi qui les ai descendus.** He's the one who carried up the luggage and I who brought it down.)

5. The past participle may also be used as an adjective.

| | |
|---|---|
| **Au dessus du lavabo il y avait une glace brisée.** | Above the washstand there was a broken mirror. |
| **Voilà une bonne maison construite en pierre.** | There is a good house built of stone. |

## REFLEXIVE VERBS

1. A verb is reflexive if its object, direct or indirect, refers to the same person (or thing) as its subject.

| | |
|---|---|
| **Je me suis habillé.** | I dressed (myself). |
| **Vous êtes-vous fait du mal?** | Did you hurt yourself? |

2. Many verbs used reflexively in French are not reflexive in English.

| | |
|---|---|
| **Je me souviens de cette nuit-là.** | I remember that night. |
| **Ils se sont bien amusés au bal.** | They had a good time at the dance. |

3. In the plural a reflexive verb may have a reciprocal meaning.

| | |
|---|---|
| **Nous nous sommes promis d'écrire.** | We promised each other to write. |
| **Embrassez-vous!** | Kiss each other! |

4. A reflexive verb in French may correspond to the passive voice in English if the subject is not a person and if no specific agent is expressed or implied. [cf. Les. 10:10–14]

5. Notice that any verb used reflexively takes the auxiliary **être** in the compound tenses. The past participle agrees with the reflexive object if it is a direct object. For reflexive pronouns see Les. 4. (See also pp. 201-203.)

## IMPERATIVE

### *A. Formation and Meanings*

The imperative forms of all verbs except **avoir**, **être**, and **savoir** are the **tu, nous**, and **vous** forms of the present indicative used without the subject pronouns. The first conjugation **(–er)** verbs drop the final **–s** of the **tu** form.*

| *2nd per. sing. (fam.)* | *1st per. plur.* | *2nd per. sing. & plur.* |
|---|---|---|
| **donne** give | **donnons** let's give | **donnez** give |
| **finis** finish | **finissons** let's finish | **finissez** finish |
| **vends** sell | **vendons** let's sell | **vendez** sell |
| **va** go | **allons** let's go | **allez** go |
| **fais** make | **faisons** let's make | **faites** make |

### *B. Irregular Imperatives*

The imperatives of **avoir**, **être**, and **savoir** are:

| | | |
|---|---|---|
| **aie** have | **ayons** let's have | **ayez** have |
| **sois** be | **soyons** let's be | **soyez** be |
| **sache** know | **sachons** let's know | **sachez** know |

It will be recognized that these three verbs derive the imperative from the present subjunctive rather than the indicative, but it should be noted that the –s of **tu aies** and of **tu saches** is dropped and that the **–i** is omitted in the **nous** and **vous** forms of **savoir.**

The verb **vouloir**, because of its meaning, really has no imperative; but the form **veuillez** *(+ infinitive)* is used with the special meaning *Please.*

* But the –s is retained before **y** and **en**: **Vas-y.** *Go there.* **Donnes-en à ta sœur.** *Give some to your sister.*

### *C. Pronoun Objects with the Imperative*

Personal pronoun objects follow the affirmative imperative but precede the negative imperative (as they do all other verb forms).

| | |
|---|---|
| **Lisons ce roman. Lisons-le.** | Let's read this novel. Let's read it. |
| **Ne le lisons pas.** | Let's not read it. |
| **Montrez cela à votre père.** | Show that to your father. |
| **Montrez-le-lui.** | Show it to him. |
| **Ne le lui montrez pas.** | Don't show it to him. |
| **Lève-toi.** | Get up. |
| **Ne te lève pas.** | Don't get up. |
| **Si vous les trouvez, donnez-m'en.** | If you find them, give me some. |

Notice the use of hyphens when pronouns follow the verb.

## CONDITIONAL SENTENCES

### *A. General Remarks*

In forming French conditional sentences, in general, the same criteria for choice of tenses are used as in other sentences.

| | |
|---|---|
| **S'il travaille, il gagne de l'argent.** | If he works, he earns money. |
| **S'il travaille bien, il gagnera plus d'argent.** | If he works well, he will earn more money. |
| **S'il travaille bien, donnez-lui l'argent.** | If he works well, give him the money. |
| **S'il travaillait bien, il gagnerait plus d'argent.** | If he worked well, he would earn more money. |
| **S'il travaillait tous les jours, il gagnait assez d'argent.** | If he worked every day, he earned enough money. |
| **S'il avait bien travaillé, il aurait gagné plus d'argent.** | If he had worked well, he would have earned more money. |

*B. Cautions*

Difficulties sometimes arise when students try to translate English sentences into French. They must remember that word meanings and tense meanings in one language seldom have a complete and exact correspondence in another language. The following cautions may be of some guidance value.

1. Remember that *will* and *would* in English are not always auxiliaries of the future and conditional. They are also used as principal verbs expressing the idea of *willingness.*

| | |
|---|---|
| If you will consent to do this, you will not regret it. | **Si vous voulez bien consentir à faire ceci, vous ne le regretterez pas.** |
| If you would consent to do this, you would not regret it. | **Si vous vouliez bien consentir à faire ceci, vous ne le regretteriez pas.** |

2. Remember that *would* is often used in English as the equivalent of *used to;* in such cases, the verb is rendered in French by the imperfect.

| | |
|---|---|
| If John would wake up first, he would call me. | **Si Jean se réveillait le premier, il m'appelait.** |

3. Remember that, in normal usage, neither the future nor the conditional is used after **si** in a conditional sentence.

## INTERROGATIVE WORD ORDER

There are examples of interrogative word order in scores of Pattern Sentences and in numerous notes and exercises throughout the book. It is by repeated imitation of such examples that the student develops facility in formulating questions in French. The following notes will be of use only if they aid in making clear the patterns formed by the practice material.

1. The basic characteristic of interrogative word order is the inversion of the subject-verb sequence of declarative sentences.

| | |
|---|---|
| **Ils ont ... Ont-ils ... ?** | They have . . . Do they have . . . ? |
| **Vous travaillez ... Travaillez-vous ... ?** | You work . . . Do you work . . .? |

2. However, in French, a noun subject cannot usually be placed after the verb; therefore the inversion must be made with a redundant pronoun subject.

| | |
|---|---|
| **Les élèves ont ... Les élèves ont-ils ... ?** | The pupils have . . . Do the pupils have . . .? |
| **Roger travaille ... Roger travaille-t-il ... ?** | Roger works . . . Does Roger work . . .? |

3. If the verb is compound, it is the subject pronoun and the auxiliary which are inverted.

| | |
|---|---|
| **Ils l'ont reçu. L'ont-ils reçu?** | They received it. Did they receive it? |
| **Roger a travaillé hier. Roger a-t-il travaillé hier?** | Roger worked yesterday. Did Roger work yesterday? |

4. This inversion is normally used after interrogative adverbs such as **quand, où, comment, combien, pourquoi.**

| | |
|---|---|
| **Quand l'ont-ils reçu?** | When did they receive it? |
| **Où travaille-t-il?** | Where does he work? |
| **Pourquoi votre père est-il sorti?** | Why did your father go out? |

With these interrogative words, except **pourquoi**, the noun subject itself is sometimes placed after the verb in short, simple questions.

| | |
|---|---|
| **Comment va votre ami aujourd'hui?** | How is your friend today? |
| **Où travaillent ces gens?** | Where do those people work? |
| **Combien coûte cette voiture?** | How much does that car cost? |

*but*

| | |
|---|---|
| **Pourquoi ces élèves rentrent-ils?** | Why are those pupils going back in? |

However, the redundant pronoun subject is generally used if the verb is compound or if it has a direct object.

| | |
|---|---|
| **Comment votre ami a-t-il voyagé?** | How did your friend travel? |
| **Où ces gens achètent-ils leurs vêtements?** | Where do those people buy their clothes? |

5. The phrase **est-ce que**, which contains an inverted subject and verb, may be used to form questions like those above with no inversion of the real subject and its verb.

| | |
|---|---|
| **Est-ce qu'ils l'ont reçu?** | Did they receive it? |
| **Est-ce que Jean travaille ce matin?** | Is John working this morning? |
| **Pourquoi est-ce que votre père est sorti?** | Why did your father go out? |

When the subject is the pronoun **je**, the **est-ce que** form is used almost exclusively.

| | |
|---|---|
| **Est-ce que je vous comprends bien?** | Do I understand you well? |
| **Est-ce que je les ai laissés chez vous?** | Did I leave them at your house? |

For examples of the interrogative word order as it applies to questions introduced by interrogative pronouns, see Lessons 6 and 7.

Of course, with French as with most other languages, in speaking, some utterances in declarative form may convey an interrogation by the inflection with which they are spoken.

## USES OF THE SUBJUNCTIVE

(These notes are supplementary to and based upon the Pattern Sentences and the Notes of Lesson 8.)

### *A. The Subjunctive after Expressions of Volition*

The most common verbs of volition are the following:

**aimer** to like
**aimer mieux** to prefer
**commander** to command
**défendre** to forbid
**demander** to ask, demand
**désirer** to desire, wish
**empêcher** to prevent, keep (from)
**ordonner** to order
**permettre** to permit
**préférer** to prefer
**souhaiter** to wish
**vouloir** to want, wish

In English, the dependent ideas following all the verbs above are generally expressed with an infinitive construction. *(I would like John to go. They prefer you to wait. He ordered us to stop.)* In French, if there are different subjects for the two verbs, the infinitive construction may be used for only six of the twelve verbs: **commander, défendre, demander, empêcher, ordonner, permettre.**

| | |
|---|---|
| **On lui a commandé de s'arrêter.** | They commanded him to stop. |
| **J'avais défendu aux élèves de parler.** | I had forbidden the pupils to talk. |
| **Demandez-lui de venir nous voir.** | Ask him to come see us. |
| **Qu'est-ce qui l'empêche de le faire?** | What keeps him from doing it? |

The subject of the infinitive is expressed as an indirect object with all of the six except **empêcher,** which takes the direct. All six require **de** before the dependent infinitive.

The verb **dire** (very similar to the English verb *to tell)* expresses volition when followed by the preposition **de** and a dependent infinitive, although it does not express volition when followed by a dependent clause. In the infinitive construction, **dire** follows the pattern of **commander, demander,** *et al.* above.

| | |
|---|---|
| **Nous leur avons dit d'attendre.** | We told them to wait. |
| **Nous leur avons dit que vous étiez en Angleterre.** | We told them that you were in England. |

Aside from the verbs just mentioned (and a few others like them), the dependent infinitive with a noun or pronoun subject is rarely possible in French. This construction – so common in English – must generally be rendered in French by a dependent clause. [See Les. 8:1, 4, 19.]

### *B. The Subjunctive after Expressions of Emotion*

The most common expressions of emotion which require the subjunctive are the following:

| | |
|---|---|
| **craindre** to fear | **être content** to be content, glad |
| **se fâcher** to get (be) angry | **être désolé** to be very sorry |
| **s'étonner** to be surprised, astonished | **être étonné** to be surprised, astonished |
| **regretter** to regret, be sorry | **être fâché** to be annoyed, angry |
| **avoir honte** to be ashamed | **être heureux** to be happy, glad |
| **avoir peur** to be afraid | **être surpris** to be surprised |
| **être bien aise** to be very glad | **être triste** to be sad |

In this category, it is common to find in English a dependent clause with the same subject as the main clause. Such sentences are rendered in French with a dependent *infinitive,* introduced by the preposition **de.**

| | |
|---|---|
| I regret that I cannot come. | **Je regrette de ne pas pouvoir venir.** |
| He is afraid that he will make a blunder. | **Il a peur de faire une gaffe.** |

### *C. The Subjunctive after Expressions of Doubt, Denial, Uncertainty*

The classification "doubt" has nothing to do with the basic accuracy or inaccuracy of the ideas expressed; it applies only to *an expression of doubt* in the governing clause with reference to the subordinate idea. Some verbs express doubt in the affirmative but not in the negative *(e.g.* **douter**). Others express doubt in the negative but not in the affirmative *(e.g.* **croire, penser).** The interrogative of these verbs may express doubt or assurance, depending upon the circumstances.

The most common expressions of doubt, denial, or uncertainty requiring the subjunctive are:

**douter** to doubt
**ignorer** not to know
**nier** to deny
**être douteux** to be doubtful
**ne pas croire** not to believe
**ne pas dire** not to say
**ne pas penser** not to think
**ne pas être certain** not to be certain
**ne pas être sûr** not to be sure

The student should remember that the notes given above and in Lesson 8 are intended as basic guides only. In this category, perhaps more than any other, the attitude of the speaker is of greater importance than the words themselves.

### *D. The Subjunctive after Impersonal Expressions of Judgment or Opinion*

This category overlaps, to some extent, the three preceding categories, since many of the impersonal expressions involve volition, emotion, or doubt. However, the separate classification is useful because it is relatively simple to develop the habit of using the subjunctive in statements beginning **Il est** *(adjective)* **que** ... The exceptions are those which express certainty or probability. **(Il est certain que vous serez élu.** *It is certain that you will be elected.)*

The most common impersonal expressions of judgment or opinion taking the subjunctive are:

**il convient** it is fitting
**il faut** it is necessary
**il se peut** it is possible
**il vaut mieux** it is better
**c'est dommage** it's too bad
**il est bon** it is good
**il est convenable** it is fitting
**il est douteux** it is doubtful
**il est heureux** it is fortunate
**il est important** it is important
**il est impossible** it is impossible
**il est juste** it is just
**il est nécessaire** it is necessary
**il est peu probable** it is improbable
**il est possible** it is possible
**il est temps** it is time

The student should remember that, if no specific subject is

*expressed,* most of the expressions above will take an infinitive. (This is true even though the context may make it clear that a specific personal reference is *intended.)*

| | |
|---|---|
| **Il faut lui écrire.** | It is necessary to write to him. (I must, we must, you must, somebody must write to him.) |
| **Il est impossible de faire cela.** | It is impossible to do that. |

### *E. The Subjunctive in Adjective Clauses*

In an adjective clause, the factor determining the mood of the verb is what is said about or felt about the noun (or pronoun) modified. If the statement is given as purely factual (and the antecedent is not a negative or indefinite pronoun), the indicative is used.

| | |
|---|---|
| **Rome est la seule ville que nous visiterons en Italie.** | Rome is the only city that we shall visit in Italy. |

If there is volition, intention, emotion, opinion, uncertainty, negation, etc. expressed in reference to the modified noun, the subjunctive is used. [See Les. 8:23–30.]

### *F. The Subjunctive in Adverbial Clauses*

The conjunctions listed in Lesson 8 (and others less common) may be classified in the following categories:

1. Concession

**bien que, quoique** although

2. Condition

**à condition que** on condition that
**à moins que** unless
**au cas que** in case that
**pourvu que** provided that
**soit que** whether
**supposé que** supposing that

3. Purpose

| | |
|---|---|
| **afin que, pour que** in order that | **de crainte que, de peur que** for fear that |

4. Time (before which . . .)

| | |
|---|---|
| **avant que** before | **en attendant que**<br>**jusqu'à ce que** } until |

5. Negation

| | |
|---|---|
| **non que** not that | **sans que** without |

The conjunction **que** is sometimes used to replace any of the conjunctions above, generally to avoid repetition. When **que** is so used, it takes the subjunctive.

| | |
|---|---|
| **Bien que vous fassiez ceci et que les autres fassent cela, je n'accepterai jamais votre offre.** | Although you may do this and the others may do that, I shall never accept your offer. |

In this category (*i.e.* subordinate ideas of an adverbial type), the dependent idea is expressed in French as an infinitive if (1) the subject of the dependent verb is the same as that of the governing verb, and (2) there exists a prepositional form of the connecting word which takes an infinitive complement (**pour – pour que, avant de – avant que**, etc.)

| | |
|---|---|
| **Nous travaillons jour et nuit pour accomplir le projet.** | We are working day and night in order to complete the project. |
| **Nous travaillons jour et nuit pour que vous puissiez accomplir le projet.** | We are working day and night in order that you will be able to complete the project. |
| **Je l'ai fait sans le savoir.** | I did it without knowing (realizing) it. |
| **Je l'ai fait sans qu'elle le sache.** | I did it without her knowing it. |
| **Il me l'a dit avant de partir.** | He told me so before leaving (before he left). |

| | |
|---|---|
| **Il me l'a dit avant que je sois parti.** | He told me so before I left. |
| **Elle monte l'échelle afin de mieux voir.** | She climbs the ladder in order to see better. |
| **Elle monte l'échelle afin que nous la voyions mieux.** | She climbs the ladder so that we may see her better. |
| **J'arriverai à l'heure à moins de manquer le train.** | I shall arrive on time unless I miss the train. |
| **J'arriverai à l'heure à moins que vous me fassiez manquer le train.** | I shall arrive on time unless you make me miss the train. |

*but*

| | |
|---|---|
| **Je le ferai pourvu que j'aie le temps.** *(no prepositional form)* | I shall do it provided that I have the time. |

### *G. Subjunctive in Indirect Commands*

When an imperative is expressed to a third person rather than directly to the person to perform the action, the subjunctive is used after the introductory conjunction **que**.

| | |
|---|---|
| **Qu'il entre!** | Have him come in! |
| **Qu'ils se taisent!** | Have them (make them) keep quiet! |

### *H. Subjunctive in Independent Clauses*

The subjunctive is used in a few fixed expressions, most of which are exclamatory in nature.

| | |
|---|---|
| **Vive l'amour!** | Long live love! (Hurrah for love!) |
| **Ainsi soit-il!** | So be it! |

### *I. Tenses of the Subjunctive*

There are four tenses of the subjunctive: the present **(qu'il prenne)**, the imperfect **(qu'il prît)**, the past [*passé composé*] **(qu'il ait pris)**,

and the pluperfect **(qu'il eût pris).** Only two of these four are commonly used in modern colloquial French: the present and the past [*passé composé*]. The other two are found only in literary or very formal language. (See pp. 161-164).
In everyday French, the past subjunctive is used when the dependent action (or condition) preceded, in time, that of the principal clause. Otherwise the present subjunctive is used. The conjunction **avant que** takes the past subjunctive whenever the dependent verb *expresses* the action as completed.

| | |
|---|---|
| **Je vous donnerai un coup de téléphone avant que vous ayez fini.** | I'll give you a (telephone) call before you have finished. |

[See Les. 8:46–52.]

## LITERARY TENSES

### *A. General Remarks*

There are four tenses in French which are not used in conversation or informal correspondence: the past definite *(passé simple),* the past anterior *(passé antérieur),* the imperfect subjunctive *(imparfait du subjonctif),* and the pluperfect subjunctive *(plus-que-parfait du subjonctif).* The intermediate student needs to recognize and understand these tenses when he reads, but he will have no *active* use for them.

### *B. Formation of Past Definite* **(passé simple)**

For all **–er** verbs, the past definite is formed by dropping the **–er** of the infinitive and adding the endings: **–ai, –as, –a, –âmes, –âtes, –èrent.**

| | |
|---|---|
| **je donnai** I gave | **nous donnâmes** we gave |
| **tu donnas** you gave | **vous donnâtes** you gave |
| **il donna** he gave | **ils donnèrent** they gave |

All other verbs have the following endings in common:

| | |
|---|---|
| **–s** | **ˆ–mes** |
| **–s** | **ˆ–tes** |
| **–t** | **–rent** |

The regular **–ir** and **–re** verbs drop the infinitive ending and add the endings above, preceded by **–i**.

| | | | |
|---|---|---|---|
| **je finis** | **nous finîmes** | **je vendis** | **nous vendîmes** |
| **tu finis** | **vous finîtes** | **tu vendis** | **vous vendîtes** |
| **il finit** | **ils finirent** | **il vendit** | **ils vendirent** |

For irregular verbs, if an active knowledge is desired, memorize the first person singular and follow the pattern above.

### *C. Meaning of the Past Definite* (passé simple)

The past definite is a narrative tense. It expresses a single unit of past action, viewed as completed.

| | |
|---|---|
| **L'armée attaqua la forteresse.** | The army attacked the fortress. |
| **Ils vendirent tous leurs biens.** | They sold all their property. |
| **Le roi reconnut-il la petite fille?** | Did the king recognize the little girl? |

### *D. The Imperfect Subjunctive*

The imperfect subjunctive for all verbs may be formed by dropping the last letter of the first person singular of the past definite and adding the following endings: **–sse, –sses, ˆ–t, –ssions, –ssiez, –ssent.**

| | | |
|---|---|---|
| **que je donnasse** | that I give | **que nous donnassions** |
| **que tu donnasses** | | **que vous donnassiez** |
| **qu'il donnât** | | **qu'ils donnassent** |

| | | |
|---|---|---|
| **que je fisse** | that I make | **que nous fissions** |
| **que tu fisses** | | **que vous fissiez** |
| **qu'il fît** | | **qu'ils fissent** |

The English translations of this tense may have numerous variations depending on the context.

| | |
|---|---|
| **Elle avait peur qu'ils ne demandassent un peu trop.** | She was afraid that they might ask (would ask) for a bit too much. |

### *E. The Compound Literary Tenses*

The past anterior and the pluperfect subjunctive are formed by the past definite and the imperfect subjunctive, respectively, of the auxiliary and the past participle of the main verb. The past anterior is used in dependent clauses introduced by **après que**, **aussitôt que**, **dès que**, **lorsque**, or **quand** to express an action which preceded that of the principal verb (expressed in the *passé simple).*

| *Past Anterior* | *Pluperfect Subjunctive* |
|---|---|
| **j'eus fini** I had finished | **que j'eusse fini** that I had finished |
| **je fus allé** I had gone | **que je fusse allé** that I had gone |

### *F. Sequence of Tenses of the Subjunctive*

In formal language, the present subjunctive is used for incompleted actions and the past subjunctive for completed actions, when the governing verb is in the present or future. The imperfect subjunctive is used for incompleted actions and the pluperfect subjunctive for completed actions, when the governing verb is in some tense other than the present or future.

| | |
|---|---|
| **Le roi ordonne que l'armée prenne la ville.** | The king orders the army to take the city. |
| **Les parents s'étonneront que les enfants aient si bien appris la leçon.** | The parents will be surprised that the children have learned the lesson so well. |
| **Le duc aurait voulu que l'amiral** | The duke would have liked (for) |

| | |
|---|---|
| **perdît la bataille.** | the admiral to lose the battle. |
| **Son père avait peur que Jeannot ne fût tombé dans l'eau.** | His father was afraid that Johnny had fallen into the water. |

## THE passé surcomposé

Since the pluperfect indicative is not used in French as the conversational equivalent of the past anterior (see p. 14), a tense called the **passé surcomposé** is used in modern colloquial usage in a dependent clause introduced by **après que, aussitôt que, dès que, lorsque,** or **quand** to express an action which preceded that of the principal verb (expressed in the **passé composé**). This tense is formed by the **passé composé** of the auxiliary and the past participle of the main verb.

| | |
|---|---|
| **Aussitôt qu'elle a eu lu sa lettre, elle a saisi le téléphone.** | As soon as she had read his letter, she seized the telephone. |

This tense is not treated in the regular lessons because the infrequency of its occurrence makes its active mastery relatively unimportant to the intermediate student.

# *Exercises Based on Supplementary Notes*

All sentences and other items in these exercises follow the patterns of the illustrative examples for each section. Each exercise is divided into two parts:

> (a) In the first group, the material is arranged in the same order as in the examples of the text.
> (b) In the second group, the arrangement is random, requiring the student to recognize the pattern or generalization which he is applying without the assistance of the corresponding sequence.

### *1. Gender of Nouns*

*Indicate the gender of each noun by supplying the proper form of the adjective indicated.*

| | | |
|---|---|---|
| (a) | (dernier) | septembre ________, lundi ________ |
| | (prochain) | mai ________, samedi ________ |
| | (ancien) | l' ________ anglais, l' ________ russe |
| | (chrétien) | bonté ________, charité ________ |
| | (oriental) | sobriété ________, valeur ________ |
| | (militant) | communisme ________, dogmatisme________ |
| | (bon) | ________ passage, ________ médicament |

| | | |
|---|---|---|
| (national) | parc ________ | , projet ________ |
| (impressionant) | structure ________ | , coiffure ________ |
| (fort) | situation ________ | , ambition ________ |
| (individuel) | croyance ________ | , imprudence ________ |
| (adoré) | patrie ________ | , rue ________ |
| (lourd) | assiette ________ | , graisse ________ |
| (b) (croissant) | pitié ________ | , pauvreté ________ |
| (américain) | idéalisme ________ | , matérialisme ________ |
| (important) | héritage ________ | , bâtiment ________ |
| (primitif) | grec ________ | , allemand ________ |
| (vert) | banc ________ | , bois ________ |
| (inattendu) | mission ________ | , explication ________ |
| (imminent) | signature ________ | , clôture ________ |
| (exact) | expérience ________ | , balance ________ |
| (nouveau) | roue ________ | , maladie ________ |
| (passé) | décembre ________ | , vendredi ________ |
| (inconnu) | aptitude ________ | , ardeur ________ |
| (léger) | canne ________ | , brosse ________ |
| (prochain) | juin ________ | , jeudi ________ |

*2. Plural of Nouns and Adjectives*

*Supply the plural forms.*

| | NOUNS | | ADJECTIVES | |
|---|---|---|---|---|
| | *singular* | *plural* | *singular* | *plural* |
| (a) | le pied | les ________ | bon | ________ |
| | l'art | les ________ | intelligent | ________ |
| | la fenêtre | les ________ | belle | ________ |
| | l'automobile | les ________ | pauvre | ________ |
| | le bas | les ________ | bas | ________ |
| | la noix | les ________ | heureux | ________ |
| | le métal | les ________ | légal | ________ |
| | le chapeau | les ________ | nouveau | ________ |
| | le chou | les ________ | mou | ________ |
| | l'œil | les ________ | bleu | ________ |
| | le bal | les ________ | naval | ________ |
| (b) | le pas | les ________ | gros | ________ |
| | le rideau | les ________ | beau | ________ |

| | | | |
|---|---|---|---|
| le hibou | les ________ | fou | ________ |
| l'usine | les ________ | riche | ________ |
| le travail | les ________ | final | ________ |
| l'armée | les ________ | élégant | ________ |
| la croix | les ________ | religieux | ________ |
| le jour | les ________ | grand | ________ |
| le ciel | les ________ | fatal | ________ |
| le rival | les ________ | fondamental | ________ |
| la voiture | les ________ | nouvelle | ________ |

### *3. Articles*

*Say in French.*

(a) 1. One cannot buy a gold watch without money. 2. Do you need any information? 3. If you don't have a car you must walk. 4. That wine glass is very beautiful. 5. My grandfather was a lawyer. 6. The other pupil is an American. 7. We met her at the beginning of the vacation. 8. "Big Charles" has many ideas. 9. I don't want to pay a hundred francs a dozen. 10. He never makes any errors. 11. California and Hawaii are states.

(b) 1. The president of the country is coming to the United States. 2. Did you know that he was a doctor? 3. She doesn't receive any letters. 4. I am learning to ride a horse. 5. They are building a new steel bridge. 6. Is that worth a thousand dollars a pound? 7. I hope that this will serve as an example. 8. Little Mary arrived late. 9. You will find it in the wastepaper basket. 10. The first inhabitant was a Frenchman. 11. Mexico is larger than Cuba.

### *4. Feminine of Adjectives*

*Supply the feminine forms.*

| (a) | | (b) | |
|---|---|---|---|
| brun | ________ | fidèle | ________ |
| blond | ________ | faible | ________ |
| intéressant | ________ | public | ________ |
| difficile | ________ | national | ________ |
| chauve | ________ | franc | ________ |
| dernier | ________ | sot | ________ |
| indiscret | ________ | vrai | ________ |
| cruel | ________ | explosif | ________ |
| violet | ________ | fameux | ________ |

| | | | |
|---|---|---|---|
| natif | ________ | mou | ________ |
| nerveux | ________ | frais | ________ |
| vieux | ________ | beau | ________ |
| épais | ________ | gentil | ________ |
| doux | ________ | muet | ________ |
| blanc | ________ | naturel | ________ |
| long | ________ | sourd | ________ |
| fou | ________ | gros | ________ |
| bon | ________ | secret | ________ |
| favori | ________ | fier | ________ |

### *5. Adjective Phrases, Adjectives Modifying* **quelque chose** *or* **rien**, *the Adjective (and Indefinite Pronoun)* **tout**

*Say in French*

(a) 1. There's our last wooden bridge! 2. I have only seven tea cups. 3. Something funny happened at the office today. 4. He didn't find anything important. 5. We'll spend the whole day there. 6. You say that every year. 7. She bought all four of them. 8. We have a test every other day. 9. Everything is calm. 10. They studied everything. 11. They all passed the exam. 12. I know them all. 13. Everybody is talking about it.

(b) 1. He never buys anything old. 2. We received all three of them. 3. They all arrived at the same time. 4. You have changed everything. 5. Bring two champagne glasses, please. 6. One can't work all the time. 7. Did you buy any nylon stockings? 8. Every pupil takes all the courses. 9. We met them all. 10. Everybody is here. 11. Here's something interesting. 12. Everything seems different. 13. They come here every other year.

### *6. Position of Descriptive Adjectives*

*Place the adjective indicated before or after the noun, as appropriate.*

| | | | |
|---|---|---|---|
| (a) noir | un chapeau | (b) orientale | la culture |
| ronde | la table | extraordinaire | une occasion |
| italienne | la cuisine | bon | un élève |

| | | | |
|---|---|---|---|
| scientifique | le monde | verte | une feuille |
| abandonnée | une maison | chers | mes amis |
| roulant | un tapis | jolie | une femme |
| désintéressée | une personne | fort mauvais | un projet |
| infatigable | un ouvrier | petit | un cadeau |
| bien méchant | un enfant | menaçant | le ton |
| tout à fait nouvelle | une idée | sphérique | une figure |
| beau | le temps | catholique | l'opinion |
| vilaine | une affaire | troués | des bas |

*Say in French.*

(aa) a former soldier
an ancient castle
a fine woman
a brave child
the last chapter
last week
the same country
the country itself
the poor millionaire
some poor people
her own car
a clean handkerchief
the only reason
reason alone

(bb) the last lesson
the same region
their own idea
the poor owner
a brave person
the war alone
a clean room
last year
a former director
some poor peasants
the very region
the only war
an ancient manuscript
a fine fellow

### *7. Comparative and Superlative of Adjectives and Adverbs*

*Say in French.*

(a) 1. Robert is more generous than Henry. 2. Robert works more assiduously than Henry. 3. You are less impulsive than I. 4. You travel less frequently than I. 5. She is as tall as her sister. 6. She understands as well as her sister. 7. They are not so rich as we. 8. This rule is the more important of the two. 9. This rule is the most important of all. 10. It's the better of the two plays, but it's not the best play of the year. 11. It's the most historic church in the state.

(b) 1. This letter seems less sincere than that one. 2. We dance as well as they. 3. Your car is the longer of the two. 4. She talks more intelligently than you. 5. He treats them less rudely than the others. 6. You are more nervous than she. 7. This is the most revolutionary period of our history. 8. John is not so stout as I. 9. She's the prettier of the two girls, but she's not the prettiest in the class. 10. Our trip was the longest of all. 11. I am as certain as he.

### *8. Formation of Adverbs*

*Supply the corresponding adverb for each adjective.*

(a) précieux ________ éperdu ________ évident ________
probable ________ impoli ________ courant ________
doux ________ mou ________ énorme ________
difficile ________

(b) nouveau ________ vif ________ indéfini ________
absolu ________ insuffisant ________ facile ________
religieux ________ possible ________ négligent ________
profond ________

### *9. Position of Adverbs*

*Say in French.*

(a) 1. Your friend writes well. 2. They finally understand. 3. Answer me frankly. 4. She doesn't often come with them. 5. We followed them blindly. 6. He has traveled everywhere. 7. I telephoned to him today. 8. You had already gone out. 9. Has she ever told you that? 10. They have not yet begun to work. 11. I always go there.

(b) 1. They placed him gently on the bed. 2. Did you see her yesterday? 3. Has he already finished the book? 4. Let's sell them quickly. 5. We have never visited that city. 6. The pianist was playing badly. 7. He hadn't seen it well. 8. You finally believe it, don't you? 9. I went everywhere before finding them. 10. She still writes to you, doesn't she? 11. They are really going to France.

### *10. Adverbs and Nouns of Quantity*

*Say in French.*

(a) 1. Americans have many good qualities. 2. How many students do you know? 3. They are demanding more privileges. 4. I have as much work as you. 5. That happens, many times. 6. Most schools close during the vacation. 7. We need a pound of butter. 8. May I offer you a bowl of soup?

(b) 1. We are receiving less money. 2. Many evenings the children are alone in the house. 3. Take a spoonful of lemon juice. 4. Most large cities have a good library. 5. They spent too many days in Marseille. 6. He ordered a litre of white wine. 7. I don't have enough time. 8. How much milk did you buy?

### *11. The Adverb* **tout**

*Say in French.*

(a) 1. The boy was quite embarrassed. 2. The girl was quite embarrassed. 3. My father will be quite tired. 4. My mother will be quite tired. 5. We were completely surprised. 6. He was there a little while ago. 7. All of a sudden they decided to leave.

(b) 1. The soldiers had been quite unhappy. 2. We shall be there in a little while. 3. You understood it immediately. 4. She seems quite excited. 5. I need six of them, at the most. 6. He will be quite anxious. 7. The young ladies would be quite unhappy.

### *12. Position of Conjunctive Pronoun Objects (including* **y** *and* **en***)*

*Say in French.*

(a) 1. Look in the drawer; you will see some there. 2. She was going to write to him. 3. We hope to send them to her. 4. They prefer to do it themselves. 5. I had them built immediately. 6. Do you like to watch us work? 7. Everybody heard them singing.

(b) 1. She wants to buy you some. 2. They were watching him eat. 3. Did you have it examined? 4. There is the store; we will find some there. 5. I used to hear you playing the piano. 6. One must study them every day. 7. When is he coming to help us?

### *13. Uses of Disjunctive (Emphatic) Pronouns*

*Say in French.* (Italics indicate emphasis.)

(a) 1. *I* don't believe it! 2. She will never choose *him!* 3. He didn't send the letter to *you!* 4. *They* don't like to do that. 5. I gave *her* all the money. 6. He, without the others, left in the middle of the night. 7. Who is going to do it? – He and I. 8. You work as well as he. 9. We ourselves wanted to see them. 10. Did you hurt yourself?

(b) 1. *You* won't believe it! 2. *They,* not knowing that, gave it to him. 3. Did you accept it yourself? 4. *He* refused to go out. 5. We are as happy as they. 6. I have told myself that many times. 7. To *them* that makes no difference. 8. Did *they* say that? 9. Everybody is looking for *her!* 10. They sent *him* all the presents!

### *14. The Demonstrative Pronoun* **ce**

*Say in French.*

(a) 1. It was you. 2. It's she. 3. It's my aunt's. 4. That's right! 5. It's John and Richard. 6. It was President de Gaulle. 7. It's a bicycle. 8. They are hats. 9. It will be a lawyer who will write it. 10. What is his nationality? – He's a German. 11. They are Catholics. 12. It isn't good. 13. My picture? – It's beautiful! 14. Spend the vacation at your house? – It's marvelous! 15. It's easy to understand. 16. It's easy to forget those details. 17. That's surprising! 18. What you believe about it is important. 19. To leave without paying is dishonest.

(b) 1. It's Mary and her brother. 2. It's an airplane. 3. It was a pharmacist who told me that. 4. They are Spaniards. 5. Her house? – It's magnificent! 6. It was he. 7. It's easy to learn. 8. What worries me is the exam. 9. It's Mr. Dupont's. 10. It isn't bad! 11. It is proper to present yourself first. 12. It isn't I. 13. What is his religion? – He's a Buddhist. 14. To write all the little details is tiresome. 15. That's too bad! 16. Pay before receiving the article? – It's ridiculous! 17. It's Lieutenant Durand. 18. They are dresses. 19. That's right!

### *15. Relative Pronouns (Special Cases)*

*Say in French.*

(a) 1. She knew all the students in the midst of whom we were sitting. 2. They took a picture of the young lady behind whom you were walking. 3. Here's the young man about whom you have heard so much. 4. We have found the student to whose mother they had spoken. 5. Here's what it's about. 6. He met René's sisters, who had just arrived. 7. Tell us what you want, please. 8. Tell us the articles which you want, please.

(b) 1. Do you like the girl with whose brother we were traveling? 2. I'm going to tell you what we must talk about. 3. They want to see Robert's mother, who knows the answer. 4. I haven't met the girl beside whom I was standing. 5. She can't tell us what they found. 6. They are the people among whom he lived for ten years. 7. I am no longer interested in those monuments of which I took so many pictures. 8. Here are the books that you lost.

### *16. Negatives*

*Say in French.*

(a) 1. That train never used to arrive on time. 2. Nothing is more important than that. 3. We can find no record of his trip. 4. They accept only the best books. 5. She is afraid that they will arrest her husband. 6. No one understands all that. 7. I haven't told them anything. 8. We can't think of anything interesting. 9. He didn't find any picture of his father. 10. No kind of vegetation is found there.

(b) 1. There were only five men in the car. 2. Nothing worries them. 3. No book is worth as much as that. 4. He has never told me that. 5. There is no country where everyone is completely happy. 6. Don't give that to anyone. 7. No one enjoys himself more than he (does). 8. You will not see anyone if you arrive late. 9. She refuses to leave for fear that you will be worried. 10. No man understands it better than he.

### *17. Numbers and Time*

*Say in French.*

(a) 18 ________ 100 ________ 4th ________
24 ________ 102 ________ 10th ________
31 ________ 251 ________ Francis 1st ________
62 ________ 385 ________ Richard 2nd ________
71 ________ 1000 ________ June 5, 1973 ________
77 ________ 2/3 ________ January 1, 1809 ________

(b) 10:00 AM ________ 11:25 PM ________ 3:40 PM ________
6:05 AM ________ 1:15 PM ________ 7:55 AM ________
2:30 PM ________ 4:45 AM ________ 12:00 ________

### *18. Special Uses of* **devoir, faire, avoir**

*Say in French.*

(a) 1. We are supposed to meet them tomorrow. 2. The bus should leave at 10:10. 3. You are the ones who were to tell them that. 4. He must have seen her when he was in Paris. 5. In spite of everything, we had to destroy it. 6. I should write more often to my mother. 7. They ought to have sent it to us yesterday. 8. The weather was beautiful, but it was windy. 9. All the students must engage in sports. 10. When they don't want to work, they pretend to be sick. 11. We used to take a bicycle ride every morning. 12. You look bored. 13. You will need a guide for that trip. 14. I don't feel like studying tonight. 15. When will the election take place? 16. Do you often have a pain in the stomach? 17. His sister is twenty years old, isn't she? 18. I believe that you are right. 19. They were all cold and sleepy.

(b) 1. We must have left our tickets at home. 2. It was sunny, but it wasn't hot. 3. Have you ever gone in for skiing? 4. I can't pretend to be surprised. 5. He is supposed to be here at nine o'clock. 6. That boy looks stupid, but really he is very intelligent. 7. She had to work, in spite of her illness. 8. What's the matter with her? 9. Why am I always wrong? 10. Who feels like going swimming? 11. She should wear her new dress. 12. The exposition took place last year.

13. Are you afraid of being late? 14. They are the ones who were to write it. 15. How old is your father? 16. I ought to have known that she would say that. 17. If you need more time, write to him. 18. Everybody is going to take a boat trip. 19. One should study every example.

### *19. Spelling Changes in the Conjugation of Verbs*

*Change the verb form to agree with the new subject indicated (keeping the same tense).*

| | | |
|---|---|---|
| (a) | 1. il croit | vous __________ |
| | 2. elles voient | nous __________ |
| | 3. vous envoyez | ils __________ |
| | 4. je commence | nous __________ |
| | 5. nous avancions | elle __________ |
| | 6. nous recevons | je __________ |
| | 7. ils ont aperçu | il __________ |
| | 8. elle mange | nous __________ |
| | 9. nous voyagions | il __________ |
| | 10. nous célébrons | ils __________ |
| | 11. vous appelez | elle __________ |
| | 12. vous achetez | tu __________ |
| | 13. je mènerai | vous __________ |
| | 14. tu répéteras | nous __________ |
| (b) | 1. elle annonce | nous __________ |
| | 2. j'ai reçu | ils __________ |
| | 3. nous mangions | je __________ |
| | 4. vous jetez | il __________ |
| | 5. il se promènera | nous nous __________ |
| | 6. elle fuit | vous __________ |
| | 7. nous espérons | elle __________ |
| | 8. vous vous levez | je me __________ |
| | 9. vous apercevez | il __________ |
| | 10. je vois | vous __________ |
| | 11. je révélerai | vous __________ |
| | 12. tu nages | nous __________ |
| | 13. nous nettoyons | tu __________ |
| | 14. vous commenciez | je __________ |

## *20. Infinitives and Participles*

*Say in French.*

(a) 1. Have you studied the verb *to do?* 2. They are beginning to speak French. 3. She has refused to answer. 4. One doesn't learn that without working. 5. Is he going to accept the prize? 6. I want to make them understand. 7. Living isn't everything. 8. After reading the book, we shall discuss it. 9. After leaving the house, he remembered the message. 10. Believing their promises, we gave them the money. 11. While looking for your friends, I met those other people. 12. Look at those rolling waves! 13. We were writing letters when she called. 14. He plays cards instead of studying. 15. At what time did you meet her? 16. There's the car that your brother bought. 17. We had already gone to bed. 18. They arrived after us. 19. Here's a letter written in 1775.

(b) 1. He often talks without thinking. 2. After receiving the message, she went home. 3. We can't let them leave now. 4. Being thirsty, we ordered some beer. 5. Have you ever seen a flying fish? 6. She talks all the time instead of listening. 7. The verb *to sleep* is similar to that other verb. 8. Mary isn't the girl I met last night. 9. He bought two books published in 1880. 10. They washed before eating. 11. Did they succeed in finding the house? 12. We have already sold them. 13. Understanding all this isn't easy. 14. She went out without saying "Good-bye." 15. I was finishing my work when they arrived. 16. We have decided to remain here. 17. While talking with the teacher, I learned that news. 18. After coming down to the dining room, she met the other students. 19. We want to arrive before the others.

## *21. Reflexive Verbs. The Imperative*

*Say in French.*

(a) 1. They dressed quickly. 2. Those children will hurt themselves. 3. She doesn't remember their visit. 4. You will have a good time during your vacation. 5. We write to each other often. 6. They used to look at each other with tenderness. 7. Give him the money; then let's finish our work. 8. Don't accept that car; ask for this one.

9. Don't sell it to her. 10. Go to bed now.

(b) 1. Sit down, please. 2. They speak to each other on the telephone *(au téléphone)* for *(pendant)* hours. 3. Keep those old pictures; don't sell them to him! 4. I used to get up early. 5. Tell them your news. 6. Have a good time next week! 7. Give me some, please. 8. You described yourself very well. 9. We often used to help each other. 10. Let's go to Europe next summer!

### *22. Conditional Sentences*

*Say in French.*

(a) 1. If one studies well, one learns well. 2. If I take the exam now, I will not pass it. 3. If she comes, tell her I have left. 4. If you understood, you wouldn't ask that question. 5. If he got up early, he used to have time to study. 6. If they had known that, they would have invited you. 7. If you will come with me, I shall explain it to you. 8. If he would accept our offer, he would not regret it. 9. If I would say "Yes," she would say "No."

(b) 1. If she went to France, she would see her relatives. 2. If you will listen to my explanation, you will understand that. 3. If they would try that method, they would finish the work sooner. 4. If everyone arrives on time, we begin on time. 5. If you had stayed in your room, you would have received the message. 6. If I don't receive the check, I will not be able to buy those things. 7. If he had his breakfast on time, he used to feel better. 8. If we would arrive late, he would make us wait outside. 9. If you don't believe me, ask the others.

### *23. Interrogative Word Order*

*Say in French.*

(a) 1. Do you believe that? 2. Do your parents live in the United States? 3. Does Mary go to that school? 4. Did you sell it today? 5. Did Charles accept the prize? 6. Why did he do that? 7. Where did the pupils find it? 8. How is the teacher this morning? 9. How much does this watch cost? 10. Why are those people leaving? 11. How did her brother arrive here? 12. Where do the students spend their vacation? 13. Did you send it to them? 14. Am I driving too fast? 15. Did I show them to you?

(b) 1. Did they buy it without bargaining? 2. How did your friends find them? 3. Where did those tourists go yesterday? 4. Do the other students understand it? 5. Did we buy them there? 6. Did Miss Dumont receive the gift? 7. How are the children this afternoon? 8. Have I already seen them? 9. Do you want them? 10. How much do those articles cost? 11. Do I have enough time? 12. When did they do that? 13. How does his brother know that? 14. Does Paul live with his parents? 15. Why are your friends waiting?

***24. Uses of the Subjunctive*** (Since these are supplementary to the material of Les. 8, they concern principally the *exceptions* to the common uses of the subjunctive.)

*Say in French.*

(a) 1. We ordered them to enter the building. 2. She had permitted the children to leave without eating. 3. Forbid them to talk about it. 4. Who will ask her to return? 5. He told me to go home. 6. I told you that it was cold today. 7. We're glad that we're back. 8. She is surprised that she feels so well. 9. It is probable that they will understand it immediately. 10. You must tell me all the details. 11. It is good to be ready before the time. 12. Miss DuVal is the first person whom we invited. 13. I will pay it, provided that the articles arrive before Friday and that they are in good condition. 14. He gets up early in order to have the time to study. 15. She gets up early in order that her husband may sleep until seven o'clock. 16. They learn that without studying. 17. You learned that without his explaining it to you. 18. I examined it carefully before buying it. 19. I discovered that before you told me (it). 20. We go there in order to hear the concerts. 21. We go there in order that the children may hear the concerts. 22. She came every day, unless she felt ill. 23. She comes every day, unless her mother doesn't allow her to leave. 24. They will help us provided that they approve the plan. 25. Have them wait outside! 26. Have her take her place! 27. Long live the President! 28. Is he going to pay you before you have completed the work?

(b) 1. I told him to wait for me at the station. 2. It is time to return home. 3. We made that trip without spending more than a hundred dollars. 4. Have her come back tomorrow. 5. We regret that we are leaving Saturday. 6. They go out every evening, unless they are too tired. 7. I pass all the exams, provided that I am interested in the subject. 8. Long live the queen! 9. Ask them to explain their plan. 10. You will learn all that before you have finished the course. 11. Do you stay here to save money? 12. It is certain that he will accept it. 13. Who ordered you to do that? 14. You had already sold it before we arrived. 15. He drives with great care in order to avoid accidents. 16. We must invite them to dinner. 17. She will be there, unless it is too hot or unless she feels ill. 18. I ate breakfast before dressing. 19. They permitted us to use their car. 20. He stays home so that we can save money. 21. You go out every evening, unless the weather is bad. 22. I can't prevent you from leaving. 23. Have them get up immediately! 24. We returned home last night without his seeing us. 25. He explains it with care in order that we may understand it. 26. This is the longest novel that we have read this year. 27. You are afraid that you will say too much. 28. He told us that she wanted to buy it.

No exercises are provided for the Literary Tenses or the *Passé Surcomposé,* because the student will have no need of the former in his own speaking and writing, and extremely rare occasions to use the latter.

# *Formation of Colloquial Verb Tenses*

## PRESENT INDICATIVE (le présent de l'indicatif)

### *A. Regular Verbs*

For the three regular conjugations, the present indicative is formed by dropping the infinitive ending and adding the present indicative endings for each conjugation as follows:

| 1ST CONJUGATION | 2ND CONJUGATION | 3RD CONJUGATION |
|---|---|---|
| **donn*er*** to give | **fin*ir*** to finish | **vend*re*** to sell |
| **je donn*e*** | **je fin*is*** | **je vend*s*** |
| **tu donn*es*** | **tu fin*is*** | **tu vend*s*** |
| **il donn*e*** | **il fin*it*** | **il vend** |
| **nous donn*ons*** | **nous fin*issons*** | **nous vend*ons*** |
| **vous donn*ez*** | **vous fin*issez*** | **vous vend*ez*** |
| **ils donn*ent*** | **ils fin*issent*** | **ils vend*ent*** |

All **–er** verbs, except **aller**, are regular in the present indicative. There are, however, certain regular changes which should be noted for the correct spelling of certain –**er** verbs. **(See pp. 143-145.)**

The number of –**ir** verbs which follow the pattern of **finir** is rather limited. The most commonly used verbs of this class are:

| | | | | | |
|---|---|---|---|---|---|
| **abolir** | to abolish | **établir** | to establish | **remplir** | to fill |
| **bâtir** | to build | **obéir** | to obey | **se réunir** | to meet |
| **choisir** | to choose | **punir** | to punish | **réussir** | to succeed |

Third conjugation verbs ending in –**pre** have the ending –**t** in the third person singular **(rompre: il rompt).**

*B. Irregular Verbs*

For irregular verbs, the whole present indicative of each verb should be memorized. This process will be simplified, however, if the following are noted.

1. Most irregular verbs (with the notable exceptions of **avoir**, **être**, **aller**, **faire**, and **dire)** have the following endings in common:

| | |
|---|---|
| **–s** | **–ons** |
| **–s** | **–ez** |
| **–t** | **–ent** |

With –**dre** verbs (regular and irregular), the third person singular ends in –**d** rather than –**t**, but when pronounced (in liaison) this –**d** has the sound of –**t.**

**prend͡-il** **comprend͡-elle**

Where the preceding vowel is –**u**, the endings of the first and second persons singular will be –**x** instead of –**s.** Since both are silent, this involves no phonetic change.

| | | |
|---|---|---|
| **je peux** | **je veux** | **je vaux** |
| **tu peux** | **tu veux** | **tu vaux** |

2. The key forms for mastering stem changes in the present indicative are the first person singular and the first person plural.

**je reçois** **nous recevons** **je prends** **nous prenons**

Since any vowel change, as in **recevoir**, is caused by a shift of stress (emphasis) from the ending to the stem, such a change does not occur in the first and second persons plural – the two forms with pronounced endings.

| | |
|---|---|
| **je reçois** | **nous** *recevons* |
| **tu reçois** | **vous** *recevez* |
| **il reçoit** | **ils reçoivent** |

Where there is a consonant change, it occurs in all three forms of the plural, because in these three forms the final consonant of the stem is pronounced.

| | |
|---|---|
| **je crains** | **nous** *craignons* |
| **tu crains** | **vous** *craignez* |
| **il craint** | **ils** *craignent* |

A few verbs have both a vowel change and a consonant change, in which case both of the preceding principles apply.

| | |
|---|---|
| **je bois** | **nous** *buvons* |
| **tu bois** | **vous** *buvez* |
| **il boit** | **ils** *boivent* |

In the three cases where the plural stem ends in **–en,** the **–n** is doubled before the mute **–e** of the third person plural ending.

| | | |
|---|---|---|
| **nous tenons** | **nous venons** | **nous prenons** |
| **vous tenez** | **vous venez** | **vous prenez** |
| **ils** *tiennent* | **ils** *viennent* | **ils** *prennent* |

This applies also to compounds of these verbs: **ils retiennent, ils deviennent, ils apprennent**, etc.

3. The following verbs are irregular in the present indicative. In order to simplify study, these verbs are listed according to the categories discussed above.

(a) Special verbs (See paradigms beginning p. 205.)

| | | |
|---|---|---|
| **avoir** to have | **aller** to go | **dire** to say, tell |
| **être** to be | **faire** to make, do | |

(b) Change in stem vowel

| | | |
|---|---|---|
| **acquérir** to acquire | **j'acquiers** | **nous acquérons** |
| **mourir** to die | **je meurs** | **nous mourons** |
| **tenir** to hold | **je tiens** | **nous tenons** |
| **venir** to come | **je viens** | **nous venons** |

(c) Change in stem consonant

| | | |
|---|---|---|
| **battre** to beat | **je bats** | **nous battons** |
| **conduire** to conduct | **je conduis** | **nous conduisons** |
| (like **conduire**: **cuire, produire)** | | |
| **connaître** to know | **je connais** | **nous connaissons** |
| (like **connaître**: all verbs ending in –**aître)** | | |
| **craindre** to fear | **je crains** | **nous craignons** |
| (like **craindre**: all verbs ending in –**aindre**, –**eindre**, –**oindre)** | | |
| **dormir** to sleep | **je dors** | **nous dormons** |
| (like **dormir**: **mentir, partir, sentir, servir, sortir)** | | |
| **écrire** to write | **j'écris** | **nous écrivons** |
| **lire** to read | **je lis** | **nous lisons** |
| **mettre** to put | **je mets** | **nous mettons** |
| **plaire** to please | **je plais** | **nous plaisons** |
| **prendre** to take | **je prends** | **nous prenons** |
| **suivre** to follow | **je suis** | **nous suivons** |
| **vaincre** to vanquish (does not have –**t** in third singular: **il vainc)** | **je vaincs** | **nous vainquons** |
| **vivre** to live | **je vis** | **nous vivons** |

(d) Change in both vowel and consonant

| | | |
|---|---|---|
| **boire** to drink | **je bois** | **nous buvons** |
| **devoir** to owe | **je dois** | **nous devons** |
| **pouvoir** to be able | **je peux** | **nous pouvons** |
| **recevoir** to receive | **je reçois** | **nous recevons** |

(like **recevoir**:
all verbs ending in –**evoir**)

| | | | |
|---|---|---|---|
| **savoir** | to know | **je sais** | **nous savons** |
| **valoir** | to be worth | **je vaux** | **nous valons** |
| **vouloir** | to want | **je veux** | **nous voulons** |

(e) **Ouvrir**-type verbs (those ending in –**ir** which follow the pattern of –**er** verbs in the present indicative)

| | | | |
|---|---|---|---|
| **ouvrir** | to open | **j'ouvre** | **nous ouvrons** |
| **couvrir** | to cover | **je couvre** | **nous couvrons** |
| **offrir** | to offer | **j'offre** | **nous offrons** |
| **souffrir** | to suffer | **je souffre** | **nous souffrons** |

(f) Defective verbs having only one form in each tense

| | | | |
|---|---|---|---|
| **falloir** | to be necessary | **il faut** | it is necessary |
| **pleuvoir** | to rain | **il pleut** | it is raining |

## IMPERFECT INDICATIVE (l'imparfait de l'indicatif)

### *A. Endings*

All verbs have regular endings in this tense.

| | |
|---|---|
| –**ais** | –**ions** |
| –**ais** | –**iez** |
| –**ait** | –**aient** |

### *B. Stem*

All verbs except **être** derive the imperfect stem from the first person plural of the present indicative by dropping the –**ons**.

| | | | |
|---|---|---|---|
| **nous donnons**: | **je donnais**, etc. | **nous sortons**: | **je sortais**, etc. |
| **nous finissons**: | **je finissais**, etc. | **nous écrivons**: | **j'écrivais**, etc. |
| **nous vendons**: | **je vendais**, etc. | **nous recevons**: | **je recevais**, etc. |

*C. The One Irregular Verb* (**être**)

| | |
|---|---|
| **j'étais** | **nous étions** |
| **tu étais** | **vous étiez** |
| **il était** | **ils étaient** |

(For the uses and meanings see Lessons 2 and 3.)

## FUTURE (le futur)

*A. Endings*

All verbs have regular endings in the future.

| | |
|---|---|
| **–ai** | **–ons** |
| **–as** | **–ez** |
| **–a** | **–ont** |

*B. Stem*

For all regular and many irregular verbs, the stem of the future is the whole infinitive. (Verbs ending in **–re** drop the final mute **–e**).

| | | | |
|---|---|---|---|
| **donner**: | **je donnerai**, etc. | **dormir**: | **je dormirai**, etc. |
| **finir**: | **je finirai**, etc. | **prendre**: | **je prendrai**, etc. |
| **vendre**: | **je vendrai**, etc. | **écrire**: | **j'écrirai**, etc. |

*C. Irregular Future Stems*

| | | | |
|---|---|---|---|
| **aller**: | **j'irai**, etc. | **tenir**: | **je tiendrai** |
| **envoyer**: | **j'enverrai** | **venir**: | **je viendrai** |
| **être**: | **je serai** | **s'asseoir**: | **je m'assiérai** |
| **faire**: | **je ferai** | **avoir**: | **j'aurai** |
| **acquérir**: | **j'acquerrai** | **devoir**: | **je devrai** |
| **courir**: | **je courrai** | **falloir**: | **il faudra** |
| **cueillir**: | **je cueillerai** | **pleuvoir**: | **il pleuvra** |
| **mourir**: | **je mourrai** | **pouvoir**: | **je pourrai** |

| | | | |
|---|---|---|---|
| **recevoir:** | **je recevrai** | **voir:** | **je verrai** |
| **savoir:** | **je saurai** | **vouloir:** | **je voudrai** |
| **valoir:** | **je vaudrai** | | |

Notice that all **–oir** verbs have irregular future stems. Only two **–er** verbs and two **–re** verbs have irregular stems.

## CONDITIONAL (le conditionnel)

The conditional of all verbs is formed by adding the imperfect endings to the future stem.

**faire**

| | |
|---|---|
| **je fer***ais* | **nous fer***ions* |
| **tu fer***ais* | **vous fer***iez* |
| **il fer***ait* | **ils fer***aient* |

## PRESENT SUBJUNCTIVE (le présent du subjonctif)

### *A. Endings*

The endings for the present subjunctive of all verbs except **avoir** and **être** are:

| | |
|---|---|
| **–e** | **–ions** |
| **–es** | **–iez** |
| **–e** | **–ent** |

### *B. Stem*

The stem of the present subjunctive for all regular verbs and most irregular verbs may be found by dropping the **–ent** of the third person plural of the present indicative.

| | | | |
|---|---|---|---|
| **ils donnent:** | **que je donne**, etc. | **ils craignent:** | **que je craigne**, etc. |
| **ils finissent:** | **que je finisse**, etc. | **ils reçoivent:** | **que je reçoive**, etc. |
| **ils vendent:** | **que je vende**, etc. | **ils boivent:** | **que je boive**, etc. |

### *C. Stem-changing Verbs*

The following verbs have the same change of stem in the first and second persons plural of the present subjunctive that they have in the present indicative.

| | | | | | |
|---|---|---|---|---|---|
| **acquérir:** | **acquière** | **acquérions** | **prendre:** | **prenne** | **prenions** |
| **boire:** | **boive** | **buvions** | **recevoir:** | **reçoive** | **recevions** |
| **devoir:** | **doive** | **devions** | **tenir:** | **tienne** | **tenions** |
| **mourir:** | **meure** | **mourions** | **venir:** | **vienne** | **venions** |

### *D. Irregular Stems*

The following verbs have irregular stems in the present subjunctive:

| | | |
|---|---|---|
| **aller:** | **que j'aille** | **que nous allions** |
| **faire:** | **que je fasse** | **que nous fassions** |
| **falloir:** | **qu'il faille** | **. . .** |
| **pouvoir:** | **que je puisse** | **que nous puissions** |
| **savoir:** | **que je sache** | **que nous sachions** |
| **valoir:** | **que je vaille** | **que nous valions** |
| **vouloir:** | **que je veuille** | **que nous voulions** |

### *E. Present Subjunctive of* avoir *and* être

| | | | |
|---|---|---|---|
| **que j'aie** | **que nous ayons** | **que je sois** | **que nous soyons** |
| **que tu aies** | **que vous ayez** | **que tu sois** | **que vous soyez** |
| **qu'il ait** | **qu'ils aient** | **qu'il soit** | **qu'ils soient** |

## COMPOUND TENSES (les temps composés)

### *A. General Remarks*

For each simple tense there is a corresponding compound tense. If the student memorizes the first person singular of the past indefinite *(passé composé)* of an irregular verb, he possesses the key to all the compound tenses – he knows the past participle and he knows which auxiliary is used. The rest is merely a matter of conjugating **avoir** or **être** in the appropriate simple tense.

### *B. Examples*

PAST INDEFINITE *(passé composé)*

| | | |
|---|---|---|
| **j'ai mis** I have put, etc. | **je suis allé** I have gone, etc. | **je me suis assis** I sat (down), etc. |
| **tu as mis** | **tu es allé** | **tu t'es assis** |
| **il a mis** | **il est allé** | **il s'est assis** |
| **nous avons mis** | **nous sommes allés** | **nous nous sommes assis** |
| **vous avez mis** | **vous êtes allé (allée, –és, –ées)** | **vous vous êtes assis (assise, –es)** |
| **ils ont mis** | **ils sont allés** | **ils se sont assis** |

PLUPERFECT INDICATIVE *(le plus-que-parfait de l'indicatif)*

| | | |
|---|---|---|
| **j'avais mis** I had put, etc. | **j'étais allé** I had gone, etc. | **je m'étais assis** I had sat (down), etc. |

FUTURE PERFECT *(le futur antérieur)*

| | | |
|---|---|---|
| **j'aurai mis** I shall have put | **je serai allé** I shall have gone | **je me serai assis** I shall have sat (down) |

PAST CONDITIONAL *(le conditionnel passé)*

| | | |
|---|---|---|
| **j'aurais mis** I would have put | **je serais allé** I would have gone | **je me serais assis** I would have sat (down) |

PAST SUBJUNCTIVE *(le passé du subjonctif)*

| | | |
|---|---|---|
| **que j'aie mis** that I have put | **que je sois allé** that I have gone | **que je me sois assis** that I have sat (down) |

## *C. Auxiliaries* **avoir** *and* **être**

The auxiliary used in the compound tenses is **avoir** except in the following two categories:

1. Any verb used reflexively takes **être**.

| | |
|---|---|
| **J'ai lavé la voiture.** | I washed the car. |
| **Je me suis lavé avant de manger.** | I washed before eating. |
| **Il ne s'est pas souvenu de l'incident.** | He didn't remember the incident. |

2. The following intransitive verbs, most of which are verbs of *going* or *coming,* take **être**.

| | |
|---|---|
| **aller** to go | **venir** to come |
| **monter** to go (come) up | **descendre** to go (come) down |
| **entrer** to go (come) in, enter | **sortir** to go (come) out |
| **partir** to go away, leave | **arriver** to arrive |
| **retourner** to go back, return | **rester** to remain |
| **naître** to be born | **mourir** to die |
| **tomber** to fall | |

Intransitive compounds of these verbs (**revenir** *to come back;* **devenir** *to become;* **rentrer** *to return [home], re-enter)* also take **être**.

The verbs **descendre, monter**, and **sortir** are sometimes used with objects. In such cases the auxiliary is **avoir**.

| | |
|---|---|
| **Le chasseur qui a descendu nos bagages n'est pas celui qui les a montés.** | The bellhop who brought down our baggage is not the one who carried it up. |

## KEY FORMS FOR MASTERY OF THE COLLOQUIAL TENSES*

### *A. Regular Verbs*

Four forms of the regular verbs provide the key to all the colloquial tenses:

(1) present infinitive
(2) 1st person singular, present indicative
(3) 1st person plural, present indicative
(4) 1st person singular, past indefinite

*Examples:*

**(1) donner**

**je donnerai**, etc. *(fut.)*
**je donnerais**, etc. *(cond.)*

**(2) je donne**

**tu donnes** *(pres. ind.)*
**il donne**

**(3) nous donnons**

**vous donnez** *(pres. ind.)*
**ils donnent**
**je donnais**, etc. *(imperf.)*
**que je donne**, etc. *(pres. subj.)*

**(4) j'ai donné**

*all compound tenses*

**(1) finir**

**je finirai**, etc. *(fut.)*
**je finirais**, etc. *(cond.)*

**(2) je finis**

**tu finis** *(pres. ind.)*
**il finit**

**(3) nous finissons**

**vous finissez** *(pres. ind.)*
**ils finissent**
**je finissais**, etc. *(imperf.)*
**que je finisse**, etc. *(pres. subj.)*

**(4) j'ai fini**

*all compound tenses*

*Note:* Imperatives are not listed because they are simply the corresponding present indicative forms used without the pronoun subjects **tu, nous,** and **vous.** In the **tu** form, the –s of –**er** verbs is dropped.

* For literary tenses see pp. 161-164.

### *B. Irregular Verbs*

The four forms listed above are a sufficient key also for the following irregular verbs, and others which follow their patterns.

| | | |
|---|---|---|
| **battre** | **dire** | **naître** |
| **conduire** | **dormir** | **plaire** |
| **connaître** | **écrire** | **rire** |
| **couvrir** | **lire** | **suivre** |
| **craindre** | **mettre** | **vivre** |

For other irregular verbs it is most useful to memorize the following nine forms.

(1-6) all forms of the present indicative
(7) 1st person singular, future
(8) 1st person singular, present subjunctive
(9) 1st person singular, past indefinite

*Examples:*

BASIC FORMS — DERIVED FORMS

**voir** to see

Present Indicative

| | | | |
|---|---|---|---|
| **je vois** | **nous voyons** | → | **voyant** *(pres. part.)* |
| **tu vois** | **vous voyez** | → | **je voyais**, etc. *(imperf. ind.)* |
| **il voit** | **ils voient** | → | **que nous voyions** *(pres. subj.)* |
| | | | **que vous voyiez** |

Future

**je verrai**, etc. — **je verrais**, etc. *(cond.)*

Present Subjunctive

**que je voie**, etc.

Past Indefinite

**j'ai vu**, etc. →
**j'avais vu**, etc. *(pluperf. ind.)*
**j'aurai vu**, etc. *(fut. perf.)*
**j'aurais vu**, etc. *(past cond.)*
**que j'aie vu**, etc. *(past subj.)*

**aller** to go

Present Indicative

| | | | |
|---|---|---|---|
| **je vais** | **nous allons** | → | **allant** *(pres. part.)* |
| **tu vas** | **vous allez** | → | **j'allais** *(imperf. ind.)* |
| **il va** | **ils vont** | → | **que nous allions** *(pres. subj.)* |
| | | | **que vous alliez** |

Future

**j'irai**, etc. — **j'irais**, etc. *(cond.)*

Present Subjunctive

**que j'aille**, etc.

Past Indefinite

**je suis allé**, etc. → **j'étais allé**, etc. *(pluperf. ind.)*
→ **je serai allé**, etc. *(fut. perf.)*
→ **je serais allé**, etc. *(past cond.)*
→ **que je sois allé**, etc. *(past subj.)*

# *Paradigms of Regular Verbs*

(For each tense, the forms within the shaded area are pronounced alike, except as they are affected by liaison. Shading is used to indicate this only where three or more forms of the same tense have the same pronunciation.)

| *First Conjugation* | *Second Conjugation* | *Third Conjugation* |
|---|---|---|
| | INFINITIVE | |
| **donner** to give | **finir** to finish | **vendre** to sell |
| | PRESENT PARTICIPLE | |
| **donnant** giving | **finissant** finishing | **vendant** selling |
| | PAST PARTICIPLE | |
| **donné** given | **fini** finished | **vendu** sold |

*Simple Tenses*

PRESENT INDICATIVE

| I give, etc. | I finish, etc. | I sell, etc. |
|---|---|---|
| je donne | je finis | je vends |
| tu donnes | tu finis | tu vends |
| il donne | il finit | il vend |
| nous donnons | nous finissons | nous vendons |
| vous donnez | vous finissez | vous vendez |
| ils donnent | ils finissent | ils vendent |

IMPERFECT INDICATIVE

| I gave, etc. | I finished, etc. | I sold, etc. |
|---|---|---|
| je donnais | je finissais | je vendais |
| tu donnais | tu finissais | tu vendais |
| il donnait | il finissait | il vendait |
| nous donnions | nous finissions | nous vendions |
| vous donniez | vous finissiez | vous vendiez |
| ils donnaient | ils finissaient | ils vendaient |

PAST DEFINITE

| I gave, etc. | I finished, etc. | I sold, etc. |
|---|---|---|
| je donnai | je finis | je vendis |
| tu donnas | tu finis | tu vendis |
| il donna | il finit | il vendit |
| nous donnâmes | nous finîmes | nous vendîmes |
| vous donnâtes | vous finîtes | vous vendîtes |
| ils donnèrent | ils finirent | ils vendirent |

FUTURE

| I shall give, etc. | I shall finish, etc. | I shall sell, etc. |
|---|---|---|
| je donnerai | je finirai | je vendrai |
| tu donneras | tu finiras | tu vendras |
| il donnera | il finira | il vendra |
| nous donnerons | nous finirons | nous vendrons |
| vous donnerez | vous finirez | vous vendrez |
| ils donneront | ils finiront | ils vendront |

CONDITIONAL

| I would give, etc. | I would finish, etc. | I would sell, etc. |
|---|---|---|
| **je donnerais** | **je finirais** | **je vendrais** |
| **tu donnerais** | **tu finirais** | **tu vendrais** |
| **il donnerait** | **il finirait** | **il vendrait** |
| **nous donnerions** | **nous finirions** | **nous vendrions** |
| **vous donneriez** | **vous finiriez** | **vous vendriez** |
| **ils donneraient** | **ils finiraient** | **ils vendraient** |

PRESENT SUBJUNCTIVE

| that I give, etc. | that I finish, etc. | that I sell, etc. |
|---|---|---|
| **que je donne** | **que je finisse** | **que je vende** |
| **que tu donnes** | **que tu finisses** | **que tu vendes** |
| **qu'il donne** | **qu'il finisse** | **qu'il vende** |
| **que nous donnions** | **que nous finissions** | **que nous vendions** |
| **que vous donniez** | **que vous finissiez** | **que vous vendiez** |
| **qu'ils donnent** | **qu'ils finissent** | **qu'ils vendent** |

IMPERFECT SUBJUNCTIVE

| that I gave, etc. | that I finished, etc. | that I sold, etc. |
|---|---|---|
| **que je donnasse** | **que je finisse** | **que je vendisse** |
| **que tu donnasses** | **que tu finisses** | **que tu vendisses** |
| **qu'il donnât** | **qu'il finît** | **qu'il vendît** |
| **que nous donnassions** | **que nous finissions** | **que nous vendissions** |
| **que vous donnassiez** | **que vous finissiez** | **que nous vendissiez** |
| **qu'ils donnassent** | **qu'ils finissent** | **qu'ils vendissent** |

IMPERATIVE

| | | |
|---|---|---|
| **donne** give *(fam.)* | **finis** finish *(fam.)* | **vends** sell *(fam.)* |
| **donnons** let's give | **finissons** let's finish | **vendons** let's sell |
| **donnez** give | **finissez** finish | **vendez** sell |

### *Compound Tenses*

PAST INDEFINITE

| I gave, etc. | I finished, etc. | I sold, etc. |
|---|---|---|
| **j'ai donné** | **j'ai fini** | **j'ai vendu** |
| **tu as donné** | **tu as fini** | **tu as vendu** |
| **il a donné** | **il a fini** | **il a vendu** |

| | | |
|---|---|---|
| **nous avons donné** | **nous avons fini** | **nous avons vendu** |
| **vous avez donné** | **vous avez fini** | **vous avez vendu** |
| **ils ont donné** | **ils ont fini** | **ils ont vendu** |

PLUPERFECT INDICATIVE

| | | |
|---|---|---|
| I had given, etc. | I had finished, etc. | I had sold, etc. |
| **j'avais donné** | **j'avais fini** | **j'avais vendu** |
| **tu avais donné** | **tu avais fini** | **tu avais vendu** |
| **il avait donné** | **il avait fini** | **il avait vendu** |
| **nous avions donné** | **nous avions fini** | **nous avions vendu** |
| **vous aviez donné** | **vous aviez fini** | **vous aviez vendu** |
| **ils avaient donné** | **ils avaient fini** | **ils avaient vendu** |

PAST ANTERIOR

| | | |
|---|---|---|
| I had given, etc. | I had finished, etc. | I had sold, etc. |
| **j'eus donné** | **j'eus fini** | **j'eus vendu** |
| **tu eus donné** | **tu eus fini** | **tu eus vendu** |
| **il eut donné** | **il eut fini** | **il eut vendu** |
| **nous eûmes donné** | **nous eûmes fini** | **nous eûmes vendu** |
| **vous eûtes donné** | **vous eûtes fini** | **vous eûtes vendu** |
| **ils eurent donné** | **ils eurent fini** | **ils eurent vendu** |

FUTURE PERFECT

| | | |
|---|---|---|
| I shall have given, etc. | I shall have finished, etc. | I shall have sold, etc. |
| **j'aurai donné** | **j'aurai fini** | **j'aurai vendu** |
| **tu auras donné** | **tu auras fini** | **tu auras vendu** |
| **il aura donné** | **il aura fini** | **il aura vendu** |
| **nous aurons donné** | **nous aurons fini** | **nous aurons vendu** |
| **vous aurez donné** | **vous aurez fini** | **vous aurez vendu** |
| **ils auront donné** | **ils auront fini** | **ils auront vendu** |

PAST CONDITIONAL

| | | |
|---|---|---|
| I would have given, etc. | I would have finished, etc. | I would have sold, etc. |
| **j'aurais donné** | **j'aurais fini** | **j'aurais vendu** |
| **tu aurais donné** | **tu aurais fini** | **tu aurais vendu** |
| **il aurait donné** | **il aurait fini** | **il aurait vendu** |

| | | |
|---|---|---|
| **nous aurions donné** | **nous aurions fini** | **nous aurions vendu** |
| **vous auriez donné** | **vous auriez fini** | **vous auriez vendu** |
| **ils auraient donné** | **ils auraient fini** | **ils auraient vendu** |

PAST SUBJUNCTIVE

| | | |
|---|---|---|
| that I have given, etc. | that I have finished, etc. | that I have sold, etc. |
| **que j'aie donné** | **que j'aie fini** | **que j'aie vendu** |
| **que tu aies donné** | **que tu aies fini** | **que tu aies vendu** |
| **qu'il ait donné** | **qu'il ait fini** | **qu'il ait vendu** |
| **que nous ayons donné** | **que nous ayons fini** | **que nous ayons vendu** |
| **que vous ayez donné** | **que vous ayez fini** | **que vous ayez vendu** |
| **qu'ils aient donné** | **qu'ils aient fini** | **qu'ils aient vendu** |

PLUPERFECT SUBJUNCTIVE

| | | |
|---|---|---|
| that I had given, etc. | that I had finished, etc. | that I had sold, etc. |
| **que j'eusse donné** | **que j'eusse fini** | **que j'eusse vendu** |
| **que tu eusses donné** | **que tu eusses fini** | **que tu eusses vendu** |
| **qu'il eût donné** | **qu'il eût fini** | **qu'il eût vendu** |
| **que nous eussions donné** | **que nous eussions fini** | **que nous eussions vendu** |
| **que vous eussiez donné** | **que vous eussiez fini** | **que vous eussiez vendu** |
| **qu'ils eussent donné** | **qu'ils eussent fini** | **qu'ils eussent vendu** |

# *Reflexive Verb*

**se laver** to wash (oneself)

*Simple Tenses*

| PRESENT INDICATIVE | IMPERFECT INDICATIVE | PAST DEFINITE |
|---|---|---|
| I wash, etc. | I washed, etc. | I washed, etc. |
| **je me lave** | **je me lavais** | **je me lavai** |
| **tu te laves** | **tu te lavais** | **tu te lavas** |
| **il se lave** | **il se lavait** | **il se lava** |
| **nous nous lavons** | **nous nous lavions** | **nous nous lavâmes** |
| **vous vous lavez** | **vous vous laviez** | **vous vous lavâtes** |
| **ils se lavent** | **ils se lavaient** | **ils se lavèrent** |

| FUTURE | CONDITIONAL | PRESENT SUBJUNCTIVE |
|---|---|---|
| I shall wash, etc. | I would wash, etc. | that I wash, etc. |
| **je me laverai** | **je me laverais** | **que je me lave** |
| **tu te laveras** | **tu te laverais** | **que tu te laves** |
| **il se lavera** | **il se laverait** | **qu'il se lave** |
| **nous nous laverons** | **nous nous laverions** | **que nous nous lavions** |
| **vous vous laverez** | **vous vous laveriez** | **que vous vous laviez** |
| **ils se laveront** | **ils se laveraient** | **qu'ils se lavent** |

IMPERFECT SUBJUNCTIVE
that I washed, etc.

**que je me lavasse**
**que tu te lavasses**
**qu'il se lavât**
**que nous nous lavassions**
**que vous vous lavassiez**
**qu'ils se lavassent**

PRESENT PARTICIPLE
**se lavant** washing

IMPERATIVE
**lave-toi** wash (yourself) *[fam.]*
**lavons-nous** let's wash (ourselves)
**lavez-vous** wash (yourself, yourselves)

*Compound Tenses*

PAST INDEFINITE
I washed, etc.

**je me suis lavé**
**tu t'es lavé**
**il s'est lavé**
**nous nous sommes lavés**
**vous vous êtes lavés**
**ils se sont lavés**

PLUPERFECT INDICATIVE
I had washed, etc.

**je m'étais lavé**
**tu t'étais lavé**
**il s'était lavé**
**nous nous étions lavés**
**vous vous étiez lavés**
**ils s'étaient lavés**

PAST ANTERIOR
I had washed, etc.

**je me fus lavé**
**tu te fus lavé**
**il se fut lavé**
**nous nous fûmes lavés**
**vous vous fûtes lavés**
**ils se furent lavés**

FUTURE PERFECT
I shall have washed, etc.

**je me serai lavé**
**tu te seras lavé**
**il se sera lavé**
**nous nous serons lavés**
**vous vous serez lavés**
**ils se seront lavés**

PAST CONDITIONAL
I would have washed, etc.

**je me serais lavé**
**tu te serais lavé**
**il se serait lavé**
**nous nous serions lavés**
**vous vous seriez lavés**
**ils se seraient lavés**

PAST SUBJUNCTIVE
that I washed, etc.

**que je me sois lavé**
**que tu te sois lavé**
**qu'il se soit lavé**
**que nous nous soyons lavés**
**que vous vous soyez lavés**
**qu'ils se soient lavés**

PLUPERFECT SUBJUNCTIVE

that I had washed, etc.

**que je me fusse lavé**
**que tu te fusses lavé**
**qu'il se fût lavé**
**que nous nous fussions lavés**
**que vous vous fussiez lavés**
**qu'ils se fussent lavés**

(*Note:* In the compound tenses, the agreement of the past participle with **nous** and **vous** will depend on the reference of those pronouns. **Nous** may be either masculine or feminine plural. **Vous** may be masculine or feminine, singular or plural.)

# *avoir* and *être*

INFINITIVE

| | |
|---|---|
| **avoir** to have | **être** to be |

PRESENT PARTICIPLE

| | |
|---|---|
| **ayant** having | **étant** being |

PAST PARTICIPLE

| | |
|---|---|
| **eu** had | **été** been |

*Simple Tenses*

PRESENT INDICATIVE

| | |
|---|---|
| **j'ai** I have, etc. | **je suis** I am, etc. |
| **tu as** | **tu es** |
| **il a** | **il est** |
| **nous avons** | **nous sommes** |
| **vous avez** | **vous êtes** |
| **ils ont** | **ils sont** |

IMPERFECT INDICATIVE

| | |
|---|---|
| **j'avais** I had, etc. | **j'étais** I was, etc. |
| **tu avais** | **tu étais** |
| **il avait** | **il était** |
| **nous avions** | **nous étions** |
| **vous aviez** | **vous étiez** |
| **ils avaient** | **ils étaient** |

PAST DEFINITE

| | |
|---|---|
| **j'eus** I had, etc. | **je fus** I was, etc. |
| **tu eus** | **tu fus** |
| **il eut** | **il fut** |
| **nous eûmes** | **nous fûmes** |
| **vous eûtes** | **vous fûtes** |
| **ils eurent** | **ils furent** |

FUTURE

| | |
|---|---|
| **j'aurai** I shall have, etc. | **je serai** I shall be, etc. |
| **tu auras** | **tu seras** |
| **il aura** | **il sera** |
| **nous aurons** | **nous serons** |
| **vous aurez** | **vous serez** |
| **ils auront** | **ils seront** |

CONDITIONAL

| | |
|---|---|
| **j'aurais** I would have, etc. | **je serais** I would be, etc. |
| **tu aurais** | **tu serais** |
| **il aurait** | **il serait** |
| **nous aurions** | **nous serions** |
| **vous auriez** | **vous seriez** |
| **ils auraient** | **ils seraient** |

PRESENT SUBJUNCTIVE

| | |
|---|---|
| **que j'aie** that I have, etc. | **que je sois** that I be, etc. |
| **que tu aies** | **que tu sois** |
| **qu'il ait** | **qu'il soit** |
| **que nous ayons** | **que nous soyons** |
| **que vous ayez** | **que vous soyez** |
| **qu'ils aient** | **qu'ils soient** |

IMPERFECT SUBJUNCTIVE

| | |
|---|---|
| **que j'eusse** that I had, etc. | **que je fusse** that I was, etc. |
| **que tu eusses** | **que tu fusses** |
| **qu'il eût** | **qu'il fût** |
| **que nous eussions** | **que nous fussions** |
| **que vous eussiez** | **que vous fussiez** |
| **qu'ils eussent** | **qu'ils fussent** |

IMPERATIVE

| | |
|---|---|
| **aie** have *(fam.)* | **sois** be *(fam.)* |
| **ayons** let's have | **soyons** let's be |
| **ayez** have | **soyez** be |

*Compound Tenses*

PAST INDEFINITE

| | |
|---|---|
| **j'ai eu** I have had, etc. | **j'ai été** I have been, etc. |

PLUPERFECT INDICATIVE

| | |
|---|---|
| **j'avais eu** I had had, etc. | **j'avais été** I had been, etc. |

PAST ANTERIOR

| | |
|---|---|
| **j'eus eu** I had had, etc. | **j'eus été** I had been, etc. |

FUTURE PERFECT

| | |
|---|---|
| **j'aurai eu** I shall have had, etc. | **j'aurai été** I shall have been, etc. |

PAST CONDITIONAL

| | |
|---|---|
| **j'aurais eu** I would have had, etc. | **j'aurais été** I would have been, etc. |

PAST SUBJUNCTIVE

| | |
|---|---|
| **que j'aie eu** that I have had, etc. | **que j'aie été** that I have been, etc. |

PLUPERFECT SUBJUNCTIVE

| | |
|---|---|
| **que j'eusse eu** that I had had, etc. | **que j'eusse été** that I had been, etc. |

# *Irregular Verbs*

## IRREGULAR VERBS NOT INCLUDED IN TABLES

These verbs are conjugated on the pattern of the sample verbs indicated to the right.

| | |
|---|---|
| **abattre** to knock down | **battre** |
| **accourir** to run up *(aux. usually* **être)** | **courir** |
| **accueillir** to welcome | **cueillir** |
| **admettre** to admit | **mettre** |
| **apercevoir** to perceive | **recevoir** |
| **apparaître** to appear *(aux. usually* **être)** | **connaître** |
| **appartenir** to belong *(aux.* **avoir)** | **venir** |
| **apprendre** to learn | **prendre** |
| **atteindre** to attain | **craindre** |
| **combattre** to combat | **battre** |
| **commettre** to commit | **mettre** |
| **comprendre** to understand | **prendre** |

| | | |
|---|---|---|
| **concevoir** | to conceive | **recevoir** |
| **conquérir** | to conquer | **acquérir** |
| **consentir** | to consent | **dormir** |
| **construire** | to construct | **conduire** |
| **contenir** (*aux.* **avoir**) | to contain | **venir** |
| **convaincre** | to convince | **vaincre** |
| **convenir** (*aux.* **avoir**) | to agree | **venir** |
| **décevoir** | to deceive | **recevoir** |
| **découvrir** | to discover | **couvrir** |
| **décrire** | to describe | **écrire** |
| **défaire** | to undo | **faire** |
| **déplaire** | to displease | **plaire** |
| **détenir** (*aux.* **avoir**) | to detain | **venir** |
| **détruire** | to destroy | **conduire** |
| **devenir** | to become | **venir** |
| **disparaître** | to disappear | **connaître** |
| **élire** | to elect | **lire** |
| **s'endormir** | to go to sleep | **dormir** |
| **s'enfuir** | to run away | **fuir** |
| **entreprendre** | to undertake | **prendre** |
| **éteindre** | to extinguish | **craindre** |
| **étreindre** | to clasp | **craindre** |
| **feindre** | to pretend | **craindre** |
| **inscrire** | to inscribe | **écrire** |
| **introduire** | to introduce | **conduire** |
| **joindre** | to join | **craindre** |
| **maintenir** (*aux.* **avoir**) | to maintain | **venir** |
| **mentir** | to lie | **dormir** |
| **obtenir** (*aux.* **avoir**) | to obtain | **venir** |
| **offrir** | to offer | **couvrir** |
| **omettre** | to omit | **mettre** |
| **ouvrir** | to open | **couvrir** |
| **paraître** | to appear | **connaître** |
| **partir** (*aux.* **être**) | to leave | **dormir** |

| | | |
|---|---|---|
| **peindre** | to paint | **craindre** |
| **permettre** | to permit | **mettre** |
| **plaindre** | to pity | **craindre** |
| **poursuivre** | to pursue | **suivre** |
| **prescrire** | to prescribe | **écrire** |
| **prévenir** (*aux.* **avoir**) | to warn | **venir** |
| **produire** | to produce | **conduire** |
| **promettre** | to promise | **mettre** |
| **reconnaître** | to recognize | **connaître** |
| **rejoindre** | to join (again) | **craindre** |
| **remettre** | to postpone | **mettre** |
| **renvoyer** | to send back | **envoyer** |
| **repartir** (*aux.* **être**) | to leave again | **dormir** |
| **se repentir** | to repent | **dormir** |
| **reprendre** | to take back | **prendre** |
| **retenir** (*aux.* **avoir**) | to hold back | **venir** |
| **revenir** | to come back | **venir** |
| **revoir** | to see again | **voir** |
| **satisfaire** | to satisfy | **faire** |
| **séduire** | to seduce | **conduire** |
| **sentir** | to feel | **dormir** |
| **servir** | to serve | **dormir** |
| **sortir** (*aux.* **être**) | to go out | **dormir** |
| **souffrir** | to suffer | **couvrir** |
| **sourire** | to smile | **rire** |
| **soutenir** (*aux.* **avoir**) | to sustain | **venir** |
| **se souvenir** | to remember | **venir** |
| **surprendre** | to surprise | **prendre** |
| **se taire** | to keep quiet | **plaire** |
| **traduire** | to translate | **conduire** |
| **transmettre** | to transmit | **mettre** |

## TABLES OF IRREGULAR VERBS

The forms given in this table are the key forms. Any forms not listed here are derived and conjugated regularly. The infinitive and present participle of each verb are given in brackets. See p. 181 ff. for details of derivations.

| PRESENT INDICATIVE | FUTURE<br>PAST DEFINITE | PAST INDEFINITE<br>PRESENT SUBJUNCTIVE *(1st sing. & pl.)* |
|---|---|---|

[**acquérir** to acquire; **acquérant**]

| | | |
|---|---|---|
| **j'acquiers** | **j'acquerrai** | **j'ai acquis** |
| **tu acquiers** | | |
| **il acquiert** | **j'acquis** | **que j'acquière** |
| **nous acquérons** | | **que nous acquérions** |
| **vous acquérez** | | |
| **ils acquièrent** | | |

[**aller** to go; **allant**]

| | | |
|---|---|---|
| **je vais** | **j'irai** | **je suis allé** |
| **tu vas** | | |
| **il va** | **j'allai** | **que j'aille** |
| **nous allons** | | **que nous allions** |
| **vous allez** | | |
| **ils vont** | | |

[**s'asseoir** to sit (down); **s'asseyant**]

| | | |
|---|---|---|
| **je m'assieds** | **je m'assiérai** | **je me suis assis** |
| **tu t'assieds** | | |
| **il s'assied** | **je m'assis** | **que je m'asseye** |
| **nous nous asseyons** | | **que nous nous asseyions** |

See pp. 209-211 for list of other irregular verbs which follow the patterns of those listed in this table.

| PRESENT INDICATIVE | FUTURE<br>PAST DEFINITE | PAST INDEFINITE<br>PRESENT SUBJUNCTIVE<br>*(1st sing. & pl.)* |
|---|---|---|
| **vous vous asseyez** | | |
| **ils s'asseyent** | | |

(**S'asseoir** also has alternate forms: *pres. part.* **assoyant**; *pres. ind.* **je m'assois**, etc; *fut.* **assoirai** or **asseyerai**, and derivatives of these forms.)

[**avoir** to have (See p. 205.)]

[**battre** to beat]

The only irregularity of **battre** is that it drops one –**t** in the singular forms of the present indicative: **je bats, tu bats, il bat.**

[**boire** to drink; **buvant**]

| | | |
|---|---|---|
| **je bois** | **je boirai** | **j'ai bu** |
| **tu bois** | | |
| **il boit** | **je bus** | **que je boive** |
| **nous buvons** | | **que nous buvions** |
| **vous buvez** | | |
| **ils boivent** | | |

[**conduire** to conduct, drive; **conduisant**]

| | | |
|---|---|---|
| **je conduis** | **je conduirai** | **j'ai conduit** |
| **tu conduis** | | |
| **il conduit** | **je conduisis** | **que je conduise** |
| **nous conduisons** | | **que nous conduisions** |
| **vous conduisez** | | |
| **ils conduisent** | | |

See pp. 209-211 for list of other irregular verbs which follow the patterns of those listed in this table.

| PRESENT INDICATIVE | FUTURE | PAST INDEFINITE |
|---|---|---|
| | PAST DEFINITE | PRESENT SUBJUNCTIVE *(1st sing. & pl.)* |

[**connaître** to know; **connaissant**]

| | | |
|---|---|---|
| **je connais** | **je connaîtrai** | **j'ai connu** |
| **tu connais** | | |
| **il connaît** | **je connus** | **que je connaisse** |
| **nous connaissons** | | **que nous connaissions** |
| **vous connaissez** | | |
| **ils connaissent** | | |

[**courir** to run; **courant**]

| | | |
|---|---|---|
| **je cours** | **je courrai** | **j'ai couru** |
| **tu cours** | | |
| **il court** | **je courus** | **que je coure** |
| **nous courons** | | **que nous courions** |
| **vous courez** | | |
| **ils courent** | | |

[**couvrir** to cover; **couvrant**]

| | | |
|---|---|---|
| **je couvre** | **je couvrirai** | **j'ai couvert** |
| **tu couvres** | | |
| **il couvre** | **je couvris** | **que je couvre** |
| **nous couvrons** | | **que nous couvrions** |
| **vous couvrez** | | |
| **ils couvrent** | | |

[**craindre** to fear; **craignant**]

| | | |
|---|---|---|
| **je crains** | **je craindrai** | **j'ai craint** |
| **tu crains** | | |
| **il craint** | **je craignis** | **que je craigne** |
| **nous craignons** | | **que nous craignions** |

See pp. 209-211 for list of other irregular verbs which follow the patterns of those listed in this table.

| PRESENT INDICATIVE | FUTURE | PAST INDEFINITE |
|---|---|---|
| | PAST DEFINITE | PRESENT SUBJUNCTIVE *(1st sing. & pl.)* |
| **vous craignez** | | |
| **ils craignent** | | |
| | **[croire** to believe; **croyant]** | |
| **je crois** | **je croirai** | **j'ai cru** |
| **tu crois** | | |
| **il croit** | **je crus** | **que je croie** |
| **nous croyons** | | **que nous croyions** |
| **vous croyez** | | |
| **ils croient** | | |
| | **[cueillir** to pick, gather; **cueillant]** | |
| **je cueille** | **je cueillerai** | **j'ai cueilli** |
| **tu cueilles** | | |
| **il cueille** | **je cueillis** | **que je cueille** |
| **nous cueillons** | | **que nous cueillions** |
| **vous cueillez** | | |
| **ils cueillent** | | |
| | **[devoir** to owe; **devant]** | |
| **je dois** | **je devrai** | **j'ai dû** |
| **tu dois** | | |
| **il doit** | **je dus** | **que je doive** |
| **nous devons** | | **que nous devions** |
| **vous devez** | | |
| **ils doivent** | | |
| | **[dire** to say, tell; **disant]** | |
| **je dis** | **je dirai** | **j'ai dit** |
| **tu dis** | | |

See pp. 209-211 for list of other irregular verbs which follow the patterns of those listed in this table.

| PRESENT INDICATIVE | FUTURE / PAST DEFINITE | PAST INDEFINITE / PRESENT SUBJUNCTIVE *(1st sing. & pl.)* |
|---|---|---|
| **il dit** | **je dis** | **que je dise** |
| **nous disons** | | **que nous disions** |
| **vous dites** | | |
| **ils disent** | | |

[**dormir** to sleep; **dormant**]

| | | |
|---|---|---|
| **je dors** | **je dormirai** | **j'ai dormi** |
| **tu dors** | | |
| **il dort** | **je dormis** | **que je dorme** |
| **nous dormons** | | **que nous dormions** |
| **vous dormez** | | |
| **ils dorment** | | |

[**écrire** to write; **écrivant**]

| | | |
|---|---|---|
| **j'écris** | **j'écrirai** | **j'ai écrit** |
| **tu écris** | | |
| **il écrit** | **j'écrivis** | **que j'écrive** |
| **nous écrivons** | | **que nous écrivions** |
| **vous écrivez** | | |
| **ils écrivent** | | |

[**envoyer to send; envoyant**]

| | | |
|---|---|---|
| **j'envoie** | **j'enverrai** | **j'ai envoyé** |
| **tu envoies** | | |
| **il envoie** | **j'envoyai** | **que j'envoie** |
| **nous envoyons** | | **que nous envoyions** |
| **vous envoyez** | | |
| **ils envoient** | | |

[**être** to be (See p. 205.)]

See pp.209-211 for list of other irregular verbs which follow the patterns of those listed in this table.

| PRESENT INDICATIVE | FUTURE / PAST DEFINITE | PAST INDEFINITE / PRESENT SUBJUNCTIVE *(1st sing. & pl.)* |
|---|---|---|
| | **[faire** to make, do; **faisant]** | |
| **je fais** | **je ferai** | **j'ai fait** |
| **tu fais** | | |
| **il fait** | **je fis** | **que je fasse** |
| **nous faisons** | | **que nous fassions** |
| **vous faites** | | |
| **ils font** | | |
| | **[falloir** to be necessary] | |
| **il faut** | **il faudra** | **il a fallu** |
| | **il fallut** | **qu'il faille** |
| | **[fuir** to flee; **fuyant]** | |
| **je fuis** | **je fuirai** | **j'ai fui** |
| **tu fuis** | | |
| **il fuit** | **je fuis** | **que je fuie** |
| **nous fuyons** | | **que nous fuyions** |
| **vous fuyez** | | |
| **ils fuient** | | |
| | **[lire** to read; **lisant]** | |
| **je lis** | **je lirai** | **j'ai lu** |
| **tu lis** | | |
| **il lit** | **je lus** | **que je lise** |
| **nous lisons** | | **que nous lisions** |
| **vous lisez** | | |
| **ils lisent** | | |

See pp. 209-211 for list of other irregular verbs which follow the patterns of those listed in this table.

| PRESENT INDICATIVE | FUTURE<br>PAST DEFINITE | PAST INDEFINITE<br>PRESENT SUBJUNCTIVE<br>*(1st sing. & pl.)* |
|---|---|---|
| | **[mettre** to put; **mettant]** | |
| **je mets** | **je mettrai** | **j'ai mis** |
| **tu mets** | | |
| **il met** | **je mis** | **que je mette** |
| **nous mettons** | | **que nous mettions** |
| **vous mettez** | | |
| **ils mettent** | | |
| | **[mourir** to die; **mourant]** | |
| **je meurs** | **je mourrai** | **je suis mort** |
| **tu meurs** | | |
| **il meurt** | **je mourus** | **que je meure** |
| **nous mourons** | | **que nous mourions** |
| **vous mourez** | | |
| **ils meurent** | | |
| | **[naître** to be born; **naissant]** | |
| **je nais** | **je naîtrai** | **je suis né** |
| **tu nais** | | |
| **il naît** | **je naquis** | **que je naisse** |
| **nous naissons** | | **que nous naissions** |
| **vous naissez** | | |
| **ils naissent** | | |
| | **[plaire** to please; **plaisant]** | |
| **je plais** | **je plairai** | **j'ai plu** |
| **tu plais** | | |
| **il plaît** | **je plus** | **que je plaise** |
| **nous plaisons** | | **que nous plaisions** |

See pp.209-211 for list of other irregular verbs which follow the patterns of those listed in this table.

| PRESENT INDICATIVE | FUTURE / PAST DEFINITE | PAST INDEFINITE / PRESENT SUBJUNCTIVE *(1st sing. & pl.)* |
|---|---|---|
| **vous plaisez** | | |
| **ils plaisent** | | |

[**pleuvoir** to rain; **pleuvant**]

| | | |
|---|---|---|
| **il pleut** | **il pleuvra** | **il a plu** |
| | **il plut** | **qu'il pleuve** |

[**pouvoir** to be able; **pouvant**]

| | | |
|---|---|---|
| **je peux (puis-je? )** | **je pourrai** | **j'ai pu** |
| **tu peux** | | |
| **il peut** | **je pus** | **que je puisse** |
| **nous pouvons** | | **que nous puissions** |
| **vous pouvez** | | |
| **ils peuvent** | | |

[**prendre** to take; **prenant**]

| | | |
|---|---|---|
| **je prends** | **je prendrai** | **j'ai pris** |
| **tu prends** | | |
| **il prend** | **je pris** | **que je prenne** |
| **nous prenons** | | **que nous prenions** |
| **vous prenez** | | |
| **ils prennent** | | |

[**recevoir** to receive; **recevant**]

| | | |
|---|---|---|
| **je reçois** | **je recevrai** | **j'ai reçu** |
| **tu reçois** | | |
| **il reçoit** | **je reçus** | **que je reçoive** |
| **nous recevons** | | **que nous recevions** |
| **vous recevez** | | |
| **ils reçoivent** | | |

See pp. 209-211 for list of other irregular verbs which follow the patterns of those listed in this table.

| PRESENT INDICATIVE | FUTURE | PAST INDEFINITE |
|---|---|---|
| | PAST DEFINITE | PRESENT SUBJUNCTIVE *(1st sing. & pl.)* |

[**rire** to laugh; **riant**]

| | | |
|---|---|---|
| **je ris** | **je rirai** | **j'ai ri** |
| **tu ris** | | |
| **il rit** | **je ris** | **que je rie** |
| **nous rions** | | **que nous riions** |
| **vous riez** | | |
| **ils rient** | | |

[**savoir** to know; **sachant**]

| | | |
|---|---|---|
| **je sais** | **je saurai** | **j'ai su** |
| **tu sais** | | |
| **il sait** | **je sus** | **que je sache** |
| **nous savons** | | **que nous sachions** |
| **vous savez** | (IMPERATIVE: **sache, sachons, sachez**) | |
| **ils savent** | | |

[**suivre** to follow; **suivant**]

| | | |
|---|---|---|
| **je suis** | **je suivrai** | **j'ai suivi** |
| **tu suis** | | |
| **il suit** | **je suivis** | **que je suive** |
| **nous suivons** | | **que nous suivions** |
| **vous suivez** | | |
| **ils suivent** | | |

[**vaincre** to conquer; **vainquant**]

| | | |
|---|---|---|
| **je vaincs** | **je vaincrai** | **j'ai vaincu** |
| **tu vaincs** | | |
| **il vainc** | **je vainquis** | **que je vainque** |
| **nous vainquons** | | **que nous vainquions** |

See pp. 209-211 for list of other irregular verbs which follow the patterns of those listed in this table.

| PRESENT INDICATIVE | FUTURE | PAST INDEFINITE |
|---|---|---|
| | PAST DEFINITE | PRESENT SUBJUNCTIVE *(1st sing. & pl.)* |
| **vous vainquez** | | |
| **ils vainquent** | | |
| | [**valoir** to be worth; **valant**] | |
| **je vaux** | **je vaudrai** | **j'ai valu** |
| **tu vaux** | | |
| **il vaut** | **je valus** | **que je vaille** |
| **nous valons** | | **que nous valions** |
| **vous valez** | | |
| **ils valent** | | |
| | [**venir** to come; **venant**] | |
| **je viens** | **je viendrai** | **je suis venu** |
| **tu viens** | | |
| **il vient** | **je vins** | **que je vienne** |
| **nous venons** | | **que nous venions** |
| **vous venez** | | |
| **ils viennent** | | |
| | [**vivre** to live; **vivant**] | |
| **je vis** | **je vivrai** | **j'ai vécu** |
| **tu vis** | | |
| **il vit** | **je vécus** | **que je vive** |
| **nous vivons** | | **que nous vivions** |
| **vous vivez** | | |
| **ils vivent** | | |
| | [**voir** to see; **voyant**] | |
| **je vois** | **je verrai** | **j'ai vu** |
| **tu vois** | | |

See pp. 209-211 for list of other irregular verbs which follow the patterns of those listed in this table.

| PRESENT INDICATIVE | FUTURE<br>PAST DEFINITE | PAST INDEFINITE<br>PRESENT SUBJUNCTIVE *(1st sing. & pl.)* |
|---|---|---|
| **il voit** | **je vis** | **que je voie** |
| **nous voyons** | | **que nous voyions** |
| **vous voyez** | | |
| **ils voient** | | |
| | [**vouloir** to want, wish; **voulant**] | |
| **je veux** | **je voudrai** | **j'ai voulu** |
| **tu veux** | | |
| **il veut** | **je voulus** | **que je veuille** |
| **nous voulons** | | **que nous voulions** |
| **vous voulez** | | |
| **ils veulent** | *(Special form:* **veuillez** please) | |

See pp. 209-211 for list of other irregular verbs which follow the patterns of those listed in this table.

*Vocabularies*

The vocabularies include all words used in the text except: (1) a few in the Supplementary Grammatical Notes for which both the English and French are given, and (2) personal pronouns, possessives, and other very elementary forms explained in the text. The * is used to indicate an aspirate *h.*

## ABBREVIATIONS

| | | | | | |
|---|---|---|---|---|---|
| *adj.* | adjective | *inf.* | infinitive | *pl.* | plural |
| *adv.* | adverb | *interr.* | interrogative | *p.p.* | past participle |
| *art.* | article | *les.* | lesson | *poss.* | possessive |
| *aux.* | auxiliary | *m.* | masculine | *prep.* | preposition |
| *comp.* | comparative | *n.* | noun | *pr.p.* | present participle |
| *conj.* | conjunction | *neg.* | negative | *pron.* | pronoun |
| *def.* | definite | *obj.* | object | *rel.* | relative |
| *dem.* | demonstrative | *p.* | page | *s.* | singular |
| *f.* | feminine | *part.* | partitive | *subj.* | subject |
| *ind.* | indefinite | *pers.* | person | *v.* | verb |

**à** to, at, in; – **deux pas** nearby, – **moins que** unless; – **pied** on foot; – **présent** now, at present
**abandonné** abandoned
**abattre** to tear down
**abord: d'–** first, at first
**absolument** absolutely
**accepter** to accept
**accident** *m.* accident
**accompagner** to accompany
**accomplissement** *m.* accomplishment
**accueillir** to welcome
**acheter** to buy
**achever** to complete, finish
**acier** *m.* steel
**acteur** *m.* actor
**actif, –ve** active
**actuel, –le** present, current
**actuellement** now, at present
**addition** *f.* check *(restaurant, etc.)*
**adieu** farewell
**admirer** to admire
**adoré** adored
**affaire** *f.* affair, matter
**afin de** *prep.* in order to; **afin que** *conj.* in order that, so that
**Afrique** *f.* Africa
**âge** *m.* age; **Quel – avez-vous?** How old are you?
**agent: – de police** *m.* policeman
**agir** to act; **s'– de** to be a question of
**agréable** agreeable, pleasant
**aider** to help, aid
**aimer** to like, love; – **mieux** to prefer
**ainsi** thus, so
**air** *m.* air, appearance; **avoir l'–** to seem, look, appear
**album** *m.* album
**Allemagne** *f.* Germany
**allemand** *n. & adj.* German
**aller** *(aux.* **être)** to go; **s'en –** to go away; **Comment allez-vous?** How are you?
**alors** then, well then, so
**américain** *n. & adj.* American
**Amérique** *f.* America; – **du Nord** North America; – **du Sud** South America
**ami** *m.,* **–e** *f.* friend
**amitié** *f.* friendship
**amour** *m.* love
**amusant** funny, amusing
**amuser: s'–** to amuse oneself, have a good time
**an** *m.* year *(used after cardinal numbers and* **tous les**; *see* **année** *below)*
**ancien, –enne** old, ancient; former
**anglais** *n. & adj.* Englishman, English
**Angleterre** *f.* England
**animal** *(pl.* **animaux)** *m.* animal
**année** *f.* year *(generally used, except in uses indicated above for* **an)**
**annoncer** to announce
**août** *m.* August
**apercevoir** to perceive, catch sight of
**appareil** *m.* apparatus; – **(photographique)** camera
**appeler** to call; **s'–** to be called, be named
**appétissant** appetizing
**apporter** to bring

**apprécier** to appreciate, esteem
**apprendre** to learn
**après** *prep. & adv.* after, afterward; – **que** *conj.* after *(see also p. 146)*
**après-midi** *m. or f.* afternoon
**aptitude** *f.* aptitude
**arbitre** *m.* referee
**arbre** *m.* tree
**architecture** *f.* architecture
**ardeur** *f.* ardor
**argent** *m.* money; silver
**Argentine** *f.* Argentina
**armée** *f.* army
**arrêter** to stop; **s'–** to stop (oneself)
**arrivée** *f.* arrival
**arriver** *(aux.* **être)** to arrive; to happen
**art** *m.* art
**article** *m.* article
**artiste** *m. or f.* artist
**Asie** *f.* Asia
**asseoir**: **s'–** to sit (down)
**assez** enough (+ **de** *before n.)*
**assiette** *f.* plate, dish
**assis** *(p.p. of* **asseoir***)* seated, sitting
**attaque** *f.* attack
**attendre** to wait (for), await
**aucun** *adj. & pron.* no, none, not any (+ **ne** *before v.)*
**aujourd'hui** today
**aussi** also, too
**aussitôt que** as soon as
**autant** as much, as many (+ **de** *before n.)*
**auteur** *m.* author
**autobus** *m.* bus
**autocar** *m.* motor coach
**automne** *m. or f.* autumn, fall
**automobile** *f.* automobile
**autre** other
**autrefois** formerly
**avance** *f.* advance; **d'–** in advance
**avancer** to advance
**avant** *adv. & prep.* before (+ **de** *before inf.); –* **que** *conj.* before
**avare** *adj.* miserly; *n.m.* miser
**avec** with
**aventure** *f.* adventure
**avenue** *f.* avenue
**avion** *m.* airplane, plane
**avocat** *m.* lawyer
**avoine** *f.* oats
**avoir** to have *(see p. 142)*
**avril** *m.* April

**bacon** [bekan] *m.* bacon
**bagage** *m.* baggage *(usually pl.)*
**bagarre** *f.* tumult, row, brawl
**bal** *m.* dance, ball
**bain** *m.* bath
**balance** *f.* balance
**banc** *m.* bench
**barbe** *f.* beard
**bas, –se** low
**bas** *m.* stocking
**baser** to base
**bateau** *m.* boat
**bâtiment** *m.* building
**battant** *m.* half of a double door; **porte à deux –s** double door
**beau, bel, belle** beautiful, handsome
**beaucoup** much, very much, many, very many, a great deal (+ **de** *before n.)*

**beauté** *f.* beauty
**bébé** *m.* baby
**bec** *m.* beak, bill *(of bird)*
**belge** *n. & adj.* Belgian
**Belgique** *f.* Belgium
**besoin** *m.* need; **avoir – de** to need, have need of
**beurre** *m.* butter
**bibliothèque** *f.* library
**bicyclette** *f.* bicycle
**bien** well; very; **vouloir –** to be willing
**bien que** although
**bientôt** soon
**bière** *f.* beer
**bijou** *m.* jewel
**billet** *m.* ticket
**blanc, blanche** white
**blesser** to wound, hurt
**bleu** blue
**blond** blond
**blue-jean** *m.* blue jeans
**boire** to drink
**bois** *m.* wood; woods
**boisson** *f.* drink
**boîte** *f.* box
**bon, bonne** good; **de bonne heure** early
**bonbon** *m.* candy
**bonheur** *m.* happiness, good fortune
**bonne** *f.* maid (servant)
**bonté** *f.* goodness, kindness
**bouche** *f.* mouth
**bouillie** *f.*: **– d'avoine** oatmeal
**boulevard** *m.* boulevard
**bout** *m.* end, tip
**bouteille** *f.* bottle
**boutique** *f.* shop, store
**bras** *m.* arm
**bref, brève** brief, short
**Brésil** *m.* Brazil
**Bretagne** *f.* Brittany
**breton** *n. & adj.* Breton
**briller** to shine, glitter
**brioche** *f.* bun, pastry roll
**brique** *f.* brick
**brosse** *f.* brush; **– à dents** toothbrush
**bruit** *m.* noise; rumor
**brun** brown
**bureau** *m.* office; desk

**ça** that *dem. pron.*; **– va?** O.K.?
**cacher** to hide
**cadeau** *m.* gift, present
**café** *m.* coffee; café
**cahier** *m.* notebook
**caillou** *m.* pebble
**calcul** *m.* calculation, arithmetic
**camarade** *m.* friend, buddy, chum
**camion** *m.* truck
**camp** *m.* camp
**campagne** *f.* country, rural area
**Canada** *m.* Canada
**canadien** *n. & adj.* Canadian
**canaille** *f.* rabble
**canne** *f.* cane
**capable** capable
**carré** square
**carte** *f.* map, chart
**cartouche** *f.* cartridge
**cas** *m.* case
**catholique** Catholic
**cause** *f.* cause
**causer** to cause; to chat
**célèbre** famous, celebrated
**célébrer** to celebrate

**certain** certain
**cesser** to stop, cease
**chacun, –e** *pron.* each one, each
**chaise** *f.* chair
**chambre** *f.* room, bedroom; – **à coucher** bedroom
**changement** *m.* change
**changer** to change
**chanson** *f.* song
**chanter** to sing
**chanteur** *m.*, **–euse** *f.* singer
**chapeau** *m.* hat
**chaque** each
**charité** *f.* charity
**château** *m.* castle, château
**châtiment** *m.* punishment, chastisement
**chaud** warm, hot; **avoir** – to be warm, hot *(persons);* **faire** – to be warm, hot *(weather) [see pp. 141-143]*
**chaussette** *f.* sock
**chaussure** *f.* footwear, shoes
**chauve** bald
**chef** *m.* head, chief; – **de cuisine** head cook
**chemin** *m.* road; – **de fer** railroad
**chemise** *f.* shirt
**cher, chère** dear; expensive
**chercher** to look for, seek; **aller** – to go get
**chétif, –ve** puny, weak
**cheval** *m.* horse
**cheveu** *m.* hair *(usually pl.* **cheveux)**
**chez** *prep.* at (in, to) the house (home, abode, office, etc.) of
**chien** *m.* dog
**chimie** *f.* chemistry
**Chine** *f.* China
**chinois** *n. & adj.* Chinese
**chocolat** *m.* chocolate
**choisir** to choose
**chose** *f.* thing; **quelque** – something
**chou** *m.* cabbage
**chrétien, –enne** Christian
**ciel** *m.* **(cieux** *pl.)* sky, heaven
**cigarette** *f.* cigarette
**cinéma** *m.* movies
**clair** clear
**classe** *f.* class; classroom
**climat** *m.* climate
**clôture** *f.* closing, closure
**club** *m.* club
**cocktail** *m.* cocktail
**cœur** *m.* heart
**coiffure** *f.* coiffure, hair arrangement
**coin** *m.* corner
**collection** *f.* collection *(stamps, etc.)*
**colonel** *m.* colonel
**colonie** *f.* colony
**combat** *m.* combat, fight
**combien** how much, how many (+ **de** *before n.)*
**commander** to order, command
**comme** like, as; – **ça** like that, in that way; – **d'habitude** as usual
**commencer** to begin, commence
**comment** how
**commerçant** *m.* merchant
**commerce** *m.* commerce, trade
**commissariat** *m.* commissioner's office; – **(de police)** police station
**communisme** *m.* communism

**compagnie** *f.* company
**complet** *m.* suit (of clothes)
**composition** *f.* composition; test
**comprendre** to understand; include
**compte** *m.* account; **se rendre — de** to realize
**compter** to count; to expect, intend
**concierge** *m. or f.* doorkeeper, concierge
**conduire** to conduct, lead, drive
**conférence** *f.* conference; lecture
**confiture** *f.* jam, preserves
**confrère** *m.* colleague
**congé** *m.* holiday, day off; **prendre — de** to take leave of
**connaissance** *f.* acquaintance
**connaître** to know, be acquainted with *(see pp. 94-95)*
**connu** known, well-known
**conscience** *f.* conscience
**consonne** *f.* consonant
**construire** to construct, build
**conte** *m.* short story
**content** content, glad, happy
**contentement** *m.* contentment
**continent** *m.* continent
**continuer** to continue
**contrat** *m.* contract
**convenable** proper, suitable
**convenir** to agree; to suit, be suitable
**corriger** to correct
**côté** *m.* side; **à — de** beside; **de l'autre —** on the other side
**cou** *m.* neck
**coucher: se —** to go to bed, lie down
**couleur** *f.* color
**couloir** *m.* corridor
**coup** *m.* blow, strike; **— de téléphone** telephone call; **tout à —** suddenly
**couper** to cut
**courant** current, present
**courir** to run
**cours** *m.* course
**court** short
**cousin** *m.*; **—e** *f.* cousin
**coûter** to cost; **— cher** to be expensive
**couvert** *m.* table setting; **mettre le —** to set the table
**cravate** *f.* necktie
**crayon** *m.* pencil
**crème** *f.* cream
**crêpe** *f.* pancake
**crime** *m.* crime
**criminel** *m.* criminal
**crise** *f.* crisis
**critique** *m.* critic; *f.* criticism, review
**croire** to believe
**croissant** *m.* crescent; crescent-shaped roll (bun)
**croissant** *adj.* increasing
**croix** *f.* cross
**croyance** *f.* credence, belief
**cruel, —le** cruel

**dame** *f.* lady
**Danemark** *m.* Denmark
**dangereux, —euse** dangerous
**dans** in, into
**danser** to dance
**date** *f.* date
**de** of, about; from

**debout** standing
**décembre** *m.* December
**décider** to decide; **se** – to make up one's mind
**déclarer** to declare
**décorer** to decorate
**découvrir** *(p.p.* **découvert)** to discover
**décrire** to describe
**défendre** to defend; to forbid
**défense** *f.* defense
**dehors** outside
**déjà** already
**déjeuner** *m.* lunch; **(petit)** – breakfast (*also v.* to lunch, breakfast)
**délicieux, –euse** delicious
**demain** tomorrow
**demander** to ask, ask for; **se** – to wonder
**demeurer** to live, dwell
**demi** half
**démolir** to demolish, wreck
**dépenser** to spend
**depuis** since, from; for
**dernier, –ère** last *(see p. 119)*
**derrière** behind
**dès que** as soon as
**descendre** to come (go) down; to get off, out; to stay, stop *(at a hotel)*
**désert** *m.* desert
**désintéressé** disinterested
**désir** *m.* desire
**désirer** to desire, want, wish
**détail** *m.* detail
**détenir** to detain, confine, hold in prison
**devant** in front of, before
**devanture** *f.* show window *(of a store)*
**devoir** *m.* duty; homework, assigned exercise
**devoir** *v.* to owe; to be obligated *(see pp. 140-141)*
**Dieu** *m.* God
**difficile** difficult
**difficulté** *f.* difficulty
**dignité** *f.* dignity
**dimanche** *m.* Sunday
**dîner** *m.* dinner (*also v.* to dine)
**dire** to say, tell; **vouloir** – to mean
**directeur** *m.* director; headmaster
**discours** *m.* speech
**discuter** to discuss
**disque** *m.* record
**docteur** *m.* doctor
**dogmatisme** *m.* dogmatism
**doigt** *m.* finger
**dommage** *m. (usually pl.)* damage; **C'est** –. That's too bad.
**donc** then, so
**donner** to give; – **sur** to face on
**dont** of whom, of which, whose *(see pp. 46-48)*
**dormir** to sleep
**doute** *m.* doubt; **sans** – probably
**douter** to doubt
**doux, douce** soft, mild, gentle, sweet
**droit** *m.* right; tax, duty
**dur** hard, firm

**eau** *f.* water
**échecs** *m. pl.* chess
**échelle** *f.* ladder
**école** *f.* school

**économique** economic
**écouter** to listen (to); to hear *(a program, concert, etc.)*
**écrire** to write
**édifice** *m.* building
**effort** *m.* effort
**égal** equal
**égaler** to equal
**église** *f.* church
**élargir** to widen
**élégant** elegant
**élémentaire** elementary
**élève** *m. or f.* pupil, student
**éloge** *m.* praise
**embarras** *m.* difficulty, mess
**empêcher** to prevent, hinder
**emplette** *f.* purchase; **faire des –s** to go shopping
**emprunter** to borrow
**en** in, to, by, while; some, any; of it, of them; from there *(see Les. 10 & 11)*
**encore** still, yet; more; **– une fois** again
**encre** *f.* ink
**endormir: s'–** to go to sleep
**endroit** *m.* place
**enfant** *m. or f.* child
**enfin** finally
**ennuyer: s'–** to be (get) bored
**ennuyeux, –euse** tiresome, boring
**énorme** enormous
**enseignement** *m.* teaching
**ensemble** together
**ensuite** then, after that
**entendre** to hear; to understand; **– dire que** to hear that
**entre** between, among
**entrée** *f.* entrance
**entrer** *(aux.* **être)** to enter, come (go) in
**envie** *f.* desire; **avoir – de** to feel like
**envoyer** to send
**épais, –se** thick
**épatant** delightful, fine, "swell"
**éperdu** bewildered, wild
**épique** epic
**épouser** to marry
**épreuve** *f.* test, examination
**esclavage** *m.* slavery
**Espagne** *f.* Spain
**espagnol** *n. & adj.* Spanish
**espèce** *f.* kind, sort
**espérer** to hope
**essayer** to try
**essentiel, –le** essential
**et** and
**établir** to establish
**étage** *m.* floor, story *(of building)*
**état** *m.* state
**Etats-Unis** *m. pl.* United States
**été** *m.* summer
**été** *p.p.* been
**étonner** to surprise, astonish; **s'–** to be surprised, astonished
**étranger, –ère** *n. & adj.* foreign; foreigner
**être** to be
**étreindre** to clasp, hold tight
**étude** *f.* study
**étudiant** *m.*, **–e** *f.* student
**étudier** to study
**Europe** *f.* Europe
**évader: s'–** to escape
**événement** *m.* event, happening
**évêque** *m.* bishop
**évident** evident

**éviter** to avoid
**exact** exact, correct
**exactement** exactly
**examen** *m.* exam, examination
**examiner** to examine
**excellent** excellent
**exemple** *m.* example
**exercice** *m.* exercise, drill
**exhibition** *f.* exhibition
**exil** *m.* exile
**expérience** *f.* experience; experiment
**explication** *f.* explanation
**expliquer** to explain
**exploit** *m.* exploit, deed
**explosif, –ve** explosive
**explosion** *f.* explosion
**exposition** *f.* exposition, fair
**extraordinaire** extraordinary

**facile** easy
**facilement** easily
**faible** weak, feeble
**faim** *f.* hunger; **avoir** – to be hungry
**faire** to make, do *(see pp. 141-142)*
**fait** *m.* fact
**falloir** to be necessary; **il faut** it is necessary, one must, etc.
**fameux, –euse** famous
**famille** *f.* family
**fatal** fatal
**fatigué** tired
**faut** *(pr. of* **falloir**): **il** – it is necessary
**faute** *f.* mistake, error
**fauteuil** *m.* armchair; seat *(theater)*
**faux, fausse** false
**favori, –te** favorite
**femme** *f.* woman, wife; – **de chambre** (chamber)maid
**fenêtre** *f.* window
**fer** *m.* iron; – **à repasser** iron *(for pressing)*
**fermer** to close; to turn off *(radio, etc.)*
**fête** *f.* holiday, celebration
**feu** *m.* fire
**février** *m.* February
**fidèle** faithful
**fier, –ère** proud
**figure** *f.* face
**fille** *f.* daughter; **(jeune)** – girl
**film** *m.* film, movie, moving picture
**fils** *m.* son
**filtrer** to filter
**fin** *f.* end
**final** final
**finir** to finish
**fleur** *f.* flower
**fleuve** *m.* river *(which empties into sea)*
**fois** *f.* time, occasion; **une** – once; **la première** – the first time
**fondamental** fundamental
**fonder** to found
**former** to form; to train, educate
**fort** *adj.* strong; *adv.* very
**fou, folle** crazy, mad
**frais, fraîche** fresh, cool; **il fait** – it is cool *(weather)*
**franc, franche** frank
**français** *n. & adj.* French
**France** *f.* France
**franchement** frankly

**frapper** to hit, strike, knock
**frère** *m.* brother
**frites** *f. pl.* French-fried potatoes
**froid** *n. & adj.* cold; **avoir** – to be cold *(persons);* **faire** – to be cold *(weather)*
**front** *m.* forehead
**frontière** *f.* frontier, boundary
**fruit** *m.* fruit
**fuir** to flee

**gagner** to gain, win, earn
**gant** *m.* glove
**garage** *m.* garage
**garçon** *m.* boy; waiter
**gare** *f.* (railroad) station
**gascon** *n. & adj.* Gascon (from Gascony in southwestern France)
**gâteau** *m.* cake
**gauche** *f.* left
**gendarme** *m.* policeman *(approximately equivalent to state trooper – not a metropolitan policeman)*
**général** *n. & adj.* general
**genou** *m.* knee
**gens** *m. pl.* people, men
**gentil, –le** nice, gentle, kind, pleasant
**gigot** *m.* leg of lamb (or mutton)
**glace** *f.* ice, ice cream
**graisse** *f.* fat, grease
**grammaire** *f.* grammar
**grand** large, big; great
**grand-mère** *f.* grandmother
**grand-père** *m.* grandfather
**grange** *f.* barn
**grave** serious, grave
**grec, grecque** *n. & adj.* Greek
**Grèce** *f.* Greece
**grillé** toasted, grilled
**gris** gray
**gros, grosse** big, stout, bulky
**groupe** *m.* group
**guerre** *f.* war
**guide** *m.* guide
**guitare** *f.* guitar

NOTE: *An asterisk indicates an aspirate* **h**, *that is one which does not take elision or liaison.*

**habile** skilled, skillful, clever
**habiller** to dress; **s'–** to get dressed
**habitant** *m.* inhabitant
**habiter** to live, dwell
**habitude** *f.* habit
* **haine** *f.* hatred
* **haut** high
**héritage** *m.* heritage
***héros** *m.* hero
**heure** *f.* hour, time; **à l'–** on time; **de bonne –** early; **tout à l'–** a little while ago; in a little while
**heureux, –euse** happy
* **hibou** *m.* owl
**hier** yesterday; – **soir** last night
**histoire** *f.* story, history
**hiver** *m.* winter
* **hollandais** *n. & adj.* Dutch
* **Hollande** *f.* Holland
**homme** *m.* man
* **honte** *f.* shame; **avoir** – to be ashamed
**hôpital** *m.* hospital
**horloger** *m.* watchmaker

**hospitalité** *f.* hospitality
**hôtel** *m.* hotel

**ici** here
**idéalisme** *m.* idealism
**idée** *f.* idea
**il y a** there is, there are; – **deux jours** two days ago
**île** *f.* island
**imiter** to imitate
**immédiatement** immediately
**immense** immense
**immeuble** *m.* building
**impoli** impolite
**important** important
**impossible** impossible
**impôt** *m.* tax
**impression** *f.* impression
**impressionnant** impressive
**impressionner** to impress
**imprudence** *f.* imprudence
**inattendu** unexpected
**incident** *m.* incident
**inconnu** unknown
**incroyable** incredible
**indéfini** indefinite
**indiquer** to indicate
**indiscret** indiscreet
**individuel, –le** individual
**infatigable** untiring, indefatigable
**infirmier** *m.*, **–ère** *f.* nurse
**informer** to inform
**ingénieur** *m.* engineer
**inhabile** incompetent
**inquiet, –ète** worried
**inquiéter** to worry; **s'–** to be worried
**insuffisant** insufficient
**intelligence** *f.* intelligence
**intelligent** intelligent
**intéressant** interesting
**intéresser: s' – (à)** to be (become) interested (in)
**interroger** to question, interrogate
**inutile** useless
**inviter** to invite
**Italie** *f.* Italy
**italien, –enne** *n. & adj.* Italian

**jamais** ever; never (+ **ne** *before v. in neg.)*
**jambe** *f.* leg
**jambon** *m.* ham
**janvier** January
**Japon** *m.* Japan
**jardin** *m.* garden
**jaune** yellow
**jeter** to throw
**jeudi** Thursday
**jeune** young
**joli** pretty
**jouer** to play; – **au bridge** to play bridge; – **du piano** to play the piano
**jour** *m.* day; **huit –s** a week; **quinze –s** two weeks
**journal** *m.* newspaper
**journée** *f.* day *(generally with emphasis on duration or activity)*
**juillet** *m.* July
**juin** *m.* June
**jus** *m.* juice
**jusqu'à** *prep.* until, up to, to
**jusqu'à ce que** *conj.* until
**justement** just now; precisely
**justice** *f.* justice

**kilomètre** *m.* kilometer (5/8 mile)

**là** there; — **-bas** over there
**lac** *m.* lake
**laisser** to allow, let; to leave
**lait** *m.* milk
**langue** *f.* language
**lard** *m.* bacon
**large** wide
**lasser** to tire; **se** — to get tired
**latin** *m.* Latin
**laver** to wash; **se** — to wash (oneself)
**leçon** *f.* lesson
**légal** legal
**léger** light, slight
**légume** *m.* vegetable
**lendemain** *m.* next day
**lentement** slowly
**lettre** *f.* letter
**lever: se** — to get up, stand up
**libre** free
**lieu** *m.* place; **au** — **de** instead of; **avoir** — to take place, happen
**lieutenant** *m.* lieutenant
**linge** *m.* linen *(table, personal, etc.)*
**lire** to read
**lit** *m.* bed
**livre** *m.* book
**livrer** to deliver
**loin** far; **au** — in the distance; **de** — from afar
**lointain** distant
**Londres** *m.* London
**long, –ue** long
**longtemps** (for) a long time
**lorsque** when
**louer** to rent, hire
**lourd** heavy
**lundi** *m.* Monday
**lunettes** *f. pl.* glasses, spectacles
**machinal** mechanical, automatic
**machine** *f.* machine; — **à écrire** typewriter; — **à laver** washing machine
**magasin** *m.* store; **grand** — department store
**magnifique** magnificent
**mai** *m.* May
**main** *f.* hand
**maintenant** now
**mais** but
**maison** *f.* house; **à la** — at home
**mal** *adv.* badly; *n.* pain, harm, trouble; **avoir** — **à** to hurt (ache) in; **faire** — to harm, hurt
**malade** *adj.* sick, ill; *n.* patient, sick person
**maladie** *f.* sickness, illness
**malgré** in spite of
**malheur** *m.* misfortune, unhappiness
**malheureux, –euse** unhappy, unfortunate
**manger** to eat; **salle à** — dining room
**manquer** to miss
**marchander** to bargain
**marchandise** *f.* merchandise, goods
**marché** *m.* market; **bon** — cheap, inexpensive; **faire le** — to do the marketing
**marcher** to walk; to run *(machinery, etc.)*
**mardi** *m.* Tuesday
**mari** *m.* husband
**marier** to marry; **se** — to get married; **se** — **avec quelqu'un** to marry someone

**marine** *f.* navy
**Maroc** *m.* Morocco
**marque** *f.* make, brand; mark
**mars** *m.* March
**masseur** *m.*, **–euse** *f.* person who gives massages
**matérialisme** *m.* materialism
**mathématiques** *m. pl.* mathematics
**matière** *f.* subject *(of study)*
**matin** *m.* morning
**mauvais** bad; **il fait** – the weather is bad
**mécanicien** *m.* mechanic
**méchant** wicked, naughty
**médecin** *m.* (medical) doctor
**médicament** *m.* medicament, medicine
**meilleur** *adj. comp.* better, best
**mêler** to mingle, mix
**membre** *m.* member
**même** same; even
*(see also p. 129)*
**menaçant** menacing, threatening
**mener** to lead
**mentionner** to mention
**menton** *m.* chin
**merci** thank you, thanks
**mercredi** *m.* Wednesday
**mère** *f.* mother
**message** *m.* message
**métal** *m.* metal
**mètre** *m.* meter (39.36 inches)
**métro** *m.* subway
**mets** *m.* dish *(of food)*
**mettre** to put, place; **se – à** to begin, set out
**Mexique** *m.* Mexico
**midi** *m.* noon
**mieux** *adv. comp.* better, best; **aimer** – to prefer
**milieu** *m.* middle, midst
**militant** militant
**ministre** *m.* minister
**minuit** *m.* midnight
**minute** *f.* minute
**miséricorde** *f.* mercy
**mission** *f.* mission
**moderne** modern
**modeste** modest
**moins** less, least; **à – que** unless
**mois** *m.* month
**moment** *m.* moment; **en ce** – now
**monde** *m.* world; **tout le** – everybody; **le beau** – polite society
**montagne** *f.* mountain
**monter** to go (come) up; **– dans** to get in, on (*a vehicle*); **– à cheval (bicyclette)** to ride a horse (bicycle)
**montre** *f.* watch
**montrer** to show
**monument** *m.* monument, historic building
**moquer: se – de** to make fun of; to not care about
**mort** *(p.p. of* **mourir)** died; dead
**Moscou** *m.* Moscow
**mot** *m.* word
**moteur** *m.* motor
**mou, molle** soft
**mouchoir** *m.* handkerchief
**mourir** *(aux.* **être)** to die
**moyen** *m.* means, manner, method
**muet, –ette** mute, dumb
**mur** *m.* wall

**murmurer** to murmur
**musée** *m.* museum
**musique** *f.* music

**nager** to swim
**naissance** *f.* birth
**naître** *(aux.* **être)** to be born
**natif, –ve** native
**nation** *f.* nation
**national** national
**naturel, –le** natural
**naval** naval
**navire** *m.* ship
**ne** *neg. particle used before v.*
**né** *p.p.* born
**nécessaire** necessary
**négligent** negligent
**neige** *f.* snow
**neiger** to snow
**nerveux, –euse** nervous
**n'est-ce pas?** is it not? *(This phrase is placed after a statement and indicates that an affirmative answer is expected. Its English version varies according to the statement which precedes it.)*
**net, nette** clear
**nettoyer** to clean
**neuf, neuve** new
**nez** *m.* nose
**ni ... ni** neither . . . nor **(+ ne** *before v.)*
**nier** to deny
**Noël** *m.* Christmas
**noir** black
**noix** *f.* nut, walnut
**nom** *m.* name; **connaître de –** to know by name
**nombre** *m.* number, quantity
**nommé** named
**nommer** to name, appoint
**non** no; not
**Norvège** *f.* Norway
**nourrissant** nourishing
**nouveau, nouvel, nouvelle** new; different
**nouvelle** *f.* news *(usually used in plural)*
**novembre** *m.* November
**nuit** *f.* night
**numéro** *m.* number; issue *(of periodical)*

**objet** *m.* object
**occasion** *f.* chance, occasion, opportunity; bargain
**occuper: s'– de** to take charge of, busy oneself with, attend to
**octobre** *m.* October
**œil** *m. (pl.* **yeux)** eye
**oeuf** *m.* egg
**oeuvre** *f.* work
**offre** *f.* offer
**offrir** to offer
**oiseau** *m.* bird
**on** *pron. 3rd pers. s.* one, we, you, they, people *(see pp. 80 and 82)*
**oncle** *m.* uncle
**or** *m.* gold
**orage** *m.* storm
**oralement** orally
**orange** *f.* orange
**ordonner** to order
**oreille** *f.* ear
**oriental** oriental
**ôter** to take off, remove
**ou** or; **ou ... ou** either . . . or
**où** where; when *(see p. 57)*

**oublier** to forget
**outil** *m.* tool
**ouvert** open
**ouvrage** *m.* work
**ouvrier** *m.*, **–ère** *f.* worker, workman
**ouvrir** (*p.p.* **ouvert**) to open

**pain** *m.* bread
**paix** *f.* peace
**panier** *m.* basket; – **à papier** wastebasket
**papier** *m.* paper
**paquet** *m.* package, parcel, bundle
**par** by, through
**paradoxe** *m.* paradox
**parapluie** *m.* umbrella
**parc** *m.* park
**parce que** because
**pardon** *m.* pardon
**parent** *m.* parent, relative
**paresseux, –euse** lazy
**parfait** perfect
**parler** to speak
**parmi** among
**participer**: – **(à)** to participate (in)
**partie** *f.* part
**partir** *(aux.* **être)** to leave, go away
**partout** everywhere
**pas** not
**pas** *m.* step; **à deux** – very near
**passage** *m.* passage
**passé** past; **lundi** – last Monday
**passer** to pass, spend (time); – **un examen** to take an exam; **se** – to happen; **un film qui passe** a movie which is showing
**pâtisserie** *f.* pastry
**patrie** *f.* country, fatherland
**patriotisme** *m.* patriotism
**pauvre** poor *(see p. 119)*
**pauvreté** *f.* poverty
**payer** to pay, pay for
**pays** *m.* country
**pêcheur** *m.* fisherman
**peindre** *(p.p.* **peint)** to paint
**peinture** *f.* painting
**pendant** during; – **que** while
**penser** to think; – **à** to think about; – + *inf.* to intend
**perdre** to lose
**père** *m.* father
**permettre** *(p.p.* **permis)** to permit, allow
**Pérou** *m.* Peru
**personne** *f.* person; nobody (+ **ne** *before v.)*
**petit** little, small
**peu** *adv.* little; – **de** few; **un** – **de** a bit of
**peur** *f.* fear; **avoir** – to be afraid; **de** – **de** for fear of
**peut-être** perhaps
**phénomène** *m.* phenomenon
**philosophie** *f.* philosophy
**photo** *f.* snapshot, picture
**phrase** *f.* sentence
**physique** *f.* physics
**piano** *m.* piano
**pièce** *f.* play; room
**pied** *m.* foot; **à** – on foot
**pitié** *f.* pity
**pittoresque** picturesque
**place** *f.* public square; seat
**plage** *f.* beach
**plaindre**: **se** – to complain
**plaire** to please, be pleasing
**plan** *m.* plan; map (of city)

**plante** *f.* plant
**plein** full, filled
**plume** *f.* feather; pen
**plupart** *f.* majority, most
**plus** more (+ **de** *before n.*), most; no more, no longer (+ **ne** *before v.*)
**plusieurs** several
**plutôt** rather
**pneumonie** *f.* pneumonia
**poche** *f.* pocket
**poème** *m.* poem
**poing** *m.* fist
**police** *f.* police (force)
**politique** political
**pomme** *f.* apple; – **de terre** potato; –**s frites** French-fried potatoes
**pont** *m.* bridge
**populaire** popular
**port** *m.* port, harbor
**porte** *f.* door
**portefeuille** *m.* wallet, pocketbook
**porter** to wear; to carry
**Portugal** *m.* Portugal
**poser** to put, place; – **une question** to ask a question
**possible** possible
**poste** *m.* job, position
**potage** *m.* soup
**poupée** *f.* doll
**pour** for, in order to, to; – **que** in order that
**pourboire** *m.* tip
**pourquoi** why
**pourvu**: – **que** provided that
**pouvoir** to be able, can
**précieux**, –**euse** precious
**précisément** precisely
**préférer** to prefer
**préfet** *m.* chief administrator of a department
**premier**, –**ère** first
**prendre** to take; to eat, drink *(when object is meal, etc.)*; – **un billet** to buy a ticket; – **congé de** to take leave of
**préparer** to prepare
**près (de)** near
**présent** *m.* present; **à** – now, at present
**présenter** to introduce, present
**président** *m.* president; judge
**presque** nearly, almost
**prêt** ready
**prêter** to lend
**primitif**, –**ve** primitive
**prince** *m.* prince
**principal** *adj.* principal
**principe** *m.* principle
**printemps** *m.* spring; **au** – in the spring
**prisonnier** *m.* prisoner
**privilège** *m.* privilege
**prix** *m.* price; prize
**probable** probable; **peu** – improbable, unlikely
**probablement** probably
**problème** *m.* problem
**prochain** next, following
**proche** near, close
**production** *f.* production
**produire** to produce
**professeur** *m.* professor, teacher
**profiter (de)** to take advantage (of)
**profond** profound, deep

**programme** *m.* program
**projet** *m.* project, plan
**promenade** *f.* walk, ride; **faire une –** to take a walk (ride)
**promener: se –** to walk, take a walk
**promesse** *f.* promise
**promettre** to promise
**prononcer** to pronounce; **– un discours** to give a speech
**propriétaire** *m. or f.* owner, proprietor, landlord
**province** *f.* province
**public, –que** public
**puis** then
**puisque** since
**pull-over** *m.* pullover (sweater)
**punir** to punish

**qualité** *f.* quality
**quand** when
**quant à** as for
**quartier** *m.* quarter, section *(of city)*
**que** *conj.* that, than; **ne ... que** only; *rel. pron.* whom, which, that; *interr. pron.* what
**quel, –le** *adj.* what, which
**quelquefois** sometimes
**quelques** *adj.* some, a few
**quelqu'un, quelqu'une** someone, somebody
**quelques-uns, quelques-unes** *pron.* some, a few
**qu'est-ce que** what *(see Les. 6 & 7)*
**qu'est-ce qui** what *(see Les. 6)*
**question** *f.* question
**questionner** to question
**qui** *rel. pron.* who, which, that; *interr. pron.* who, whom
**quitter** to leave; **se –** to separate, leave each other
**quoi** what *(see Les. 6 & p. 133)*; **– que** whatever
**quoique** although

**rabattre** to knock down, pull down
**raconter** to tell, relate
**raisin** *m.* grape
**raison** *f.* reason; **avoir –** to be right
**ramener** to take back, bring back
**rappeler** to recall, remind; **se –** to remember
**rat** *m.* rat
**rayon** *m.* counter, department *(in store)*
**réaction** *f.* reaction; **avion à –** jet plane
**réalisme** *m.* realism
**récent** recent
**recevoir** to receive
**recherche** *f.* research
**récit** *m.* account, story
**recommander** to recommend
**reconnaître** to recognize
**refuser** to refuse
**regarder** to look (at)
**région** *f.* region, section
**regretter** to regret; to miss
**rejoindre (quelqu'un)** to meet (someone)
**religieux, –euse** religious
**relire** to re-read, read again
**remarque** *f.* remark
**remarquer** to notice, remark
**remercier** to thank

**remplir** to fill
**rencontrer** to meet
**rendre** to give back, return, render; **se – compte de** to realize
**renseignement** *m.* information *(usually used in pl.)*
**rentrer** *(aux.* **être)** to go (come) back in, return (home)
**réparation** *f.* repair
**réparer** to repair
**repas** *m.* meal
**répéter** to repeat
**répondre (à)** to answer, respond
**réponse** *f.* response, answer
**repos** *m.* rest, repose
**reposer: se –** to rest
**responsable** responsible
**restaurant** *m.* restaurant
**reste** *m.* rest, remainder
**rester** *(aux.* **être)** to remain, stay
**retard** *m.* delay; **en –** late
**retirer** to draw back, withdraw; **se –** to retire, go home, go to bed
**retour** *m.* return; **être de –** to be back
**retourner** *(aux.* **être)** to return, go back
**réunir** to gather, assemble; **se –** to meet
**réussir (à)** to succeed (in); **– à un examen** to pass an exam
**réveiller: se –** to wake up
**révéler** to reveal
**revenir** *(aux.* **être)** to come back, return
**revue** *f.* magazine; review
**riche** rich
**rideau** *m.* curtain
**rien** nothing (+ **ne** *before v.)*
**risque** *m.* risk
**rival** *m.* rival
**rivière** *f.* river, stream
**robe** *f.* dress
**roi** *m.* king
**rôle** *m.* role, part
**romain** *n. & adj.* Roman
**roman** *m.* novel
**rompre** to break
**rose** *f.* rose
**rouge** red
**roulant** rolling; **tapis –** conveyor belt
**route** *f.* road, way, route; **en –** on the way
**roux, rousse** red(-haired); russet
**rue** *f.* street
**russe** *n. & adj.* Russian
**Russie** *f.* Russia

**sagesse** *f.* wisdom
**saison** *f.* season
**salade** *f.* salad
**salle** *f.* room; **– à manger** dining room; **– de bain** bathroom
**salon** *m.* living room
**samedi** *m.* Saturday
**sandwich** *m.* sandwich
**sans** without; **– doute** probably; **– que** without *(conj.)*
**sauce** *f.* sauce, gravy
**saucisse** *f.* sausage
**sauvage** wild
**savant** *adj.* learned, scholarly; *n.* scholar, scientist
**savoir** to know, know how to
**savon** *m.* soap
**science** *f.* science

**scientifique** scientific
**sec, sèche** dry
**secret, –ète** secret
**secrétaire** *m. or f.* secretary
**séjour** *m.* stay, sojourn
**sel** *m.* salt
**selon** according to
**semaine** *f.* week; **la – dernière** last week
**semblable** similar
**sembler** to seem
**sentir: se –** to feel *(health)*
**septembre** *m.* September
**sérieux, –euse** serious, grave
**serviette** *f.* towel; napkin
**servir** to serve; **– de** to serve as; **se – de** to use
**seul** *adj.* only; alone; single
**seulement** *adv.* only
**si** *conj.* if, whether; *adv.* so; yes *(when answering neg.)*
**siècle** *m.* century
**signaler** to point out
**signature** *f.* signature
**signer** to sign
**s'il vous plaît** please
**simple** simple
**situation** *f.* situation
**sobriété** *f.* sobriety
**soeur** *f.* sister
**soif** *f.* thirst; **avoir –** to be thirsty
**soir** *m.* evening; **demain –** tomorrow night; **hier –** last night
**soldat** *m.* soldier
**soleil** *m.* sun, sunshine; **il fait du –** it is sunny
**solution** *f.* solution
**sonner** to ring, sound
**sorte** *f.* sort, kind
**sortir** *(aux.* **être)** to go (come) out, leave; *transitive v. (aux.* **avoir)** to take out
**sot, sotte** silly, foolish
**souffrir** *(p.p.* **souffert)** to suffer
**soulier** *m.* shoe
**soupçon** *m.* suspicion
**soupe** *f.* soup
**sourd** deaf
**sourire** to smile
**sous** under
**souvenir** *m.* souvenir, remembrance; *v.* **se – de** to remember
**souvent** often
**sphérique** spherical
**stable** *adj.* stable
**station** *f.* station *(not railroad station, which =* **gare)**
**statue** *f.* statue
**structure** *f.* structure
**stupide** stupid
**stylo** *m.* (fountain) pen; **–-bille** ball-point pen
**succursale** *f.* branch (office)
**sud** *m.* south
**suisse** *n. & adj.* Swiss; **la Suisse** Switzerland
**suite: tout de –** immediately
**sujet** *m.* subject
**sur** on, upon
**sûr** sure, certain
**surtout** especially, above all
**symbole** *m.* symbol
**système** *m.* system

**table** *f.* table
**tableau** *m.* picture; **– (noir)** blackboard

**tant** so, so much, so many **(+ de** *before n.); –* **que** so long as
**tante** *f.* aunt
**tapis** *m.* rug, carpet; – **roulant** conveyor belt
**tard** late
**tasse** *f.* cup
**taxi** *m.* taxi
**télégramme** *m.* telegram
**téléphone** *m.* telephone
**téléphoner** to telephone
**téléviseur** *m.* television (set)
**télévision** *f.* television
**température** *f.* temperature
**temps** *m.* time; weather; **à** – on time; **en même** – at the same time
**tenir: se** – to stand, be standing
**testament** *m.* will, testament
**tête** *f.* head
**thé** *m.* tea
**théâtre** *m.* theater
**timbre** *m.* stamp
**tiroir** *m.* drawer
**titre** *m.* title
**tomber** *(aux.* **être)** to fall
**toucher** to touch; – **un chèque** to cash a check
**toujours** always; still
**tour** *f.* tower
**touriste** *m. or f.* tourist
**tout** *adj. (m. pl.* **tous)** all, every; whole; – **le monde** everybody
**tout** *adv.* very, quite; – **à coup** suddenly; – **à fait** completely; – **de suite** immediately
**tout** *pron.* everything
**tracteur** *m.* tractor
**train** *m.* train
**traité** *m.* treaty
**traiter (de)** to treat (of), deal (with)
**travail** *m. (pl.* **travaux)** work
**très** very
**triste** sad
**trop** too, too much, too many (+ **de** *before n.)*
**trottoir** *m.* sidewalk
**troué** having holes, full of holes
**trouver** to find; **se** – to find oneself; to be located; to be standing
**Tunisie** *f.* Tunisia

**usine** *f.* factory
**utile** useful

**vacances** *f. pl.* vacation
**valeur** *f.* value; valor
**valise** *f.* suitcase, valise
**valoir** to be worth
**vélo** *m.* bike
**vendeur** *m.,* **–euse** *f.* clerk, salesman, saleswoman
**vendre** to sell
**vendredi** *m.* Friday
**venir** *(aux.* **être)** to come; – **de** + *inf.* to have just + *p.p.*
**vent** *m.* wind; **il fait du** – it is windy
**vérité** *f.* truth
**verre** *m.* glass
**vers** toward
**vert** green
**vertu** *f.* virtue
**vêtement** *m.* garment; *pl.* clothes
**viande** *f.* meat

**vice** *m.* vice
**vie** *f.* life
**vieux, vieil, vieille** old; **mon vieux** pal, chum, buddy
**vif, vive** alive; lively
**vilain** ugly
**village** *m.* village
**ville** *f.* city, town
**vin** *m.* wine
**vinaigre** *m.* vinegar
**violet, –ette** violet
**visage** *m.* face
**visite** *f.* visit, call; **faire une –** to visit, call on *(a person)*
**visiter** to visit *(a place)*
**visiteur** *m.*, **–euse** *f.* caller, visitor
**vite** quickly, fast
**vivant** living; **une langue –e** a modern language
**vivre** to live
**voici** here is (are)
**voilà** there is (are) *(when pointing out)*
**voir** to see
**voiture** *f.* car, automobile
**voix** *f.* voice
**volonté** *f.* will, desire
**vouloir** to want, wish; **– bien** to be willing; **– dire** to mean
**voyage** *m.* trip, voyage; **faire un –** to take a trip
**voyager** to travel
**voyageur** *m.* traveler
**vrai** true, real
**vraiment** really, truly
**vue** *f.* sight, view; **connaître de –** to know by sight

**y** there, in it, on it *(see pp. 80-82)*
**yeux** *m.* eyes *(pl. of* **œil)**
**Yougoslavie** *f.* Yugoslavia

## English-French Vocabulary

**a (an)** un, une
**able** capable; **to be –** pouvoir
**about** de; **– it, – them** en *(with v)*; **it is about . . .** il s'agit de ...
**above: – all** surtout
**absolutely** absolument
**accept** accepter
**accident** accident *m.*
**accompany** accompagner
**according to** selon
**account** récit *m.*
**acquaintance** connaissance *f.*
**actor** acteur *m.*, actrice *f.*
**address** adresse *f.*
**admire** admirer
**advance** avance *f.*; **in –** d'avance
**advice** conseil *m.*
**affair** affaire *f.*
**afraid: be –** avoir peur
**Africa** Afrique *f.*
**after** après *prep.*; après que *conj.*
**afternoon** après-midi *m. or f.*
**afterwards** après
**again** encore (une fois)
**age** âge *m.*
**ago** il y a; **two years –** il y a deux ans
**agreeable** agréable
**aid** aider
**airplane** avion *m.*
**album** album *m.*
**all** tout, toute, tous, toutes; **not at –** pas du tout
**allow** permettre, laisser
**almost** presque
**alone** seul
**already** déjà
**also** aussi
**although** bien que, quoique
**always** toujours
**America** Amérique *f.*
**American** américain *n. & adj.*
**among** entre, parmi
**amusing** amusant
**ancient** ancien, –enne
**and** et
**animal** animal *m.*
**announce** annoncer
**another** un autre, une autre
**answer** réponse *f.*; répondre (à) *v.*
**any** de, du, de la, de l', des *(as part. art.)*; en *pron.* *(see pp. 80-83)*
**anything** quelque chose; **not –** rien *(+ ne before v.)*
**apparatus** appareil *m.*
**appear** avoir l'air
**appearance** air *m.*
**appreciate** apprécier
**approve** approuver
**April** avril *m.*
**architecture** architecture *f.*
**Argentina** Argentine *f.*
**arm** bras *m.*
**armchair** fauteuil *m.*
**army** armée *f.*
**arrest** arrêter
**arrival** arrivée *f.*
**arrive** arriver *(aux.* être)
**article** article *m.*
**artist** artiste *m. or f.*
**as** comme; **– good –** aussi bon que; **– much –** autant que; **– soon –** aussitôt que
**ashamed: be –** avoir honte
**Asia** Asie *f.*
**ask** demander; **– a question** poser une question
**assiduously** assidûment

**at** à; – **the home of** chez
**attack** attaque *f.*
**attend**: – **to** s'occuper de
**August** août *m.*
**aunt** tante *f.*
**author** auteur *m.*
**auto(mobile)** voiture *f.*, auto *f.*, automobile *f.*
**autumn** automne *m. or f.*
**avenue** avenue *f.*
**avoid** éviter
**awaken** se réveiller

**baby** bébé *m.*
**back** *m.* dos; **to be** être de retour
**bacon** bacon *m.*
**bad** mauvais; **the weather is** – il fait mauvais; **it's too** – c'est dommage
**badly** mal
**ball** bal *m. (dance)*
**bargain** *v.* marchander
**base** baser
**basket** panier *m.*
**be** être; – **back** être de retour; – **located** se trouver; – **well** aller bien *(see also pp. 141-143)*
**beach** plage *f.*
**beak** bec *m.*
**beard** barbe *f.*
**beautiful** beau (bel), belle
**beauty** beauté *f.*
**because** parce que; – **of** à cause de
**bed** lit *m.*; **go to** – se coucher
**bedroom** chambre à coucher *f.*
**beer** bière *f.*
**before** avant *prep.* (+ de *before inf.);* avant que *conj.;* devant **(in front of)**
**begin** commencer, se mettre à
**beginning** commencement *m.*
**behind** derrière
**Belgian** belge *n. & adj.*
**Belgium** Belgique *f.*
**believe** croire
**beside** à côté de
**besides** d'ailleurs
**best** meilleur *adj.;* mieux *adv.*
**better** meilleur *adj.;* mieux *adv.*
**between** entre
**bicycle** bicyclette *f.*, vélo *m.*
**big** grand
**bill** note *f.*; bec *m. (of bird)*
**bird** oiseau *m.*
**birth** naissance *f.*
**bit**: **a** – **of** un peu de
**blackboard** tableau (noir) *m.*
**blind** aveugle
**blindly** aveuglément
**blond** blond
**blow** coup *m.*
**blue** bleu
**boat** bateau *m.*
**book** livre *m.*
**bore** ennuyer; **be bored** s'ennuyer
**born** né; **to be** – naître
**borrow** emprunter
**both** (tous) les deux
**bottle** bouteille *f.*
**boulevard** boulevard *m.*
**boundary** frontière *f.*
**bowl** bol *m.*, jatte *f.*
**box** boîte *f.*
**boy** garçon *m.*
**brand** marque *f.*

**brave** courageux, –euse, brave
**Brazil** Brésil *m.*
**bread** pain *m.*
**breakfast** (petit) déjeuner *m.*
**brick** brique *f.*
**bridge** pont *m.;* bridge *m. (game)*
**bring** apporter
**Brittany** Bretagne *f.*
**brother** frère *m.*
**brush** brosse *f.*
**Buddhist** bouddhiste
**build** construire
**building** bâtiment *m.,* édifice *m.,* immeuble *m.*
**bundle** paquet *m.*
**bus** autobus *m.;* autocar *m. (motor coach)*
**busy** occupé; **to – oneself with** s'occuper de
**but** mais
**butter** beurre *m.*
**buy** acheter
**by** par; de; – **working** en travaillant

**café** café *m.*
**cake** gâteau *m.*
**call** appeler; **be –ed** s'appeler; a **telephone –** un coup de téléphone
**calm** calme
**camera** appareil (photographique) *m.;* caméra *m.* **(moving picture)**
**camp** camp *m.*
**can** pouvoir
**Canada** Canada *m.*
**Canadian** canadien *m.,* –enne *f., n. & adj.*
**candy** bonbon *m.*
**capable** capable
**car** voiture *f.,* auto *f.,* automobile *f.*
**card** carte *f.;* **play cards** jouer aux cartes
**care** soin *m.*
**carefully** avec soin
**cartridge** cartouche *f.*
**case** cas *m.*
**castle** château *m.*
**catch** attraper; – **sight of** apercevoir
**Catholic** catholique
**cause** cause *n. f.;* causer *v.*
**century** siècle *m.*
**certain** certain, sûr
**chair** chaise *f.;* **arm–** fauteuil *m.*
**change** changement *m.*; changer *v.*
**chapter** chapitre *m.*
**check** chèque *m.*
**chemistry** chimie *f.*
**chess** échecs *m. pl.;* **to play –** jouer aux échecs
**chief** chef *m.*
**child** enfant *m. or f.*
**China** Chine *f.*
**Chinese** chinois *n. & adj.*
**chocolate** chocolat *m.*
**choose** choisir
**Christmas** Noël *m.*
**church** église *f.*
**cigarette** cigarette *f.*
**city** ville *f.*
**clasp** étreindre
**class** classe *f.*
**clean** *adj.* propre
**clean** nettoyer
**clear** clair; évident

**climate** climat *m.*
**close** fermer
**clothes** habits, vêtements *m. pl.*
**club** club *m.*, cercle *m.*
**cocktail** cocktail *m.*
**coffee** café *m.*
**cold** froid; **to be** – *(persons)* avoir froid; **it is** – *(the weather)* il fait froid
**colleague** confrère *m.*
**collection** collection *f.* *(stamps, etc.)*
**colonel** colonel *m.*
**colony** colonie *f.*
**color** couleur *f.*
**come** venir *(aux.* être); – **back** revenir; – **in** entrer
**company** compagnie *f.*
**complain** se plaindre
**complete** achever
**completely** tout à fait, complètement
**comrade** camarade *m.*
**concert** concert *m.*
**condition** condition *f.*, état *m.*; **in good** – en bon état
**consonant** consonne *f.*
**construct** construire
**contentment** contentement *m.*
**continent** continent *m.*
**continue** continuer
**cook** cuisinier *m.*, –ère *f.*; **head** – chef de cuisine
**cool** frais, fraîche; **the weather is** – il fait frais
**correct** corriger
**corridor** couloir *m.*
**cost** coûter
**count** compter
**counter** *(store)* rayon *m.*
**country** pays *m.*; campagne *f.* *(rural area)*
**course** cours *m.*
**cousin** cousin *m.*, –e *f.*
**cream** crème *f.*
**crime** crime *m.*
**criminal** criminel *m.*
**crisis** crise *f.*
**criticize** critiquer
**cup** tasse *f.*
**cut** couper

**damage** dommage *m.* *(usually pl.)*
**dance** bal *m.*; danser *v.*
**date** date *f.*
**daughter** fille *f.*
**day** jour *m.*, journée *f.*; **every** – tous les jours; **the next** – le lendemain; **today** aujourd'hui; **the – before** la veille
**deal**: **a great** – beaucoup (+ de *before n.)*
**dear** cher, chère
**December** décembre *m.*
**decide** décider (de)
**declare** déclarer
**decorate** décorer
**defense** défense *f.*
**delay** retard *m.*
**delicious** délicieux, –euse
**delightful** délicieux, –euse; épatant *(colloquial)*
**deliver** livrer
**demand** demander, réclamer
**demolish** démolir
**Denmark** Danemark *m.*
**deny** nier
**describe** décrire

**desert** désert *m.*
**desire** désirer, vouloir
**desk** bureau *m.;* pupitre *m. (pupil's desk)*
**destroy** détruire
**detail** détail *m.*
**die** mourir *(aux.* être)
**difficult** difficile
**difficulty** difficulté *f.;* embarras *m.*
**dine** dîner
**dining room** salle à manger *f.*
**dinner** dîner *m.*
**director** directeur *m.*
**discover** découvrir
**discuss** discuter
**disease** maladie *f.*
**dishonest** malhonnête
**distance** distance *f.;* **a short – away** à peu de distance, à deux pas
**distant** lointain
**do** faire; **how do you – ?** comment allez-vous?
**doctor** médecin *m.;* docteur *m.*
**dog** chien *m.*
**doll** poupée *f.*
**door** porte *f.*
**doubt** doute *m.;* douter *v.*
**dozen** douzaine *f.*
**drawer** tiroir *m.*
**dress** robe *f.;* habiller *v.;* **get –ed** s'habiller
**drill** exercice *m.*
**drink** boire; **– some wine** prendre du vin
**drive** conduire
**during** pendant
**Dutch** hollandais *n. & adj.*
**dwell** habiter, demeurer

**each** chaque; **– one** chacun, –e
**ear** oreille *f.*
**early** de bonne heure
**earn** gagner
**easily** facilement
**easy** facile
**eat** manger; **– lunch** prendre le déjeuner
**economic** économique
**effort** effort *m.*
**egg** œuf *m.*
**either . . . or** ou ... ou
**election** élection *f.*
**elementary** élémentaire
**embarrassed** embarrassé
**end** fin *f.;* bout *m. (of stick, etc.)*
**engage in** faire du (de la, etc.)
**engineer** ingénieur *m.*
**England** Angleterre *f.*
**English** anglais *n. & adj.*
**enjoy oneself** s'amuser
**enough** assez (+ de *before n.)*
**enter** entrer *(aux.* être) *(requires prep. before complement)*
**entrance** entrée *f.*
**epic** épique
**equal** égal *adj.;* égaler *v.*
**error** faute *f.,* erreur *f.*
**especially** surtout
**essential** essentiel, –le
**establish** établir
**esteem** apprécier
**Europe** Europe *f.*
**even** même
**evening** soir *m.,* soirée *f.*
**event** événement *m.*
**ever** jamais; **not –** jamais (+ne

*before v.)*

**every** chaque; tous les, toutes les

**everybody** tout le monde

**everything** tout

**everywhere** partout

**exactly** exactement, précisément

**exam(ination)** examen *m.*, épreuve *f.*

**examine** examiner

**example** exemple *m.*

**excellent** excellent

**except** excepté, sauf

**excited** ému

**exercise** exercice *m.*, devoir *m.*

**exhibition** exhibition *f.*

**exile** exil *m.*

**expect** attendre; compter; s'attendre à

**expensive** cher, chère

**experiment** expérience *f.*

**explain** expliquer

**explanation** explication *f.*

**exposition** exposition *f.*

**eye** œil *m.* (yeux *pl.)*

**face** figure *f.*

**fact** fait *m.*

**factory** usine *f.*

**fall** automne *m. or f.*

**fall** tomber *(aux.* être)

**family** famille *f.*

**famous** célèbre; fameux, –euse

**far (off)** loin; **–from** loin de; **from – off** de loin

**fast** vite *adj. & adv.;* rapide *adj.*

**father** père *m.*

**fear** peur *f.;* **for – that** de peur que

**February** février *m.*

**feel** sentir; *(health)* se sentir; **– like** avoir envie de

**fellow** *(colloquial)* type *m.*

**few** peu de; **a –** quelques *adj.;* quelques-uns, quelques-unes *pron.*

**fight** combat *m.*

**fill** remplir

**filter** filtrer

**finally** enfin

**find** trouver

**fine** *(excellent)* excellent, bon; **a – boy** un brave garçon

**finger** doigt *m.*

**finish** finir, achever

**fire** feu *m.*

**first** premier, –ère; **at –** d'abord

**fish** poisson *m.*

**fisherman** pêcheur *m.*

**floor** plancher *m.;* **first –** le rez de chaussée; **second –** le premier étage

**flower** fleur *f.*

**fly** voler

**follow** suivre

**foot** pied *m.;* **on –** à pied

**for** pour; pendant; depuis *(see p. 21)*

**forbid** défendre

**foreign** étranger

**forget** oublier

**form** former

**former** ancien, –enne *adj.;* celui-là, celle-là, ceux-là, celles-là *pron.*

**formerly** autrefois

**found** fonder

**fountain pen** stylo *m.*

**frankly** franchement

**free** libre; gratis *(no cost)*

**French** français *n. & adj.*
**frequently** fréquemment
**Friday** vendredi *m.*
**friend** ami *m.*, –e *f.*; camarade *m. or f.*
**friendship** amitié *f.*
**from** de; **(starting)** – depuis
**front: in – of** devant
**frontier** frontière *f.*
**fruit** fruit *m.*
**full** plein *(+* de *before n.)*
**funny** amusant

**gain** gagner
**garage** garage *m.*
**garden** jardin *m.*
**general** général *n. & adj.*
**generous** généreux, –euse
**gentle** doux, douce
**gently** doucement
**gentleman** monsieur *m.*
**German** allemand *n. & adj.*
**Germany** Allemagne *f.*
**get: – up** se lever
**gift** cadeau *m.*
**girl** (jeune) fille *f.*
**give** donner; **– a speech** prononcer un discours; **– back** rendre
**glad** heureux, –euse; content
**glass** verre *m.*
**glasses** lunettes *f. pl.*
**glitter** briller
**glove** gant *m.*
**go** aller *(aux.* être); **– away** s'en aller, partir; **– back** retourner; **– out** sortir; **– up** monter; **– to bed** se coucher
**gold** or *m.*
**good** bon, bonne
**goodbye** au revoir
**goodness** bonté *f.*
**grammar** grammaire *f.*
**grandfather** grand-père *m.*
**grandmother** grand-mère *f.*
**grape** raisin *m.*
**gravy** jus *m.*, sauce *f.*
**great** grand; **a – deal, a – many** beaucoup (+ de *before n.)*
**Greece** Grèce *f.*
**Greek** grec, grecque *n. & adj*
**green** vert
**group** groupe *m.*
**guide** guide *m.*
**guitar** guitare *f.*

**habit** habitude *f.*
**hair** cheveux *m. pl.*
**ham** jambon *m.*
**hand** main *f.*
**handkerchief** mouchoir *m.*
**happen** arriver *(aux.* être), se passer, avoir lieu
**happiness** bonheur *m.*
**happy** heureux, –euse; content
**hard** difficile; dur; **study –** étudier beaucoup
**harm** mal *m.*
**hat** chapeau *m.*
**hatred** *haine *f.*
**have** avoir; **– just done something** venir de faire quelque chose *(see p. 97)*; **– lunch** prendre le déjeuner; **– something done** faire faire quelque chose *(see pp. 97-98)*; **– to do something** devoir faire quelque chose *(see pp. 140-141)*

**head** tête *f.;* chef *m. (person in charge)*
**headmaster** directeur *m.*
**hear** entendre; écouter *(program, concert, etc.);* – **that** entendre dire que
**heavy** lourd
**help** aider
**here** ici; – **is (are)** voici
**hero** *héros *m.*
**heroine** héroïne *f.*
**hide** cacher
**high** haut, élevé
**highly**: – **esteemed** bien apprécié
**historic** historique
**history** histoire *f.*
**hit** frapper
**hold** tenir; – **tight (close)** étreindre
**home** maison *f. (There is no real equivalent in French for the English word* **home**, *but* maison *is reasonably approximate in most uses.)* **at** – à la maison; **at the – of** chez
**homework** devoir *m.*
**hope** espérer
**horse** cheval *m.*
**hospital** hôpital *m.*
**hospitality** hospitalité *f.*
**hot** chaud; **to be** – avoir chaud *(persons),* faire chaud *(weather)*
**hotel** hôtel *m.*
**hour** heure *f.*
**house** maison *f.;* **at the – of** chez; **at his** – chez lui
**how** comment; – **long** combien de temps, depuis quand *(with the "have been doing" construction; see p. 21);* – **much,** – **many** combien *(+* de *before n.)*
**however** cependant
**hungry**: **be** – avoir faim
**hurry** se dépêcher
**hurt** avoir mal à; **my arm** –s j'ai mal au bras
**husband** mari *m.*

**ice** glace *f.;* – **cream** glace *f.*
**idea** idée *f.*
**if** si
**ill** malade
**illness** maladie *f.*
**immediately** immédiatement, tout de suite
**immense** immense
**important** important
**impress** impressioner
**improbable** peu probable
**impulsive** impulsif
**in** dans, en, à; de *(after superlatives);* – **order to** pour; – **order that** pour que, afin que
**incompetent** inhabile
**incredible** incroyable
**indicate** indiquer
**indolent** indolent
**inform** informer
**information** renseignement *m. (generally used in pl.)*
**inhabitant** habitant *m.*
**ink** encre *f.*
**instead**: – **of** au lieu de
**intelligent** intelligent
**intelligently** intelligemment
**interest** *v.* intéresser
**interested**: **be** – **(in)** s'intéresser (à)

**interesting** intéressant
**into** dans, en
**introduce** présenter
**invite** inviter
**iron** fer *m.;* fer à repasser *(for pressing)*
**island** île *f.*
**Italian** italien, –enne *n. & adj.*
**Italy** Italie *f.*

**January** janvier *m.*
**Japan** Japon *m.*
**job** poste *m.*
**juice** jus *m.*
**June** juin *m.*
**July** juillet *m.*
**just** juste *adj.;* justement *adv;* **to have – done something** venir de faire quelque chose
**justice** justice *f.*

**keep** garder
**kind** type *m.*, sorte *f.*
**kindness** bonté *f.*
**king** roi *m.*
**kitchen** cuisine *f.*
**knock** frapper
**know** connaître *(persons, places, etc.);* savoir *(facts, subjects, etc.);* – **how to** savoir *(see also p. 97)*
**known** connu; **well –** célèbre

**ladder** échelle *f.*
**lady** dame *f.*, femme *f.*
**lake** lac *m.*
**lamb** agneau *m.;* **leg of –** gigot *m.*
**language** langue *f.*
**large** grand
**last** dernier, –ère *(see p. 119);* – **night (evening)** hier soir
**late** tard; en retard *(not on time)*
**Latin** latin *n. & adj.*
**latter** celui-ci, celle-ci, ceux-ci, celles-ci *pron.*
**lawyer** avocat *m.*
**learn** apprendre
**learned** savant
**least** le moins
**leave** partir *(aux.* être **go away);** sortir *(aux.* être **go out);** quitter *(always takes obj.* **go away from)**· laisser **(leave behind)** *(see also p. 98)*
**lecture** conférence *f.*
**left** gauche
**leg** jambe *f.;* – **of lamb** gigot *m.*
**lemon** citron *m.*
**lend** prêter
**less** moins
**lesson** leçon *f.*
**let** laisser
**letter** lettre *f.*
**library** bibliothèque *f.*
**lieutenant** lieutenant *m.*
**life** vie *f.*
**light** lumière *f.*
**like** aimer; **feel –** avoir envie de
**like** comme *conj. & prep.*
**linen** linge *m.*
**listen (to)** écouter
**litre** litre *m. (a little more than a quart)*
**little** petit *adj.;* peu *adv.*
**live** vivre; **(dwell)** habiter, demeurer
**living room** salon *m.*, living-room *m.*

**London** Londres *m.*
**long** long, longue; **a – time** longtemps; **as – as** tant que; **how –** combien de temps, depuis quand *(see p. 21)*
**longer: no –** plus (+ ne *before v.)*
**look (at)** regarder; **– for** chercher; **– tired** avoir l'air fatigué
**lose** perdre
**lost** perdu
**love** amour *m.;* aimer *v.*
**lunch** déjeuner *m.*

**machine** machine *f.*
**magazine** revue *f.*, magazine *m.*
**magnificent** magnifique
**maid** bonne *f.;* **lady's –** femme de chambre *f.*
**majority** la plupart (+ de + *def. art. before n.)*
**make** marque *f. (make of car, etc.)*
**make** faire; **– up one's mind** se décider (à + *inf.)*
**man** homme *m.*
**manuscript** manuscrit *m.*
**many** beaucoup; **as –** autant; **how –** combien; **too –** trop *(all require* de *before n.)*
**map** carte *f.*
**March** mars *m.*
**market** marché *m.*
**marketing: to do the –** faire le marché
**marry** épouser; se marier (avec)
**marvelous** merveilleux, –euse
**mathematics** mathématiques *f. pl.*
**matter** matière *f.;* **What's the – ?** Qu'est-ce qu'il y a? **What's the matter with you?** Qu'avez-vous?
**may** pouvoir; **that – be** cela se peut
**May** mai *m.*
**meal** repas *m.*
**mean** vouloir dire
**means** moyen *m.*
**meat** viande *f.*
**mechanical** machinal
**meet** rencontrer; faire la connaissance de **(become acquainted with)**; se réunir **(assemble)**
**member** membre *m.*
**men** gens *m. pl.;* hommes *m. pl.*
**mention** mentionner
**merchant** commerçant *m.*
**mercy** miséricorde *f.*
**message** message *m.*
**method** méthode *f.*
**Mexico** Mexique *m.*
**middle** milieu *m.*
**midnight** minuit *m.*
**midst: in the – of** au milieu de
**milk** lait *m.*
**millionaire** millionnaire
**minister** ministre *m.*
**minute** minute *f.*
**misfortune** malheur *m.*
**miss** manquer
**mistake** faute *f.*, erreur *f.*
**modern** moderne; **– language** langue vivante
**modest** modeste
**Monday** lundi *m.*
**money** argent *m.*
**month** mois *m.*
**monument** monument *m.*

**more** plus; – **and** – de plus en plus
**morning** matin *m.*
**Morocco** Maroc *m.*
**Moscow** Moscou *m.*
**most** la plupart (+ de + *def. art. before n.); adv.* plus
**mother** mère *f.*
**motor** moteur *m.*
**mountain** montagne *f.*
**movie** film *m.*
**movies (movie theater)** cinéma *m.*
**much** beaucoup; **as** – autant; **how** – combien; **so** – tant; **too** – trop *(all require* de *before n.)*
**murmur** murmurer
**museum** musée *m.*
**music** musique *f.*
**must** falloir; devoir *(see pp. 140-141)*

**name** nom *m.;* nommer *v.*
**napkin** serviette *f.*
**nation** nation *f.;* peuple *m.*
**nationality** nationalité *f.*
**near** près *adv.;* près de *prep.;* proche *adj.*
**necessary** nécessaire; **it is** – il faut
**necktie** cravate *f.*
**need** besoin *m.; v.* avoir besoin de
**neither . . . nor** ni ... ni (+ ne *before v.)*
**nervous** nerveux, –euse
**never** jamais (+ ne *before v.)*
**new** nouveau (nouvel), nouvelle
**news** nouvelle *f. (usually used in plural)*
**newspaper** journal *m.*
**next** prochain
**nice** bon, gentil; **the weather is** – il fait beau
**night** nuit *f.;* **last** – hier soir
**no** non; pas, aucun *(both require* ne *before v.)*
**nobody** personne (+ ne *before v.)*
**noon** midi *m.*
**Norway** Norvège *f.*
**nose** nez *m.*
**not** pas (+ ne *before v.)*
**notebook** cahier *m.*
**nothing** rien (+ ne *before v.)*
**notice** remarquer
**nourishing** nourrissant
**novel** roman *m.*
**November** novembre *m.*
**now** maintenant, à présent, actuellement, en ce moment
**number** numéro *m.;* nombre *m. (quantity)*
**nurse** infirmier *m.,* –ère *f.*
**nylon** nylon *m.*

**oatmeal** bouillie d'avoine *f.*
**obey** obéir (à)
**occasion** occasion *f.;* fois *f.*
**October** octobre *m.*
**of** de
**offer** offre *f.;* offrir *v.*
**office** bureau *m.*
**often** souvent
**old** vieux (vieil), vieille; ancien, –enne; **How** – **are you?** Quel âge avez-vous?
**on** sur; *also* à, en, dans *in various special locutions:* **on time** à l'heure, **on leaving** en sortant, etc.

**only** seul *adj.;* seulement *adv.*; ne ... que
**open** ouvrir
**or** ou
**orally** oralement
**orange** orange *f.*
**order** ordonner; *(meals)* commander; **in – to** pour; **in – that** pour que, afin que
**other** autre
**ought** *see* devoir *pp. 140-141*
**outside** en dehors
**over**: – **there** là-bas
**own** *adj.* propre
**owner** propriétaire *m. or f.*

**package** paquet *m.*, colis *m.*
**pain** mal *m. (see pp. 142-143)*
**paint** peindre
**painting** peinture *f.*
**pancake** crêpe *f.*
**paper** papier *m.;* **news–** journal *m.*
**parcel** paquet *m.*, colis *m.*
**pardon** pardon *m.*
**parent** parent *m.*
**part** partie *f.*
**participate** participer
**pass** passer; – **an examination** réussir à un examen
**past** passé
**pastry** pâtisserie *f.*
**patriotism** patriotisme *m.*
**pay** *v.* payer
**peace** paix *f.*
**peasant** paysan *m.*
**pebble** caillou *m.*
**pen** plume *f.;* **fountain** – stylo *m..;* **ball-point** – stylo-bille *m.*
**people** gens *m. pl.*
**perceive** apercevoir
**perfect** parfait
**perhaps** peut-être
**period** période, époque *f.*
**permit** permettre
**person** personne *f.*
**Peru** Pérou *m.*
**pharmacist** pharmacien *m.*
**phenomenon** phénomène *m.*
**philosophy** philosophie *f.*
**pianist** pianiste *m. & f.*
**piano** piano *m.*
**picture** photo *f.;* tableau *m.;* **moving** – film *m.*
**picturesque** pittoresque
**pity** plaindre
**place** endroit *m.*, lieu *m.;* **to take** – avoir lieu; **Take your places.** Prenez vos places.; *v.* mettre
**plan** plan *m.;* projet *m.*
**plane** avion *m.*
**plant** plante *f.*
**play** pièce *f.*, comédie *f.*
**play** jouer; – **bridge** jouer au bridge; – **the piano** jouer du piano
**pleasant** agréable
**please, be pleasing** plaire
**please** s'il vous plaît; veuillez + *inf.*
**pleasure** plaisir *m.*
**pocket** poche *f.*
**poem** poème *m.*
**point out** signaler
**police (force)** police *f.*
**policeman** agent (de police) *m.*
**political** politique
**poor** pauvre *(see p. 119)*

**popular** populaire
**port** port *m.*
**Portugal** Portugal *m.*
**position** position *f.;* poste *m.* *(job)*
**possible** possible
**potato** pomme (de terre) *f.*
**pound** livre *f.*
**poverty** pauvreté *f.*
**powerful** puissant
**praise** éloge *m.*
**prefect** préfet *m.*
**prefer** préférer, aimer mieux
**prepare** préparer
**present (gift)** cadeau *m.*
**present** présenter
**president** président *m.*
**pretend** faire semblant *(see p. 142)*
**pretty** joli
**price** prix *m.*
**prince** prince *m.*
**principal** principal *adj.*
**principle** principe *m.*
**privilege** privilège *m.*
**prize** prix *m.*
**probable** probable
**probably** probablement, sans doute
**problem** problème *m.*
**product** produit *m.*
**production** production *f.*
**professor** professeur *m.*
**program** programme *m.*
**project** projet *m.*
**promise** promesse *f.;* promettre *v.*
**pronounce** prononcer
**proper** convenable
**proud** fier, –ère
**provided: – that** pourvu que
**province** province *f.*
**publish** publier
**punish** punir
**punishment** punition *f.;* châtiment *m.*
**pupil** élève *m. or f.*
**purchase** emplette *f.*
**put** mettre

**quality** qualité *f.*
**queen** reine *f.*
**question** question *f.;* interroger, questionner *v.;* **to ask a –** poser une question
**quickly** vite
**quite** très, tout

**radio** radio *f.;* **– set** appareil (de radio) *m.*
**railroad** chemin de fer *m.;* **– station** gare *f.*
**read** lire
**ready** prêt
**real** vrai
**realism** réalisme *m.*
**really** vraiment
**reason** raison *f.*
**receive** recevoir
**recent** récent
**recognize** reconnaître
**recommend** recommander
**record** disque *m.;* mention *f. (notation)*
**red** rouge
**referee** arbitre *m.*
**refuse** refuser
**region** région *f.*
**regret** regretter

**relate** raconter
**relative** parent *m.*
**religion** religion *f.*
**remain** rester *(aux.* être)
**remark** remarquer
**remember** se rappeler, se souvenir (de)
**rent** louer
**repair** réparer
**repeat** répéter
**reply** répondre (à)
**re-read** relire
**research** recherche *f.*
**resemble** ressembler (à)
**responsibility** responsabilité *f.*
**responsible** responsable
**rest** reste *m.* **(remainder)**; repos *m.* **(repose)**; se reposer *v.*
**restaurant** restaurant *m.*
**retire** se retirer
**return** revenir *(aux.* être **come back)**; retourner *(aux.* être **go back)**; rentrer *(aux.* être **go home, come home)**; rendre **(give back)**; être de retour **(be back)**
**reveal** révéler
**revolutionary** révolutionnaire
**rich** riche
**ride**: – **a horse, bicycle, etc.** monter à cheval, bicyclette, etc.; – **in a car, boat, etc.** se promener en voiture, bateau, etc.
**ridiculous** ridicule
**right** droite *f. (right side);* **to be** – avoir raison
**ring** sonner
**river** fleuve *m. (empties into sea);* rivière *f.*
**road** chemin *m.;* route *f.*
**roll** petit pain *m.;* brioche *f.*, croissant *m.;* rouler *v.*
**Roman** romain *n. & adj.*
**room** pièce *f.;* salle *f.;* **bath**– salle de bain; **bed**– chambre (à coucher) *f.;* **dining** – salle à manger; **living** – salon *m.*
**rose** rose *f.*
**rude** grossier
**rudely** grossièrement
**rule** règle *f.*
**run** courir
**Russia** Russie *f.*
**Russian** russe *n. & adj.*

**salad** salade *f.*
**salesman** vendeur *m.*
**saleswoman** vendeuse *f.*
**salt** sel *m.*
**same** même
**sandwich** sandwich *m.*
**Saturday** samedi *m.*
**sausage** saucisse *f.*
**savage** sauvage
**save** *(money)* économiser, faire des économies
**say** dire
**scholar** savant *m.*
**school** école *f.*
**science** science *f.*
**scientific** scientifique
**scientist** savant *m.*
**season** saison *f.*
**seat** place *f.;* fauteuil *m. (orchestra seat in theater)*
**secretary** secrétaire *m. or f.*
**section** région *f. (of country);* quartier *m. (of city)*

**see** voir
**seem** avoir l'air; sembler
**sell** vendre
**send** envoyer; **to — for** faire venir
**sentence** phrase *f.*
**separate** se quitter **(leave each other)**
**September** septembre *m.*
**serious** sérieux, –euse; grave
**serve** servir; **to — as** servir de
**set** mettre; **— the table** mettre le couvert
**several** plusieurs
**shine** briller
**ship** navire *m.*
**shirt** chemise *f.*
**shoe** soulier *m.*
**shop** boutique *f.*
**short** court; **— story** conte *m.*
**show** montrer
**sick** malade
**sickness** maladie *f.*
**sidewalk** trottoir *m.*
**sight** vue *f.*; **to know by —** connaître de vue
**sign** signer
**similar** semblable
**since** puisque; depuis *(time)*
**sincere** sincère
**sing** chanter
**singer** chanteur *m.*, –euse *f.*
**sister** sœur *f.*
**sit (down)** s'asseoir
**situation** situation *f.*
**skiing: go (in for) —** faire du ski
**skilled** habile
**skillful** habile
**slavery** esclavage *m.*
**sleep** dormir; **to go to —** s'endormir
**sleepy: be** avoir sommeil
**slowly** lentement
**small** petit
**smile** sourire
**so** si; **— much, — many** tant (+ de *before n.)*; **— long as** tant que; **— that** pour que, afin que
**soap** savon *m.*
**society** monde *m.*
**sock** chaussette *f.*
**soft** doux, douce
**soldier** soldat *m.*
**solution** solution *f.*
**some** du, de la, de l', des, de *(part. art.)*; en *(part. pron.)*; quelques *adj.*; quelques-uns, quelques-unes *pron.*
**somebody** quelqu'un
**something** quelque chose
**sometimes** quelquefois
**somewhere** quelque part
**son** fils *m.*
**song** chanson *f.*
**soon** bientôt; **as — as** aussitôt que
**sooner** plus tôt
**sorry: be —** regretter
**soup** soupe *f.*, potage *m.*
**south** sud *m.*
**South America** l'Amérique du Sud *f.*
**souvenir** souvenir *m.*
**Spain** Espagne *f.*
**Spaniard** Espagnol *m.*, Espagnole *f.*
**speak** parler
**speech** discours *m.*

**spend** passer *(time)*; dépenser *(money)*
**spite: in — of** malgré
**spoon** cuiller *f.*
**spoonful** cuillerée *f.*
**spring** printemps *m.*
**square** carré *adj.*; place *n.f.*
**stable** stable *adj.*
**stamp** timbre *m.*
**stand (up)** se lever
**standing: be** — être debout; se tenir, se trouver
**state** état *m.*
**station** gare *f. (railroad)*; station *f.*
**stay** rester; **to — at the . . . hotel** descendre à l'hôtel . . .
**steel** acier *m.*
**step** pas *m.*
**still** encore, toujours
**stocking** bas *m.*
**stomach** estomac *m.*
**stop (oneself)** s'arrêter
**store** magasin *m.*
**storm** orage *m.*
**story** histoire *f.*; **short —** conte *m.*; étage *m. (building)*
**stout** gros, corpulent
**street** rue *f.*
**strong** fort
**student** élève *m. or f.*; étudiant *m.*,–e *f.*
**study** étude *f.*; étudier *v.*
**stupid** stupide
**subject** sujet *m.*; **(study)** matière *f.*
**subway** métro *m.*
**succeed** réussir (à)
**sudden: all of a —** tout d'un coup
**suddenly** tout à coup
**suffer** souffrir
**suit** complet *m.*
**suit (to be suitable)** convenir
**suitable** convenable
**suitcase** valise *f.*
**summer** été *m.*
**sun** soleil *m.*
**Sunday** dimanche *m.*
**sunny: the weather is —** il fait du soleil
**supposed** *see* devoir *pp. 140-141*
**sure** sûr, certain
**surprise** surprise *f.*; s'étonner *v.*
**surprised: to be —** s'étonner, être étonné
**surprising** étonnant
**suspicion** soupçon *m.*
**swim** nager
**Swiss** suisse *n. & adj.*
**Switzerland** Suisse *f.*
**symbol** symbole *m.*

**table** table *f.*; **to set the —** mettre le couvert
**take** prendre; **— an exam** passer un examen; **— someone somewhere** conduire (accompagner) quelqu'un quelque part; **— a trip** faire un voyage; **— a walk (ride)** faire une promenade; **— place** avoir lieu
**talk** parler
**tall** grand
**tax** impôt *m.*
**taxi** taxi *m.*
**tea** thé *m.*
**teach** enseigner
**teacher** professeur *m.*
**teaching** enseignement *m.*

**telegram** télégramme *m.*
**telephone** téléphone *m.;* téléphoner *v.*
**television** télévision *f.;* téléviseur *m. (set)*
**tell** dire; raconter
**temperature** température *f.*
**tenderness** tendresse *f.*
**test** examen *m.*, épreuve *f.*
**than** que
**thank** remercier
**thanks** merci
**theater** théâtre *m.;* **movie –** cinéma *m.*
**then** puis, ensuite, alors
**there** là; y *(before v. only);* **from –** en *(before v. only);* **– is (are)** il y a; voilà *(pointing out)*
**thing** chose *f.*
**think** penser; **to – about** penser à
**thirsty: be –** avoir soif
**through** par
**Thursday** jeudi *m.*
**thus** ainsi
**ticket** billet *m.*
**tie** cravate *f.*
**time** temps *m.;* heure *f. (of clock);* **on –** à l'heure, en temps voulu; **a long –** longtemps; **the first –** la première fois; **the next –** la prochaine fois; **the – when** l'occasion où
**tip** bout *m.*
**tired** fatigué
**tiresome** ennuyeux, –euse
**title** titre *m.*
**to** à; en
**toast** pain grillé *m.*
**today** aujourd'hui
**together** ensemble
**tomorrow** demain
**tonight** ce soir
**too (also)** aussi; – + *adj. or adv.* trop: – **much (many)** trop (+ de *before n.*); **it's – bad** c'est dommage
**tool** outil *m.*
**toothbrush** brosse à dents *f.*
**tourist** touriste *m. or f.*
**toward(s)** vers
**towel** serviette *f.*
**tower** tour *f.*
**town** (petite) ville *f.*
**train** train *m.*
**travel** voyager
**treat** traiter
**treaty** traité *m.*
**tree** arbre *m.*
**trip** voyage *m.;* **take a –** faire un voyage
**truck** camion *m.*
**true** vrai
**truly** vraiment
**truth** vérité *f.*
**try** essayer
**Tuesday** mardi *m.*
**Tunisia** Tunisie *f.*
**turn: – off** fermer, éteindre
**typewriter** machine à écrire *f.*

**ugly** vilain
**uncle** oncle *m.*
**understand** comprendre
**undress** (se) déshabiller
**unhappy** malheureux, –euse
**United States** Etats-Unis *m. pl.*

**university** université *f.*
**unless** à moins que
**unlikely** peu probable
**until** jusqu'à *prep.;* jusqu'à ce que *conj.*
**upon** sur
**use** employer, se servir de
**useful** utile
**useless** inutile
**usual: as –** comme d'habitude

**vacation** vacances *f. pl.*
**valise** valise *f.*
**vegetable** légume *m.*
**vegetation** végétation *f.*
**verb** verbe *m.*
**very** très, bien; **– much, – many** beaucoup (+ de *before n.);* **the – day** le jour même
**vice** vice *m.*
**village** village *m.*
**vinegar** vinaigre *m.*
**virtue** vertu *f.*
**visit** visite *f.;* visiter *v. (places);* faire (rendre) une visite à *(persons)*
**visitor** visiteur *m.*
**voice** voix *f.*
**voyage** voyage *m.*

**wait (for)** attendre
**waiter** garçon *m.*
**wake up** (se) réveiller
**walk** marcher, aller à pied; **to take a –** faire une promenade
**wallet** portefeuille *m.*
**want** vouloir, désirer
**war** guerre *f.*
**warm** chaud; **to be –** avoir chaud *(persons);* faire chaud *(weather)*
**wash** laver; **– (oneself)** se laver
**washing: – machine** machine à laver *f.*
**wastepaper basket** panier *(m.)* à papier
**watch** montre *f.;* regarder *v.*
**watchmaker** horloger *m.*
**water** eau *f.*
**wave** vague *f.*
**wear** porter
**weather** temps *m. (see p. 141)*
**Wednesday** mercredi *m.*
**week** semaine *f.*
**welcome** accueillir
**well** bien; **feel –** se sentir bien
**what** que, qu'est-ce qui, qu'est-ce que, quoi *interr. pron.;* quel *interr. adj.;* ce qui, ce que *rel. pron.*
**when** quand, lorsque; où *(after nouns of time)*
**where** où
**whether** si
**which** quel *adj.;* qui, que, lequel *pron.;* **– one** lequel
**while** pendant que; en *(see pp. 146-147);* **a little – ago** tout à l'heure
**white** blanc, blanche
**who** qui
**whole** tout
**whom** qui *interr.;* qui, que *rel.*
**whose** dont *rel. (see pp. 46-48);* à qui *interr. (see pp. 75-76)*
**why** pourquoi
**wide** large
**widen** élargir

**wife** femme *f.*
**will** volonté *f.;* testament *m. (legal document)*
**win** gagner
**wind** vent *m.*
**window** fenêtre *f.*
**windy: to be –** faire du vent
**wine** vin *m.*
**winter** hiver *m.*
**wisdom** sagesse *f.*
**wish** vouloir, désirer; souhaiter
**with** avec; **filled –** rempli de; **the man – the beard** l'homme à la barbe *(see p. 91)*
**withdraw** (se) retirer
**without** sans *prep.;* sans que *conj.*
**woman** femme *f.*
**wonder** se demander
**work** travail *m.;* ouvrage *m.;* travailler *v.*
**workman** ouvrier *m.*
**world** monde *m.*
**worry** inquiéter; **be worried** s'inquiéter
**wreck** démolir
**write** écrire
**wrong: to be –** avoir tort

**year** an *m.,* année *f.* (an *is used principally after cardinal numbers and* tous les)
**yellow** jaune
**yes** oui
**yesterday** hier
**yet** encore
**young** jeune
**Yugoslavia** Yougoslavie *f.*

# *Index*

*(Numbers refer to pages)*

## Common Verbs Which Require *à* or *de* Before a Dependent Infinitive

### Verbs followed by à

**aider à** to help to
**s'amuser à** to amuse oneself by
**apprendre à** to learn to
**s'attendre à** to expect to
**chercher à** to try to
**commencer à** to begin to
**consentir à** to consent to
**continuer à** to continue to
se **décider à** to make up one's mind to
**demander à** to ask to
**encourager à** to encourage (someone) to
**s'ennuyer à** to be bored by (with)
**enseigner à** to teach to
**s'habituer à** to get accustomed to
**hésiter à** to hesitate to
**s'intéresser à** to be interested in
**inviter à** to invite (someone) to
**se mettre à** to start to
**s'occuper à** to busy oneself in
**parvenir à** to succeed in
**persister à** to persist in
**se préparer à** to get ready to
**réussir à** to succeed in
**songer à** to think of
**tarder à** to be long in
**tenir à** to insist upon

### Verbs followed by de

**achever de** to finish
**s'arrêter de** to stop, cease
**cesser de** to stop, cease
**se charger de** to undertake to
**commander de** to order (someone) to
**commencer de** to begin to
**conseiller de** to advise (someone) to
se **contenter de** to content oneself with
**continuer de** to continue
**craindre de** to be afraid to
**décider de** to decide to
**défendre de** to forbid (someone) to
**demander de** to ask (someone) to
**se dépêcher de** to hasten to
**dire de** to tell (someone) to
**écrire de** to write (someone) to
**empêcher de** to prevent (someone) from
**s'ennuyer de** to tire of
**essayer de** to try to
**s'étonner de** to be surprised to
**éviter de** to avoid
**s'excuser de** to excuse oneself from
**finir de** to finish
**se hâter de** to hasten to
**manquer de** to fail to, to almost
**menacer de** to threaten to
**mériter de** to deserve to
**offrir de** to offer to
**ordonner de** to order (someone) to
**oublier de** to forget to
**permettre de** to allow (someone) to
**persuader de** to persuade (someone) to
**prier de** to beg (someone) to
**promettre de** to promise (someone) to
**proposer de** to propose to
**refuser de** to refuse to
**regretter de** to regret to
**remercier de** to thank (someone) for
**risquer de** to risk
**se souvenir de** to remember (to)
**suggérer de** to suggest (to someone) to